Microcosmos

From Robert Fludd's *Utriusque Cosmi Historia* (1617)
Courtesy of the Folger Shakespeare Library

MICROCOSMOS

The Shape
of the
Elizabethan Play

THOMAS B. STROUP

University of Kentucky Press, Lexington

1965

Copyright © *1965* *by the University of Kentucky Press*
Manufactured in the United States of America
Library of Congress Catalog Card No.
65-27010

To Annie Mary

FOR whose patience "it were pity but she should suffer salvation, body and soul."

Preface

When the idea out of which this work has developed first occurred to me fifteen years ago, it seemed to be quite a new one—although one any student of Elizabethan drama should have been struck by. Though the commonplace was well known, little had appeared, if indeed anything, concerning the Elizabethan play's relation to the concept of the world as stage; little if anything had been said about the Elizabethan stage as built to represent the world in little; and little had been written to show that the metaphor had something to do with the nature of the Elizabethan drama. But as time has gone on, others have observed a relationship between the idea that "The world's a stage, / And all the men and women merely players" and certain phenomena in this drama, and many have written about certain aspects of this relationship. Also as time has gone on, I have studied the corpus of Elizabethan drama with this concept in mind. The result has been that I am convinced the basic structure of the Elizabethan play of whatever kind lies in this ancient observation. I present here my reasons for thinking so.

Few if any of the scholars who have touched upon the idea have gone so far; most have seen only a few aspects of the notion. But all have been helpful, and I have tried to give credit at the proper place to all who have anticipated me in print.

They have often helped me clarify my thinking; often they have confirmed beliefs held long before their writings appeared. I gratefully acknowledge their help.

I also acknowledge much other help. In addition to all the numerous little unremembered acts, suggestions, and comments from this one and that whom I held (at least for a moment) with my tale, I have these to thank: The Folger Shakespeare Library for a fellowship in the summer of 1957, the University of Kentucky for a half-year sabbatical which I spent reading in the British Museum; the University of Kentucky Research Fund for the cost of typing and of travel; and the editors of *Studies in English Literature* and *All These to Teach: Essays in Honor of C. A. Robertson* for permission to reprint (with considerable revision) parts of two chapters. I am especially grateful to Professor Mary Ellen Rickey for reading the manuscript and offering her kind and most helpful criticisms. From all these nothing but well and fair, nothing but good; the faults, the errors of judgment, the lack of perception, and the excesses of enthusiasm must, unless "your indulgence set me free," be mine alone to regret.

17 January, 1965

Contents

A Note on Practices

§ THROUGHOUT THIS STUDY I have used the short titles of the plays as given in modern spelling (usually) by Chambers in *The Elizabethan Stage* and Bentley in *The Jacobean and Caroline Stage*. My authority for the dates included with the titles of the plays has likewise been these two works. I have included dates where I thought they might be a convenience and might show changes, indicate development, or reveal decline in certain practices. In my notes I have named the particular editions of the plays I have cited. Texts have not been of paramount importance in this work (though I have made an effort to use the best available); my concern is with large practices, patterns, and designs, not often with textual matters. I have relied at times upon the elaboration of stage directions made by editors; in each case I have found the addition justified by the dialogue. The same is true of the editors' identification of the places of scenes.

If my dependence upon Shakespeare's plays for illustration and analysis seems out of proportion, I may claim in justification that his work is not only typical of the period but far more familiar to readers than that of others: references to his work come easily to mind.

I have followed the loose but general and convenient practice of referring to the drama produced from the beginning of the reign of Elizabeth I until the closing of the theatres in 1642 as Elizabethan drama. To be always dividing and discriminating where little division or discrimination exists is to feed one of the peccant humors of learning merely.

Introduction

§ The structure of the Elizabethan play has puzzled critics from Sir Philip Sidney to T. S. Eliot.[1] It is frequently noted that, though Shakespeare might write a brilliant scene, he could not put scenes together into a well-made play [2] and that, whereas Marlowe's mighty line might thunder down the centuries and his Tamburlaine and Faustus stalk the stage of the world, the vehicles for both lines and characters are rather shapeless things, created of scraps and hastily stuck together, likely to break down at any turn. The wonder is that, with so much knowledge of the Roman plays, the Elizabethan playwright paid so little attention to their form; that with no little regard for the dramatic criticism of the Ancients and the Italians in his own day, he failed to make much use of it when he wrought out the plots of his plays, especially those designed for the public theatre.

Though many others have written of it, Professor T. W. Baldwin's work alone, especially the exhaustive (and exhausting) study of Shakespeare's five-act structure,[3] is sufficient to demonstrate the playwrights' knowledge of dramatic form as derived from the Ancients and their commentators. Any dramatist of the period who had got through the fourth form at grammar school knew Terence, and to know Terence was to know not only the purity of his language but the five-act structure of

1

his plays as it was explained by the commentators from Donatus onward. But knowledge does not always warrant practice. And Professor Baldwin with all his analysis, does not, I think, find out any frequent adherence to the five-act structure, even among the most academic playwrights such as Lyly or in the early work of Shakespeare fresh from the grammar school at Stratford. He does not get to Marlowe. Recently Professor Henry L. Snuggs has effectively disposed of Baldwin's arguments, showing that the five-act structure never did exist and that five-act division (quite another matter) developed largely after 1610.[4] On the whole, if we forget the often arbitrarily imposed act divisions of the printed texts, we find nothing more than protasis, epitasis, and catastrophe, the natural divisions of any sort of literary invention and especially necessary to drama. But granted a rough sort of neoclassical five-act pattern in some plays, we still look in vain for a tightly woven plot of classic design, or for a "well-made" play, concentrated, logical, and coherent in form. Elizabethan plays were more complicated in structure than such five-act division suggests.

Several reasons, all close akin, for this disregard of both neoclassical or Horatian precept and occasional example have been given. Although Dryden attacks the Elizabethan playwright's disregard for the rules in his essay on *The Dramatic Poetry of the Last Age*, in his *An Essay of Dramatic Poesy* he defends any English playwright's practice of ignoring them. Neander maintains that the English genius as opposed to the French requires subplots, numerous characters, and much action, even though these make for loose construction and a loss of concentration and logical, coherent development. The English require variety. Realizing this, the dramatist, though he may be well aware of classical form and neoclassical rules, disregards them when he chooses. Related to this reason is one of more recent development: since the Elizabethan theatre was a popular theatre catering to citizen, apprentice, and countryman as well as to courtier, gentleman, and lady, it required a bustling drama in which all sorts and conditions of men must appear in every play; in other words, since all London went to the public playhouse, all of London society from king to clown should be represented on the stage—and in almost every play. Playwrights had to provide plots to accommodate all: hence the multiple plot; numerous characters, scenes, pageants, processions, and ceremonies; violent and swift action; and bombastic rhetoric. It has been alleged from Dryden on, moreover, that many were ignorant of the rules and practices of dramatic art who attempted it. The chronicle plays and historical pageants, popular in the extreme, rather took their shape, we are told, from their narrative sources than from the proper rules of dramatic poetry, the dramatists being either ignorant or disregardful.

Doubtless each of these reasons—and more like them—has some validity. But I have not found them adequate. Many Elizabethan dramatists seem to have had sufficient stature to lead their patrons and public, rather than to be led by them, in the production of their art. The English playwright, though quite well aware of the unities, for example, had never regarded adherence to them as a *sine qua non* of a good play; and, although equally well aware of the rather spurious doctrine of the five-act structure, he felt little or no compulsion to follow it. It is true that the public theatre was a popular one and that it depended much upon popular taste for its support. This fact does not explain either the peculiar shape of the Elizabethan play, or the disregard for the rules and practices of the classics.

One may very well ask whether the Elizabethan dramatist did not have another structural pattern to follow, another source for the form of his work. When the new drama was born in the Middle Ages, its mother was the Church. It had no kinship, no direct relationship at least, with what had been produced in the theatres scattered over the Roman Empire. As it grew up in grace, but not always in comeliness, it found its own form, awkward according to some, but it owed little if anything at all to its predecessor among the Greeks and the Romans. With the coming of the new learning, or the revival of the old, all that was medieval was not suddenly broken off or quickly forgotten.

This was not less true of the drama than of the other arts; in fact, the traditions of the theatre are persistent, and playwrights are slow to modify their practices or to change, especially a popular form. Imitated and translated in academic circles, Plautus, Terence, and Seneca were slow to affect the popular stage. Their gains were grudgingly allowed, seldom dissociated altogether from the native tradition, and largely restricted to academic circles. The glib generality once often heard that the "regular drama" gave shape to the Elizabethan play implies that the native and medieval had either no proper shape or that the Elizabethan took over classical structure in its entirety, dropping its connection with the earlier native tradition. But this generalization is now seldom heard.

Within the last three decades it has been pretty well discredited. The plays of the public theatres especially, the great popular drama of the period 1585 to 1642 which I refer to as "Elizabethan," grew out of the medieval tradition and were for the most part a continuation of it; hence they owed much to the medieval, especially in their structure. Though Professor Willard Farnham [5] emphasizes the debt Elizabethan tragedy owes to the medieval narrative verse tragedy, he observes also its structural debt to the morality play, as does Professor Howard Baker (who on the other hand minimizes far too much the Senecan influence).[6] Miss Catherine Dunn [7] shows that the chronicle play has antecedents in the mystery cycles, as does Miss Effie MacKinnon.[8] Professor Irving Ribner [9] has linked Shakespeare's tragedies with the moralities, especially as they reveal the basic religious experience. Professor Bernard Spivack [10] has dealt with structure, especially the impact of the *psychomachia*, as he makes the connection between the Vice of the morality play and the Shakespearean villain. And Professor David M. Bevington [11] has analyzed the linear structure of the moralities and their pattern of soul-struggle as they emerge in Marlowe's plays. These are some of the important studies—by no means all—connecting the medieval play and its structure with the Elizabethan. As I go forward with this study, I shall frequently rely upon them, as upon others which touch less directly upon structure.

For my concern with the structure of the Elizabethan play has to do with the medieval heritage. But not with the medieval play only. Before the cycles were, the concept of cosmic drama was. The Fathers of the Church as well as the Neoplatonists and Renaissance humanists, repeating a classical metaphor, had likened the world to a stage on which the Christian is tested, and this figure of speech is basic to the medieval drama, whether mystery or morality. The cycles were each a series of pageants presenting the story of the salvation of the race. The place of action was the cosmos and the time was all time. The morality, especially the early morality play, as is so frequently said, was concerned with the salvation of the individual soul, the representative of all the race, as he is beset by the world, the flesh, and the devil. This struggle for salvation provided a pattern, gave structure to the action. As time went on, the stage became more restricted and the allegorical characters more circumscribed, until both place and person were individualized. The breakdown begins in the moralities themselves and continues throughout the period, or until the closing of the theatres, so that in these later times of realism, as T. S. Eliot would say, the flow of spirit "ends its course in the desert of exact likeness to the reality which is perceived by the most commonplace mind." Not so with the Elizabethan (though Eliot apparently thought so); he does not lose sight of his cosmic concept; he did not discard his universalizing machinery got from the earlier drama. As he individualized his characters and particularized his time and place, he did not allow them to lose contact with the whole, nor did he forget that their action took place within the temporal parentheses of eternity.[12] He adapted from the classical certain qualities; but he was eclectic, making use of what fit his basic medieval pattern. The world, except in the later years of the period, remained his stage, as he so often said, and the structure of his plays was based ultimately upon this concept, I believe.

It is the purpose of the following study to explore how this metaphor was a force in shaping the Elizabethan play. It will bring together for the first time much that has been discovered already; it will, I hope, also reveal some aspects of Elizabethan drama not hitherto observed or fully realized. And perhaps it may even suggest something of the fundamental nature of drama itself, especially those qualities which make it most effective and enduring. For however great and eternal the verity, it is the form, the shape of the thing, which enables it to catch the conscience of the King—and of Everyman.

ONE

The World as Stage

ᔑ JAQUES'S METAPHOR in *As You Like It* that "All the
world's a stage, / And all the men and women merely players" is
a memorable utterance of one of the most common of Elizabethan commonplaces. It goes back at least as far as Democritus,
in one of whose Fragments we find this: " Ὁ κόσμος σκηνή. ὁ βίος
πάροδος. ἦλθες, εἶδες, ἀπῆλθες" (The world's a stage, life a
play. / You come, you look, you go away). As has been often
observed, Sir Edmund Chambers quoted these words as epigraph for his celebrated biography of William Shakespeare,
but did not go further, as might have been expected, to suggest
their implications in the development of Shakespeare's art. Professor T. W. Baldwin and Sister Miriam Joseph, as well as various editors of *As You Like It,* have indicated their appearance in
the works of several writers between Democritus and Shakespeare, but have not suggested that they might reveal something
of the nature of the Elizabethan play. Recently, however, M.
Jean Jacquot has investigated thoroughly their origins, development, and modifications up through the sixteenth century and
has shown one or two of their implications as a possible shaping
force in Renaissance drama; and even more recently Anne
Righter has shown it as basic to the stage imagery and a structural force in Shakespeare's plays.[1] Others have seen the possi-
bilities of a connection between this metaphor and the shape of

7

the Elizabethan playhouse, but they have made little of the matter. As M. Jacquot has thoroughly traced the early appearances
of the figure from its origin through the works of the humanists, I shall here need only to review its more notable expressions, especially those which may reflect a concept of the nature
of drama or the shape of a play. I shall be chiefly concerned,
therefore—far more so than M. Jacquot—with showing how
widespread was the idea among the Elizabethans, especially the
dramatists and with demonstrating its part in shaping the Elizabethan theatre, before I turn in my succeeding chapters to its
very important implications in the structure of the plays. The
humanists may well serve as our Janus.

Sir Thomas More and Erasmus in 1506 translated Lucian's
Dialogues, in one of which, the *Menippus or Necromantia*, they
found as elaborate a statement of the metaphor as is known:

> So as I [Menippus] looked at them [the dead] it seemed
> to me that human life is like a long pageant, and that all its
> trappings are supplied and distributed by Fortune, who arrays
> the participants in various costumes of many colours. Taking
> one person, it may be, she attires him royally, placing a tiara
> upon his head, giving him body-guards, and encircling his brow
> with the diadem; but upon another she puts the costume of a
> slave. Again, she makes up one person so that he is handsome,
> but causes another to be ugly and ridiculous. I suppose that
> the show must needs be diversified. And often, in the very
> middle of the pageant, she exchanges the costumes of several
> players; instead of allowing them to finish the pageant in the
> parts that had been assigned to them, she reapparels them,
> forcing Croesus to assume the dress of a slave and a captive,
> and shifting Maeandrius, who formerly paraded among the
> servants, into the imperial habit of Polycrates. For a brief space
> she lets them use their costumes, but when the time of the
> pageant is over, each gives back the properties and lays off
> the costume along with his body, becoming what he was be-
> fore birth, no different from his neighbor. . . .
> I suppose you have often seen these stage-folk who act
> in tragedies, and according to the demands of the play become

at one moment Creons, and again Priams and Agamemnons; the very one, it may be, who a short time ago assumed with great dignity the part of Crecops, or of Erectheus soon appears as a servant at the bidding of the poet. And when at length the play comes to an end, each of them strips off his gold-bespangled robe, lays aside his mask, steps out of his buskins, and goes about in poverty and humility. . . . That is what human affairs are like, it seemed to me as I looked.[2]

The passage made its impression on Erasmus, for three years after the translation he incorporated its substance into *The Praise of Folly* (1509). Our life according to Folly is "but a kind of stage play through which men pass in various disguises, each going on to play his part until he is led off by the director." [3] Often, she says, the same actor plays several parts, the king at one time, the slave at another, and Fortune directs the whole. "Thus everything is pretense; yet this play is performed in no other way." However subtle he may have been in putting the words into Folly's mouth, Erasmus nevertheless finds much truth in the notion that life is a pageant, a drama in which men play their various parts. Like the Stoic, the actor in his obedience to the director submits himself to the world's order. Indeed the humanist found ample warrant for his use of the figure in the Stoics, who themselves found it a ready means for expressing their moral imperative of conformity to the scheme of things. As M. Jacquot points out,[4] Epictetus employed the figure more than once, noting especially that God judges the actor's performance, and the author of *Damon and Pythias* (1571), Robert Edwards, thought Pythagoras the source of the metaphor. Sir Thomas More compares a commonwealth to a play in his *Utopia*. Some of the humanists thus acknowledged indebtedness for the figure to the early physical philosophers, the Stoics, and the satirists.

But others acknowledged other sources, and it certainly reached the Renaissance writers by still other routes. In Philip Mornay's *A Woorke concerning the Trewnesse of the Christian Religion*, translated by Sir Philip Sidney and Arthur Golding and published in 1587, we discover that Plotinus was the source.

Having described Plotinus' ladder of Being, Mornay has this to say:

> Unto the ordinarie complaynt concerning the prosperitie of the wicked, and the aduersitie of the vertuous, he [Plotinus] answereth that the prosperitie of the wicked is but a Stage-play, and the aduersitie of the godly as a gaming exercise, wherein they bee tyed to a streight dyet, that they may win the prize for which they contend.[5]

So Plotinus (and Mornay, Sidney, and Golding) would account for adversity and the existence of evil in the world by way of the metaphor: the world is a stage whereon we play our role as if it were a game to see whether we can win the prize of salvation. On it we are tested by God, the director, as were Job or Jonah. A new emphasis comes into the metaphor here.

In another connection, Mornay, still deriving his explanation from the Neoplatonic source, gives the point thorough treatment, saying that God as director of the play allows the wicked to walk at large upon the stage of the world and the godly to lie in prison, yet can provide also for the punishment of the one and the triumph of the other. Furthermore, "When a Tragedie is played afore thee, thou art not offended at any thing which thou hearest," for the playgoer trusts the director's art to bring the play to a just and proper conclusion.

> How much more oughtest thou to resreine [restreine ?] thy mislyking, if thou considerest that the world is a kind of Stageplay, conueied to a certeine end by a most excellent maker: And what an excellent order wouldest thou see there, if thou mightest behold all the ages and alterations thereof as in a Comedie, all in one day: yea or but the successe of some one onely Nation for an hundred yeres, which were lesse than the interuiewe of two Seruants in a Comedy.[6]

The actors in the play, no more than the audience, know the end. They too must trust the director and the author. If they could all see and know the end, they would not only understand divine justice but be able to observe clearly the divine plan. They might also find out the nature of human freedom or the extent of the freedom of the will, for a little later Mornay relates it to the dramatic scheme of things. We are told that "God . . . guydeth all things to the performance of his will, . . . the things indewed with sence, by their appetites, and the reasonable things, by their willes; . . ." and these which have wills "yeeld freely to obedience by gentle handling" and thus render God's glory the greater, being not haled about by force and compulsion.[7]

Now, as Professor Roy W. Battenhouse has pointed out, before Mornay, Ficino had picked up the metaphor in his translation of Plotinus; [8] and as M. Jacquot has shown, Ficino used the figure in his translation of Plato's *Laws*,[9] thus deriving it from Plato himself. Indeed the opening sentence of Pico's *Oratio de hominis dignitate* (1486) contains the commonplace: "in haec quasi mundana scaena." It thus became especially popular among the Neoplatonists of the sixteenth century. And it is out of this Neoplatonic tradition, now merging with the Christian, that John Colet comments on the *Hierarchies* of Dionysius the Areopagite, finding that it is through a poetic fiction, "a sort of stage, a rude show, and indistinct representation," [10] that one shall understand theology, which is the revelation of the divine. The *Hierarchies* themselves are to him a cosmic stage by which sort of fiction the human understanding is accommodated to the divine. By such figures of speech the Neoplatonists were always to work, and it takes little imagination to see their method as an extension of Plato's doctrine of ideas. The very figure itself was to be found in his *Laws*. If the world of substance is in truth only a shadow of the real, then it may easily be thought of as a play, a pageant, only a representation of ultimate reality. Man's struggle here to achieve the perfection by which he may return to that from which he came, moreover, forms the conflict of that drama; it is a testing of man provided by the gods. To anticipate a little, one finds perhaps the noblest expression of the concept of God as cosmic dramatist in the Preface to Sir Walter

Ralegh's *History of the World* (pointed out by both Batten-house and Jacquot):

> God, who is the Author of all our tragedies, hath written out for vs, and appointed vs all the parts we play: and hath not in their distribution, beene partiall to the most mighty Princes of the world.[11]

And his poem *On the Life of Man* develops the figure fully, lik-ening the particulars of our lives to the theatre; our graves are, for example, "like drawn curtaynes when the play is done." And "Heauen the Iudicious sharpe spectator is, / That sits and markes still who doth act amisse." Professor Marjorie Hope Nicolson also notices that the Cambridge Platonist Henry More, of a much later time, employed as a favorite metaphor "God as the Great Dramatist," [12] especially in his *Divine Dialogues* (1668). The concept of God as producer is inherent in almost all uses of the figure, and it came early into the Christian tradition.

Neoplatonist or not, a seminal purveyor of the concept was St. Augustine. In *The City of God* he uses the metaphor, as M. Jacquot points out,[13] to demonstrate that each age of our life dies to the next, and every generation drives each of us to take his place on the stage of the world, a suggestion of Jaques's seven ages of man. Nor did St. Augustine stand alone among the Fathers of the Church in the use of this image. In his *Arte of Rhetorique* (1553) Thomas Wilson reminds us that "Among the learned men of the Church, no one vseth this figure more than *Chrisotome*, whose writings the rather seeme more pleasant and sweet." St. Chrysostom used the comparison at least three times, developing it fully, as M. Jacquot has shown, and always to the effect that our life is a tale and a dream as well as a play:

> Fabula quaedā est, & somniū vita: sicut enim in scena aulaeo sublato varietates dissoluntuur, & omnia coruscante luce somnia auolāt: ita nūc quoque cōsummatione veniēte tam cōmuni, qua vniuscuiusque, dissoluuntur & euanescunt.[14]

His two other uses are much the same as this one. Getting thus early into the Christian tradition, the figure served well as a means for explaining why evil exists in the world and for accepting the *contemptus mundi* and the transitory nature of this life. It was to suggest, however transmuted, Prospero's conclusion to his memorable comment on this insubstantial pageant, perhaps even Hamlet's "to sleep, perchance to dream."

Professor Baldwin thinks, however, that Shakespeare, no student of ancient philosophy or of the Fathers' doctrine, was rather more directly dependent upon his school textbooks for his repetitions of the figure. In Barnaby Googe's translation of Palengenius' *Zodiacke of Life* (1565) it is given this expression:

> Wherefore if thou dost well discerne, thou shalt behold and sée
> This mortal lyfe that here you leade, a Pageant for to bee.
> The diuers partes therein declarde, the chaunging world to showe,
> The maskers are eche one of them with liuely breth that blowe.
> For almost euery man now is desguised from his kinde,
> And vnderneth a false pretence they sely soules doe blinde,
> So moue they Goddes aboue to laugh with toyes and trifles vayne,
> Which here in Pageants fond they passe while they do lyfe retayne.[15]

Baldwin thinks this passage came directly from Vives' *Satellitium* (1524) into Palengenius, but with an addition from the celebrated figure in Democritus' *Fragment*. And he thinks also that Shakespeare may well have had the whole from John Withals' *Little Dictionarie*, wherein it is copied, widely used in the grammar schools of the day. However that may be, by Shakespeare's day the figure through wide and varied usage had achieved aphoristic place in the language of the learned as a means for expressing a special sort of truth. It came down from the laughing philosopher and the classical satirists on the one side and the Platonists and Christian Fathers on the other to the Renaissance humanists and English schoolmasters. Its tone changed from one writer to another, and it took on different coloring and associations, but the basic concept remained: the world is a stage, all men are actors upon this stage, and God (or the gods, including Fortune) serves as author, director, and spectator, judging the performance of the actors and taking pleasure in the production.

But the new humanists were not content to let things be; they also added to and changed their metaphor. Roger Ascham, for example, says in *The Schoolmaster* (1563) that "The whole doctrine of Comedies and Tragedies is a perfite imitation of a faire liuelie painted picture of the life of euerie degree of man." [16] Here the figure is turned about: if the world is a stage, then the stage becomes a little world, and we are now getting into the realm of dramatic criticism. The play, however, should present all degrees of men and in a lively picture, a moving pageant, as it were. Thus the basic structure of the Elizabethan play is suggested.

A further elaboration of the notion of the world as stage is given in the remarkable *Theatrum Mundi* of Pierre Boaistuau, translated into English by John Alday and published as early as 1566. In the "Epistle Dedicatorie" addressed to the Archbishop of Glasgow and ambassador of Scotland to France, Boaistuau writes:

> and if we will be equal Iudges in humane actiõs: what else is this world but a Theatre? Whereas some playe or vse the state of Artificers and men of base condition and calling, & others do represēt the state of Kings, Dukes, Earls, Marquises, Barons, and others, constituted in dignities. And neverthelesse whē al these haue cast of their visards & masking garments, and that death commeth and maketh an end of this bloudie tragedy, thē they acknowledge themselues al to be mortal men. And then the Lord that is in heauen laugheth at their foolish enterprizes & vanities (as the Prophet Dauid witnesseth) but with such a fearefull and terrible laughter, that hee maketh us tremble and quake for feare, and the earth also. [17]

Here particularization has taken place: all orders and degrees of men must appear; the Lord laughs not merely at man but at man's enterprizes and vanities.

Similarly the remarks of "The Printer to the Reader" tell us of the famous theatre built by "Adrian the Emperour" in Rome, contrasting it with the theatre which is this book, made by a faithful Christian, in which "thou maist see and beholde all the universall world." In it "thou maist first see thy selfe what thou art, and what miseries all humane creatures are subject to." Next, the reader may see the clergy and then the governors and magistrates of the world, then the lawyers and merchants, then the fathers and mothers, and finally the procession of man's whole life as he passes from cradle to grave.[18] Here is an outline of the degrees of society and the occupations of men. At the center is the individual, the microcosm ("thy selfe what thou art"), shown as he passes through the several ages of his life, such as Jaques gives us. Moreover, in some anonymous verses "In praise of the booke" the world is not only "Most like a Theater, a game or gameplace if ye will," but a place where one "aloft in princely state may be brought down" by fortune.[19] And finally in the fourth book of the *Theatrum* man, a creature endowed with freedom of will and hence corruptible, is subject to many miseries by which his pride is checked. His early life especially is a testing and a trial, and his ability to pass the tests and stand the trials, to act his role properly on the great stage through God's grace, may bring him salvation *ad gloriam Dei.*[20] Thus in Boaistuau's work the metaphor is fully wrought out and elaborated. Most, if not all, of its facets are examined, and new particulars are added. Besides, the title itself indicates much.[21] The soul-struggle of man is especially evident.

It is also evident in John Davies of Hereford's *Microcosmos* (1603), wherein the soul of every man is a little theatre. Davies calls us to

> View this *VVorlds Stage*, and they that play thereon,
> And see if thou canst one espie,

> That plaies the *wanton* being wo-begon;
> Or in *VVealth* wall'wing, plaies not the VVanton.

And he ends the stanza next following with what Bacon would call the blessing of the New Testament:

> *Affliction* thus to God doth Soules *indeere*,
> When welfare makes them to the Devill deere.[22]

In a similar, slightly earlier work Sir John Davies associates the figure with the three kinds of soul, observing in his *Nosce Teipsum* (1599) that men, in passing through the evolutionary process from the vegetative (quickening to life in the womb) to the sensible (becoming aware of the world through the senses) and to the reasonable, are tested as they move ahead: "When he has pass'd some time upon the stage, / His *reason* then a little seems to wake." [23] Since he combines in himself all that is in the whole and since the whole is a theatre or stage, the individual human being must himself be a little theatre.

And we learn from a very popular courtesy book that God places this little world within the greater as a manifestation of His divine Providence. One finds in Pierre de la Primaudaye's *French Academie*, originally translated by Thomas Bowes (1586), an eloquent statement of the idea. After telling us that this world is like a school and also like a rich shop, he says it is likewise

> a temple, wherein there is no creature so little, but it is a similitude and resemblance of the creator thereof, to shew and manifest him vnto vs. In a word, it is a Theatre, where the diuine essence, his iustice, his prouidence, his loue, his wisdome haue their working by a wonderful vertue in euery creature, euen from the highest heauen to the center of the earth.[24]

Appearing in the "forespeech" to Part II, this passage serves to direct the reader to the *nosce teipsum* theme of the book. It makes clear God's scheme of things and sets forth the principle of the unity of all. It suggests that upon the stage of any theatre one may expect to see God's justice and providence worked out among men.

A repetition and another elaboration of the similitude appeared in the same year (1586) in *The Diamant of Devotion, Cut and Squared into Six Severall Points* by Abraham Fleming, one of the sources frequently cited for Jaques's speech. In Part I the reader finds that man was not placed in this world to stay; he is merely a traveler and sojourner in it:

> Heere we walke like plaiers uppon a stage, one representing the person of a king, another of a lorde, the third of a plowman, the fourth of an artificer, and so foorth, as the course and order of the interlude requireth; everie acte whereof being plaide, there is no more to doe, but open the gates and dismisse the assemblie. Even so fareth it with us; for what other thing is the compasse of the world, beautified with varietie of creatures, reasonable and unreasonable, but an ample and large theatre wherein all things are appointed to play their pageants, which when they have done, they die, and their glorie ceaseth.[25]

Fleming would thus insist on the representation of the various orders of society, and his use of the word "pageants" suggests he had in mind the cyclic drama and its immediate descendants, a connection well worth noting.

Again in the same year, Spenser says that his friend Gabriel Harvey "sitting like a looker-on / Of this worldes stage, doest note with critique pen / The sharpe dislikes of each condition" and neither fawns for favor nor fears reprehension. Like a god, Harvey sits outside the fret and turmoil of the world-drama and looks on. And later, in the *Amoretti* Spenser speaks similarly of his beloved, who "Of this worlds theatre in which we stay" like a spectator sits beholding him "that all the pageants play."

In the lovely litany of *Summer's Last Will and Testament* Thomas Nashe summarizes several implications of the figure in few words, emphasizing especially the *contemptus mundi* or the *Weltschmerz* motif:

Autumn hath all the summer's fruitful treasure.
 Haste therefore each degree
 To welcome destiny:
 Heaven is our heritage,
 Earth but a player's stage;
 Mount we unto the sky.

Often the work of the less well-known writers reveals the fullest expression of a commonplace, if not the most unusual. As did Primaudaye, the devout Henry Lok includes all creatures as actors upon his stage of the world. His whole sonnet deserves quotation:

This stately stage where we players stande,
To represent the part to vs assignde,
Was built by God, that He might pleasure finde,
In beautie of the worke of His owne hand;
All creatures of the ayre, the sea and land,
Are players at His appointment of some thing,
Which to the world a proper vse may bring,
And may not breake assigned bownds or band:
Some do in ioy still forth His praises sing,
Some mourne and make their mone with heauy mind;
Some shew the frutes of Nature weake and blind,
Some shew how grace base sin away doth fling;
 God—like a king—beholds; Christ doth attire
 The plaiers with the shape, their states require.[26]

Lok places emphasis upon degree and order in his world theatre. Apparently all degrees must appear, and it is every creature's obligation to maintain his place, not to step out of character, as it were. The whole was built for the builder's pleasure, who like a king sits outside the action, enjoying and judging it; Christ, the activating force in the Godhead, is the producer. Yet the actors are all tested: some through false doctrine and wilfulness fail; others through diligence and effort, but not without grace, achieve salvation.

As one might expect, Geoffrey Goodman employs the metaphor as a means for explaining the fall of man.[27] And Bacon repeatedly refers to it.[28] Perhaps more important are John Donne's frequent references to it, the best known being that in *The Second Anniversary*. Here to lend universality to her character he speaks of Elizabeth Drury as an actor on the stage of the world:

> Shee to whom all this world was but a stage,
> Where all sat harkning how her youthful age
> Should be emploi'd, because in all she did,
> Some figure of the Golden time was hid.

And one of the *Holy Sonnets* (1617) links the metaphor of life's pilgrimage to that of life's drama: "This is my play's last scene; here heavens appoint / My pilgrimage's last mile." The linking suggests Bunyan's later treatment of the figure. But Donne states it far more elaborately in his sermon of March 24, 1616/17, preached at Paul's Cross:

> Hath God made this World his Theatre, *ut exhibeatur ludus deorum*, that man may represent God in his conversation; and wilt thou play no part? But think that thou wast made to pass thy time merrily, and to be the only spectator upon this Theatre? Is the world a great and harmonious Organ, where all parts are play'd, and all play parts; and must thou only sit idle and hear it? [29]

In the margin opposite this passage appears the name "Plato." Donne knew at least one source of the figure. Shortly thereafter he links up these two figures with others: the world is a "great Body" and man a member of that body, and on the next page he refers to man as a "link in God's Chain."

Discussing man's reluctance to leave this life, William Drummond in his *Cypresse Grove* (1623) remarks that perhaps what "anguisheth Thee most, is to haue this glorious Pageant of the World remoued from thee. . . ." [30] Sir Thomas Browne reflects in his *Religio Medici* (1635) that "The World to mee is but a dream or mock-show, and we all therein but Pantalones and Anticks. . . ." And later in the same work he says doomsday "shall include and comprehend all that went before it; wherein as in the last scene, all Actors must enter, to compleat and make up the Catastrophe of this great piece," [31] indicating thereby some knowledge of the structure of the Elizabethan play. Herrick, who alludes to the figure several times, in one place rings a notable change. In one of the Noble Numbers entitled *Good Friday: Rex Tragicus, or Christ Going to the Cross*, he writes:

> The Crosse shall be Thy Stage; and Thou shalt there
> The spacious field have for Thy Theater.
> Thou art that Roscius, and that markt-out man,
> That must this day act the Tragedian,
> To wonder and affrightment.

Here the greatest of heroes furnishes the Christian spectator the required katharsis. The nations may look upon the suffering god as he acts out the cosmic passion. For Phineas Fletcher the world stage is also a tragic one. In the *Purple Island* (1633) he comments

> How like's the world unto a tragick stage:
> Where every changing scene the actours change;
> Some subjects crouch and fawn; some reigne and rage:
> And strange new plots bring scenes as new & strange
>   Till most are slain; the rest their parts have done.
>   (Canto I. 37)

For George Daniel

> The World's a tottring Stage; and Mankind All
> Is but one Antike Individuall;
> From time to Time, the Same; now Age can boast
> The better Interlude.[32]

And in elaborating the figure, he says that in this "Mockshow" man is a degenerate being and the play in which he acts a tragedy which hinders "Natures first made Harmonie." Perhaps he has Goodman in mind.

John Milton alludes to the figure at least four times, the earliest being in *The Passion*, where he relates that poem to his *Nativity Ode*, indicating that he consciously set the action of the *Ode* upon the stage of the world:

> Ere-while of Music and Etherial mirth,
> Wherewith the stage of Air and Earth did ring,
> And joyous news of heav'nly Infant's birth,
> My muse with Angels did divide to sing.

At the end of his arguments in *Colasterion* he wishes that "since the life of man is likn'd to a Scene," his actions in his play might be mixed only with such as are actors of tragedy, not wth "Clowns and Vices." In the *Second Defence* he writes of Charles's having made his exit from the stage of the world, and in his *Familiar Letters* he writes to Richard Jones about "that theatre of the world on which you have enter'd" as a testing place.[33] One might expect Milton to think in terms of the world stage, on which he deliberately set the action of his greatest poems.

But one might not expect John Bunyan to think in such terms. He maintains, however, in his *Advice to Sufferers* "that a man when he suffereth for Christ, is set upon a hill, upon a stage, as in a theatre to play a part for God in the world." Actors in a play, he says, are more desirous of bringing credit to their master, their art, and to themselves than in ordinary life, for every eye is upon them. So with men in this life if they would realize that God is looking upon them. "Yea, he laugheth, as being pleased to see a good behaviour attending the trial of the innocent."[34] And in his poem called *Prison Meditations* he writes:

> Here [on earth] we can see how all men play
> Their parts, as on a stage,
> How good men suffer for God's way
> And bad men at them rage.[35]

It seems a far cry from Plotinus to Ficino to John Bunyan, but it is a clear one: the same figure has for all of them the same meanings and value. God the artist, stage-builder, and producer, puts on his cosmic drama and tests his creature, man. In this way they explain the presence of evil in the world and the suffering of the innocent. In these the ancient satirical laughter of the gods of Democritus becomes the joyous laughter of the Christian God as he watches the triumph of his god-like creature.

So far it has been my purpose to demonstrate from non-dramatic literature the fact and the nature of the commonplace, to sketch briefly its history, and to indicate the meanings associated with it. M. Jacquot's thorough work has made it unnecessary to treat in detail the earlier uses or to list a great many of them. I believe I have presented enough instances, however, to show that it was a metaphor quite as widespread as the Great Chain of Being, quite as fully developed and far more frequently used.

But my concern is with its impact upon the structure of the Elizabethan play. However varied its meanings and however widespread its appearance in the writings of others, we must be sure the dramatists were in some degree at least guided in the shaping of their plays by the concept of the world as stage.

As I have already indicated, they did know it. They referred to it in their non-dramatic works as well as in their plays. In the prefatory poems for Thomas Heywood's *An Apology for Actors* (1612) Arthur Hopton and John Taylor say that upon the stage, as in a mirror of the world, one may see all degrees and professions of men. Heywood in his own preliminary poem gives one of the fullest and most important statements of the figure. By it, one gathers, he and his contemporaries were guided in the writing of their plays:

> THe world's a Theater, the earth a Stage
> Which God, and nature doth with Actors fill   { So compared
> Kings haue their entrance in due equipage,   { by the Fathers.
> And some their parts play well and others ill.
> The best no better are (in this Theater,)

Where euery humor's fitted in his kinde,
This a true subiect acts, and that a Traitor,
The first applauded, and the last confin'd
This plaies an honest man, and that a knaue
A gentle person this, and he a clowne
One man is ragged, and another braue.
All men haue parts, and each man acts his owne.

Here follows a long list of the kinds of characters to be found in plays, the various degrees and conditions of men, from the wanton to the soldier, sailor, shepherd, and the rest, after which Heywood comments on the nature of this world theatre:

If then the world a Theater present,
As by the roundnesse it appeares most fit,
Built with the starre-galleries of hye ascent,
In which Iehoue doth as spectator sit.
And chief determiner to applaud the best,
And their indeuours crowne with more than merit.
But by their euill actions doomes the rest,
To end disgrac't whilst other praise inherit.
  He that denyes then Theaters should be
  He may as well deny a world to me.[36]

Devout and learned man that he was, Heywood notices in the margin that the Fathers had made the comparison and themselves thought of this world as a theatre. Perhaps he had Chrysostom particularly in mind. Later we shall see how the figure became a shaping force in the creation of his plays and of those of other dramatists as well. Frequently they did little more than allude to it; for, aside from the fact that the subject matter of a play does not often lend itself to the discussion of dramatic theory or theatrical performance, the allusion, being commonplace, was sufficient.

And yet Shakespeare managed to state the metaphor or allude to it directly at least fourteen times in his plays and once in his sonnets.[37] Of these Jaques's reference is best known. In *As You Like It* he picks up the Duke's allusion and elaborates it

with the ages of man, another commonplace already associated
with the world as stage by Chrysostom and others. Familiar as
the passage is, it still deserves quotation, at least in part:

> *Duke S.* Thou seest we are not all alone unhappy.
> This wide and universal theatre
> Presents more woeful pageants than the scene
> Wherein we play in.
> *Jaq.*   All the world's a stage,
> And all the men and women merely players.
> They have their exits and their entrances,
> And one man in his time plays many parts,
> His acts being seven ages.
>
> (II.vii.136–43)

Then follows the familiar description of the seven ages—infant,
schoolboy, lover, soldier, justice, the "pantaloon," and finally
doddering second childhood. Shakespeare here notes the pageantry, the many roles to be played, and the universality of the
whole. In *The Merchant of Venice* he had already made off-
hand but revealing allusion to the figure, in which Antonio had
told Gratiano (I.i.77–79) that he regarded the world "but as the
world," a stage on which every man plays a part, his a sad one.
Gratiano, agreeing, asks that he in contrast may play the fool.
That the world is not reality, only an imitation of reality (that it
is the Neoplatonic God's art), is more than suggested.

In *Henry IV*, Part II, Northumberland, to be echoed later
by Ulysses, attacks the age in which he lives as one where order
is lost and chaos come again; and he associates the world with
the stage, a place where order should prevail:

> *North.*   Let order die!
> And let this world no longer be a stage
> To feed contention in a ling'ring act;
> But let one spirit of the first-born Cain
> Reign in all bosoms, that, each heart being set
> On bloody courses, the rude scene may end,
> And darkness be the burier of the dead!
>
> (I.i.154–60)

Cain, the symbol of disorder, the ancient and basic evil, is here the prototype of all villainy as it occurs upon the world-stage.

Among Shakespeare's remaining allusions that in *The Tempest* is the most memorable and informative, as M. Jacquot has noted. Speaking to Ferdinand, whom he has just tested severely, Prospero describes the masque he as cosmic dramatist has produced, punning upon "globe" and emphasizing the pageantry of the drama, its universal nature, and its Neoplatonic quality— this world the divine *objet d'art*.

> Our revels now are ended. These our actors,
> As I foretold you, were all spirits and
> Are melted into air, into thin air;
> And, like the baseless fabric of this vision,
> The cloud-capp'd towers, the gorgeous palaces,
> The solemn temples, the great globe itself,
> Yea, all which it inherit, shall dissolve,
> And, like this insubstantial pageant faded,
> Leave not a rack behind. We are such stuff
> As dreams are made on, and our little life
> Is rounded with a sleep.
>   (IV.i.148–58)

Thus the world we call reality, like the pageant of the playhouse, shall fade away. The ultimate reality lies with the spirits fled, and we like them will find it elsewhere, being such stuff as dreams are made on.

One further reference reveals still another meaning in the figure. Coriolanus, his mother having dissuaded him from destroying his native Rome, cries out,

> What have you done? Behold the heavens do ope,
> The gods look down, and this unnatural scene
> They laugh at.
>   (V.iii.183–85)

He is here thinking of the gods as spectators and directors of the world's drama and the testers of men. From their point of view

Coriolanus has failed the test and made himself a laughingstock. The gods create the actors, give them their roles with freedom to play as they will, whether comedy or tragedy, and judge the performance.

These references are sufficient to show how fully aware of the various meanings of the metaphor Shakespeare was. As indicated in his other allusions to it, he assumes that his audience was likewise aware of them.[38] The pageant of life, the testing of man, the gods as spectators and producers watching the private, national, and international scene emerge in which are men of all degrees, orders, and professions, the world as an orderly stage on which is represented every kind of scene—all are implied, suggested, or stated outright.

Perhaps less frequently, though no less fully, other dramatists make use of the metaphor. One of the most interesting because of the classical reference in it is found in Chapman's *The Revenge of Bussy d'Ambois*. In the first scene, Guise, speaking of the court characters and their doings, says that he "would have these things / Brought upon stages." To which Clermont replies that nowadays nothing is "brought upon stages / But puppetry." Then Baligny replies, "Why, is not all the world esteem'd a stage?" And Clermont answers at some length about the function of the stage:

> Yes, and right worthily; and stages too
> Have a respect due to them, if but only,
> For what the good Greek moralist says of them.
> (I.i.332–34)

The Greek moralist turns out to be Epictetus from whose *Discourses* (IV.vii.13) he adapts a passage in which the actor is called on to show how a man proud of greatness or riches is but a man "fray'd with poverty and lowness." The actor on the stage, he contends, is made to show what small cause such man has "to be so blown up." Thus the world-stage becomes a moral agent for the correction of human pride, as it was for Coriolanus.[39]

Although the titles of Middleton's *A Mad World, My Masters* and *The World Tost at Tennis* both imply the world as their proper stage, it is not till one comes to his and William Rowley's *A Fair Quarrel* (1615?–1617) that one finds the notion set forth explicitly. In his dedicatory letter to Robert Gray, Rowley elaborates the notion:

> yet if it be (as some philosophers have left behind 'em), that this megacosm, this great world, is no more than a stage, where everyone must act his part, you shall of necessity have many partakers, some long, some short, some indifferent, all some; whilst indeed the players themselves have the least part of it, for I know few that have lands (which are a part of the world), and therefore no grounded men; but howsoever they serve for mutes, happily they must wear good clothes for attendance, yet all have exits, and must all be stript in the tiring-house (viz. the grave), for none must carry anything out of the stock.

Thus the analogy is elaborated: if the great world is a megacosm, the stage must be an epitome of the great world. Moreover, in Middleton's *A Game at Chess* (1624) the chessboard becomes the stage on which the international drama is enacted. Indeed, the White Queen's Pawn alludes directly to the world as stage and continues her metaphor throughout some eighteen lines, discussing especially the necessity for decorum in handling the characters:

> The world's a stage on which all parts are play'd;
> You'd think it most absurd to see a devil
> Presented there not in a devil's shape,
> Or, wanting one, to send him out in yours.
> (V.ii.19–22)

And in his poem *The Blacke Booke* Middleton has "Lucifer ascending, as Prologue to his own play," saying,

> Now hell is landed here upon the earth,
> When Lucifer, in limbs of burning gold,

> Ascends this dusty theatre of the world,
> To join his powers.

Later he returns to the same figure:

> And now that I have vaulted up so high
> Above the stage-rails of this earthen globe,
> I must turn actor and join companies
> To share my comic sleek-ey'd villaines.

And for Middleton this world-stage is man's testing place, where Lucifer plays the villain, trying always to seduce man from good and bring about his fall. Throughout his plays Middleton seems constantly aware of the metaphor and deliberate in following it as a principle of composition.[40]

Although Ben Jonson alludes to or implies the world as stage, or the stage as world, in a number of places, he is never more explicit than in one of the Host's speeches in *The New Inn* (1629):

> If I be honest, and that all the cheat
> Be of myself, in keeping this Light Heart,
> Where, I imagine all the world's a play:
> The state, and all men's affairs, all passages
> Of life, to spring new *scenes;* come in, go out,
> And shift, and vanish; and if I have got
> A seat to sit at ease here, in mine inn,
> To see the comedy; and laugh, and chuck
> At the variety and throng of humours
> And dispositions, that come justling in,
> And out still, as they drove hence another;
> Why will you envy me my happiness?
>
> (I.i)

Goodstock, the Host, would sit like a god on the outside of the action, look at the cosmic spectacle played out in his inn, and laugh at men's follies. He follows the satirical tradition of Democritus and Lucian, as one might expect Jonson's characters to do. In the Induction to *The Magnetic Lady* the playhouse itself becomes the microcosm. It is conceived of as a shop where plays are sold, and the apprentice asks the audience what they lack, offering them any kind of character they want: "Waiting-women, parasites, knights, captains, courtiers, lawyers." The play is designed to present in its pageant of life all degrees and conditions of men. The audience are thought of as the whole body of mankind, Probee and Damplay being their representatives. Not only are the inn in *The New Inn* and the stage in *The Magnetic Lady* (1632) chosen as little worlds, but so are the fair in *Bartholomew Fair* (1614) and the hoax world of London in *Epicoene* (1609).[41] *Every Man in His Humor* and *Every Man Out* by their very titles make the world their stage.

The Duchess of Malfi, tortured by what purports to be the severed hand of her husband and then the dead bodies of husband and children, is comforted in bitter words by soul-torn Bosola and asked, since she is a Christian, not to despair but to bear her grief and live. To his counsel she replies that he might as well persuade one who has been broken on the wheel to have his bones set so that he may be executed a second time. Then she comments: "I account this world a tedious theatre, / For I do play a part in 't 'gainst my will" [42] (IV.i. 82–83). Her mortal life is a testing.

In Fletcher's *Thierry & Theodoret*, Thierry grieves over his impotence, throws himself on the ground in despair, and exclaims:

Oh, such a scene of grief,
And so set down, the world the stage to act on,
May challenge a tragedian better practiced
Than I am to express it! For my cause
Of passion is so strong, and my performance
So weak, that though the part be good, I fear
The ill acting of it will defraud it of
The poor reward it may deserve, men's pity.
                                        (IV.ii)

Thierry is conscious of his role in the world-tragedy and fears he is incapable of rousing the pity of mankind required of the tragedian.[43]

One of the fuller statements of the metaphor within a play is found in Massinger's *The Roman Actor* (1626). The actors Paris, Aesophus, and Latinus are apprehended and brought before the Senate for trial on a charge of treason. Paris, the tragedian, makes the defense. Aretinus charges him with speaking out too boldly, asking whether he thinks he is on the stage. To his question, Paris replies:

> The whole world being one [a stage]
> This place is not exempted, and I am
> So confident in the iustice of our cause,
> That I could wish *Caesar* (in whose great name
> All kings are comprehended) sate as judge,
> To hear our Plea, and then determine of vs.
> (I.iii.50–55)

Later he says that philosophers present cold precepts, seldom read, about the nature of virtue; but these do not "swell the veins with emulation / To be both good and great, equal to that / Which is presented on our Theaters?" (I.iii.81–83)[44] The world theatre is both a place of judgment and a place to persuade men to virtuous deeds.

Among the numerous other examples is that found in the strange German version of *Hamlet, Tragoedia Der Bestrafte Brudermord oder: Prinz Hamlet aus Daennenmark*, played in Dresden as early as 1626. Justifying the art of the actor, Hamlet instructs Corambus to treat the players well, for

> If they are treated well in one place, they cannot praise it enough in another; for their theatre is a little world wherein they represent nearly all that happens in the great world. They revive the old forgotten histories, and set before us good and bad examples; they publish abroad the justice and praiseworthy government of princes; they punish vices and exalt virtues;

they praise the good, and show how tyranny is punished. (III.ix) [45]

Anything that happens in the world may also happen in the microcosm, and what is represented is for the edification of the onlookers: histories are presented to furnish examples of good and bad; thus the punishment of wickedness and tyranny is published and the proper use made of the story of the past. The players become a moral force in the state.

Henry Chettle is as conscious of this force as the writer of the German *Hamlet*. Hoffman says at the end of the first scene of his *Tragedy* that the scene has been but the prologue to his play: his life and deeds, his revenge, constitute a play. Or one might cite the same concept in the much earlier *Book of Sir Thomas More* (1594-1595?), in which Sir Thomas, as he goes to the block, observes that his life has been a play and that he has now finished the role prepared for him. The playgoer will think he has acted well (Scene xvii). In the Induction to *The First Part of Antonio and Mellida* (1599?) Alberto tells Antonio that on the stage of this world every man must play at least two parts. And in Act II of Dekker's *The Noble Spanish Soldier* (S.R. 1631) Balthazar describes the battle he has fought in terms of the stage, with the cannon furnishing the music, the field the stage, the Furies the actors, blood and vengeance the scene, and death the story. And toward the end of the piece, he tells the King that he thinks the great day is really a new play wherein "all men are but Actors" and where the King, if he should be out of his part, it were a lamentable business. (II.i.66-70; V.iv.27-32).[46] Among the Elizabethan dramatists, then, the figure was widely known and frequently referred to—even in their plays.

In Spain, as one would expect, Calderon, later than the Elizabethans, found the figure fundamental to his art, especially in his *autos sacramentales*. M. Jacquot has shown its obvious function in *El Gran Teatro del Mundo* and in *La Vida es Sueño* and says, "Le personnage du Monde figure dans une vingtaine d'*autos* de

Calderón où le monde est représenté tantôt comme un théâtre, tantôt une prison, un labyrinthe, etc." [47] And in the secular *La Vida es Sueño* the scheme is almost as obvious as in the *autos*, which are really belated moralities designed for the feast of Corpus Christi. The metaphor is used by Lope de Vega and in France by such dramatists as Georges de Scudéry and Corneille, especially in their plays within plays. So dramatists other than English and later than the Elizabethans not only show their knowledge of the figure but make it useful in the writing of their plays.

Further multiplication of instances—and the multiplication would be easy—will add little that is new, if indeed anything at all. The playwrights themselves, no less than the ancient philosophers and rhetoricians, the Fathers and the Neoplatonists, and the Elizabethan poets and prose writers refer to the world as a stage and life as a play. The figure had become a part of their thinking. They allude to it frequently and often quite casually, as if it conveyed a generally accepted truth; and the playwrights give good evidence that, with all its cluster of associated meanings, it was a force in the shaping of their plays.

It was likewise a basic force in the shaping of the playhouses in which the drama was produced. If the world is a stage, then the converse would be expected: the stage would represent the world. And so it did. The Elizabethan dramatists and theatergoers, we can be sure, recognized the playhouse as a little world. The "Cockpit or wooden O" of the Prologue of *Henry V* comes at once to mind, and, as Professor Ribner and others have noted, the Globe was so named not merely because of the sign the builder gave it. It was indeed a place where Anthony might almost literally light up "The little O, the earth," and where his voice "propertied / As all the tuned spheres . . . might shake the Orbe."

If we can be at all sure of anything about the public theaters —about the Curtain, the Rose, the Red Bull, the Globe, and the others—it is that each had a "scaffold," two or three galleries, and a "heavens" over the scaffold. Out of the floor of the scaffold hell could and did break loose, and from the heavens could, but less frequently did, descend angels or gods. Upon the scaffold, in the houses or the battlements represented at the rear and upon the upper levels moved man, the actor, the lesser microcosm—a creature walking between heaven and hell. And however puny a person, whether Christian or not, he might expect on this stage to face the tests and trials the warfaring Christian usually faced. We have learned a great deal about the various parts of the stage from the painstaking work of the historians; and though the details yet remain much in doubt, we can be reasonably sure of the general structure of theatre and stage. Contemporary references are sufficient for that, and several have already been noticed which reflect the notion (almost all imply it) that the world is a stage and that the stage represents a world. It is implicit especially in the passage cited from *The Tempest*, one cited from *The Revenge of Bussy d'Ambois*, one from the Induction to Jonson's *Magnetic Lady*, and one from Heywood's poem prefixed to his *Apology for Actors*. In the *Apology* itself is another, fuller statement, his oft-cited account of the theatre he says was built in Rome by Julius Caesar. Thomas Nashe has a similar account in *The Unfortunate Traveler*. Since neither Nashe nor Heywood seems to have been in Rome, we can be pretty sure they are describing, not what someone had seen in Rome, but what both had seen at the Rose or the Globe or the Swan or some other public theatre. It has a "heavens," he says "(where upon any occasion their Gods descended) which (heavens) were geometrically supported by a Giant-like Atlas, whom the poets for his Astrology, feign to bear heauen on his shoulders. . . ." The description is of the very sign of the Globe Theatre! Later he says, "In briefe, in that little compasse were comprehended the perfect modell of the firmament, the whole frame of the heauens, with all the grounds of Astronomical coniecture." In this theatre, or on its stage, sat the emperor, the nobles, the soldiers, the multitude, every man according to his degree. It is a place for presenting all that goes on in the world and a place where everyone may come to see what the world affords. Whatever special shape any one of them had, the theatres of Elizabethan London were so designed as to provide a place where the earth and its vast surroundings could be realized and its orderly arrangements viewed. Even Mr. Leslie Hotson in that strangest of all studies of the Elizabethan theatre grants that, whatever else it may have been, this stage was one "embracing . . . the 'World' or 'Court' for the trial of man's soul." [48]

And the critic Mr. Hotson chooses as chief adversary, paradoxically, comes to much the same conclusion. Approaching the subject of the Elizabethan stage from an entirely different point of view, Professor George Kernodle shows that the medieval and Renaissance painters were able to unify their complex paintings by placing their subjects before architectural screens, usually one or more arches, remarkably like the doors of the palace that stood at the back of the Greek stage.[49] Interiors as such do not appear in their art: the viewer sees the interior from the outside, or he may see the outside from an interior. The exterior is always represented. Let us supply a familiar example. The Nativity was often painted with the front wall of the stable open, the roof showing from outside and the landscape and background well accounted for, the heavenly hosts singing from the clouds, the shepherds and the Magi worshiping from within and without, and the devils slinking off to hell below. Sometimes God the Father sits benign above. Now, Professor Kernodle maintains that the stage illustrates this same concept of art, followed much the same pattern, presenting especially both exterior and interior. The particularized ranges outward in its setting to the infinite. If he is correct, then the cosmic nature of the Elizabethan stage is apparent, as it was in the art that preceded it. What is more, the central figures of the plays, no less than the central figures of the paintings, are related to the whole—to the room, to the street, to the garden, to the city where the house is located, to the state with its international surroundings, to the earth and hell below, and to the heavens above with the good God reigning there. And one can realize at once on this stage that the characters who play here are *at once, at one and the same time,* present in each of these places. But Professor Kernodle is not directly interested in the world as stage and is never quite explicit.

Professor Francis Fergusson is, however, explicit on the point. In his essay on *Hamlet,* he says that "The Elizabethan stage itself, that central mirror of the life of the time, was a symbolic representation of this traditional cosmos: it was taken both as the physical and the metaphysical 'scene' of man's life." [50] But at this point Fergusson is much interested in proving that *Hamlet* is a ritualistic play. (Since T. S. Eliot read Miss Jessie Weston, many a critic has seen the Grail.) He thinks of the stage as especially symbolic. Now, any sort of stage is symbolic in that it represents something. And it may represent realistically and in much detail, or it may suggest merely and make use of only a few conventional details. As best I can judge, the Elizabethan stage was as realistic as it could easily be in the representation of what it was pretty obviously designed to represent: a little world where men could see themselves represented, as in Sidney's speaking picture, strutting, fretting, torn and tested, but always maintaining their proper place in the world and their proper relationship with the whole of creation. And whether or not we think of the stage as a "round," as Mr. Hotson does, or as a conventionalized scaffold with background arches, as Professor Kernodle does, nothing less than a little world is here represented. Whatever its shape, it was so designed as to enable the playwright to relate the events that take place in his play to the world as a whole.

And this had been true of the mystery plays and the moralities of earlier times. In the mystery plays the series of pageants showed the story of the trial and salvation of humanity in time and space, set within the framework of the divine and the eternal. In the moralities the representative of all the race, as an individual, consciously and designedly plays out his temporal existence on the cosmic stage, tested as a Christian and ultimately brought to salvation. In the mystery plays, scenes are often localized, but the whole series of scenes taken together spread themselves from Eden to Jerusalem, to Bethlehem, to Egypt, to Mt. Sinai, to Rome, enough places to represent the world. In the moralities, the place is seldom so localized: heaven is above, the earth below, and hell beneath. With such settings and places popular drama, moralities and mysteries, continued through Shakespeare's lifetime, played no doubt at times on platforms in the inn yards.

It was perhaps not altogether because of the physical inheritance from the inn yard or the bear garden or the need for daylight that the pit of the Elizabethan public playhouse went roofless. One may find ample reason for the shape in the basic theories of art and drama of its past—and of its own time. If the stage was so designed as to represent the world, and if the play acted upon it represented action as wide as life itself, indicating in this action the Elizabethan concept of the cosmos, then we have something more than a clue to the shape and the shaping force of the Elizabethan play. On this basis we may the better explain the disregard for classical precepts and practices such as the mixture of tragic and comic, or the better realize the encompassing actions of the plays, or the better account for the remarkable amount of pageantry and ritual in them, or explain why all estates and degrees of men are found in almost all plays, or why the scenes of any one play, often quite indefinitely indicated, may reach from heaven to hell or be scattered over the face of the earth, or why the motif of testing the Christian hero is so prevalent in both tragedy and comedy. These explanations will be offered in the remaining chapters of this work.

TWO

Encompassing Actions

SOME EXPLANATION of the world order as the Elizabethans knew it is then necessary to our discussion of the structure of Elizabethan drama. If we think of the plays as contrived from a conception of men living in an ordered universe, themselves a part of that order, if we think of the plays as designed to present men in their various degrees, representative of social orders and occupations upon this universal stage, we may begin to discover a design hitherto not generally observed. Elizabethan plays were not constructed to set forth highly selected events cut off in time and space from all other events and specially contrived with a few carefully selected characters (as in *Antigone,* say, or in *Ghosts*); on the contrary, they were designed to set forth a series of events in relation to all preceding events and all events to come in the ever-moving pageant of time. The presenters, choruses, and speakers of soliloquies indicate as much. The search was for the greater order and unity, however much to some it might seem to be breaking up, and the model was the cosmic plan.

That plan, moreover, was pretty widely if not universally recognized. Writers kept their world picture in mind as they wrote, their notion of the scheme of things, and they believed that such schemes did exist. The vertical metaphor of the Great Chain of Being was not destroyed or twisted or greatly blurred by the horizontal metaphor of a series of corresponding planes. In fact, the two were merely different ways of envisioning the same idea. And the latter illustrates best for us the enveloping actions or encircling forces or "plots" in the plays. Drawing upon Ulysses' famous speech on order and degree in *Troilus and Cressida* as an indication of the correspondence of macrocosm and commonwealth, Professor Tillyard says that "The different planes were the divine and angelic, the universe or macrocosm, the commonwealth or body politic, man or the microcosm, and the lower creation." [1] He adds that Shakespeare must have been thoroughly familiar with this network of correspondences. (And if Shakespeare, then the other playwrights of the time.) In *Shakespeare's History Plays* he comments also that "when Shakespeare deals with the concrete facts of English history he never forgets the principle of order behind all the terrible manifestations of disorder, a principle sometimes fulfilled, however imperfectly, even in the kingdoms of this world." [2] It is almost precisely the order thus indicated in the metaphor of the "corresponding planes" that one may observe in the plays; and it is the observance of this order, opposed and shattered at times, that furnishes a general plan for the plays and provides for each of them the spread of characters throughout the social spectrum. The concept was being questioned, it is true; the old order, the old metaphor, was passing. And perhaps the story of the Elizabethan drama is the story of its loss—the bitter allegory of *Troilus and Cressida*. Yet it is this scheme of things that enables the dramatist to set his action on the stage of the world and give it cosmic significance.

Miss Una Ellis-Fermor realized something of this significance. In her essay "The Nature of Plot in Drama," left unpublished at her death, she observed the phenomenon of what she called "plot perspective." In *Antony and Cleopatra*, for example, she found that "the grandeur of the chief characters, the multiplicity of figures and events witness to the vastness of its design and the cosmic imagery leads the imagination on to a universe beyond, into which the immediate world of the play seems limitlessly extended." [3] She found the same sort of limitless extension in *A Midsummer Night's Dream*, where the Theseus-Hippolyta plot holds all together and the Titania-Oberon plot suggests the relation of all events to timelessness itself. But Miss Ellis-Fermor went no further.

On the other hand, Theodore Spencer did go further. He showed that the Elizabethan dramatist, drawing upon the morality plays and the early interludes, saw man "in relation to truth." Bale's *King John* he thought a "very interesting example of how the particular and the general, the historical and the universal were brought together in the same dramatic structure." [4] As the chronicle plays rose and as the *dramatis personae* became less abstract or allegorical and more human, the dramatists "continued to think of the individual situation invariably in relation to some universal power." [5] The playwright consciously and regularly interweaves three domains: "the cosmos, the state, and the individual." [6] Even in such a human-centered play as *Romeo and Juliet*, Friar Laurence acts as chorus for the emotions of Romeo, and the prince of Verona as chorus to the feud: the Prince must keep order in the state and see that orderly processes of government are not destroyed by the quarrel of the Montagues and Capulets. And the quarrel, be it noted, ranges from the lowliest servants upward to the heads of households, ultimately involving the head of state. [7] And, I might add, outside this earthly action moves the force of the stars. (Incidentally, this concept of the structure was well brought out in Zeffirelli's production of the play in 1960 at the Old Vic.)

In still another place Spencer recognizes that "Hamlet's thought like that of so many men of his time, involves the world, the state, and the individual." [8] Hamlet's mind runs to the rottenness of all three areas: individual, state, and world. But it seems to me that Spencer fails to observe, as Jean Paris does not fail to observe in his brilliant essay on *Hamlet*, [9] that the Prince has looked beyond the rottenness of this world to the ultimate requirements of justice necessary to the re-establishment of universal order. Spencer fails to observe, though again Paris does not fail to observe, that the structure of the play is determined to a great extent by the spiritual force of the Ghost come from Purgatory. But neither Spencer nor Paris recognizes this or the other areas with which Hamlet's mind is involved as encompassing forces of action.

Professor Harry Levin in his analysis of the player's speech in *Hamlet* [10] does, however, recognize the emotional relationship which reaches from the central characters outward as something of a structural determinant. He comments upon the relationship existing between player, Hamlet, and audience, saying that "There the reality lodges, in the *reaction* of the AUDIENCE: the empathy that links our outlook with a chain of being which sooner or later extends all the way from the actors to the gods." He does not mark out the areas of the forces within the play proper. Rather, he is concerned with the relationship existing between players in the play-within-the-play, players in *Hamlet* proper, and the *personae* of the audience in the theatre. His perceptive reading requires that Shakespeare's stage be a world and all his actors men and women to whom Hecuba or any other unfortunate is of concern.

As I see it, the spiritual domain of the Ghost, an area beyond thought where is the divinity that shapes his end, lies outside the earthly and international domain of Norway, England, and rotten Denmark; the international domain surrounds the rottenness that is Denmark, and that domain surrounds and affects the personal domain and private affairs of Hamlet, Ophelia, Laertes, Gertrude, and Claudius. Within these and central to all is the soul of the Prince. The characters' affairs cannot be kept personal or restricted to the home; they range outward from each other to state, to world, to spirit again, and "no man is an Island, entire of itself." We cannot remove from the action either the Ghost or the Fortinbras plot, nor can we restrict Hamlet's struggle with the King to a fight with Claudius.

Both Spencer and Paris come close, but since they are more interested in the nature of man than in the shape of plays, they do not observe the structure which rests upon this nature. Nor does Professor Levin precisely, though he suggests much. More explicitly the structure is this: the Elizabethan playwrights representing a little world of action on a stage well devised for the purpose, place the individual and private person and private or personal action at the center, surround that action with the action belonging to the city or state, and that public action with an international action, and finally that whole earthly action (not always, but often) with an unearthly action or area for action, which may be an abstract concept or a ghostly or metaphysical force, or simply the gods looking on. Each of these might loosely be termed a "plot," but perhaps the term "spheres of force" or "spheres of action" more accurately describes them: the sphere of the individual, who is himself a microcosm, the sphere of private affairs, the sphere of public affairs, the sphere of world affairs, and the sphere of spiritual affairs. Often, though not always, each of these is explicitly realized on stage; each is represented by characters; each occupies a certain place or represents a certain space. Whereas in later drama we are usually made aware of only one or two of these spheres, in the Elizabethan we are usually made sharply aware of all. Human action thus ranges outward from the single person to a small group of intimates, to society, to the state, to the world, to a metaphysical or a divine force beyond, even at times to the human achievement of spirit itself. Indeed the scheme suggests, as it appropriately should, the concentric spheres of the Ptolemaic system. And Dryden makes the comparison for us. Neander in *An Essay of Dramatic Poesy* says that the plots of English plays are like the movements of the planets in relation to the *primum mobile* and "That similitude expresses much of the English stage." [11]

No one would claim that all Elizabethan plays follow this pattern exactly, or that all parts of it are to be found in all plays, or that numerous changes and modifications did not furnish variety in its use, or that it did not fade perceptibly before 1642, or that as a working concept it was not pretty well lost to later ages. But it was basic to most plays, observed by most playwrights. Such observation is now our concern.

These encompassing actions or forces (I shall use the terms interchangeably) emerge from the medieval drama. Even in the mystery plays men walked close to God, and yet they were mindful that Satan went to and fro in the world and walked up and down in it. Thus man's little world was rounded with both hope and fear. The first of the pageants in the cycles was the fall of Lucifer, and the second, the fall of man. Thence we come to the more human and family play: the killing of Abel, wherein God metes out punishment to Cain. Later Abraham, at the command of the Lord, takes Isaac as a sacrifice to the top of Mount Moriah, where an angel furnishes a substitute and the son is saved; but the center of this drama is the *psychomachia*, the struggle within the soul of Abraham. The microcosmic play, such as the morality, is suggested. Still later the complaining shepherds on their ever-so-Yorkshire-like moor and the sheep-stealing Mak conclude their folktale kneeling before the manger-throne of the King of Heaven as "*Angelus cantat 'Gloria in Excelsis.'* " And not only did the Epiphany come to the shepherds but also to the three kings of this world, who had their pageant too. Thus the mystery plays range from the vast cosmic action set in the heavens to the struggle of the individual soul, and all are related.

The morality plays, the later ones especially, tend to telescope the pattern. One sees it "in little." At the play's center is the whole wrapped up into one man, or all men—Mankind, Everyman, *Humanum Genus*. Within his soul the action of the drama takes place. But to get this action before an audience the dramatist must somehow objectify it. This he does by means of his allegorical characters. And however clumsy or paradoxical it may seem, Confession, Knowledge, and Good Deeds, or Faith, Hope, and Charity appear on the same footing as the character of whom they are really only extensions, or parts. The dramatist's purpose is to show the way to salvation through the soul-struggle of the protagonist, to set up for his audience the universal pattern or some variant of it: after temptation and sin come threat of despair, then confession, penance, sacrament, good deeds, salvation. And though as time went on and as logic would require, the protagonists became more individualized, their action, nevertheless, was held to much the same basic pattern. If not their character, their experience remained universal. Thus Wit represents us all in his effort to gain the hand of Science, and the pattern of the effort is only a variant of that by which Everyman accomplished his salvation. Whether in the early or the late moralities, the protagonists in their struggle between their good and evil angels, between reason and passion, between wit and will reveal themselves as little worlds. In each is symbolized not only mankind, the representative of the race, but the world as well. For the very expressions of these struggles reflect the peculiar nature of the microcosm that is man. In him live at one and the same time the vegetable, the beast, the human, and the angel; in him lives reason giving freedom of choice; but in him lives passion too. Deficient in each, he is subject to the strife consequent upon their natural opposition.[12] Every man is indeed Everyman. No man is free from the cosmic conflict; and the more he realizes himself, the more acutely aware of it he becomes. Yet paradoxically it is personal, inner, his very own.

It is from this inner yet cosmic conflict of the central figure of the morality play that the soul-struggle of the Elizabethan characters, especially the tragic heroes, emerges. As the main characters of the moralities strove to realize themselves in terms of salvation, so the Elizabethans strove to know themselves in much the same terms. Whereas in the moralities the whole play sets forth the conflict within the one representative or universal soul, in the Elizabethan play the individualized characters more often reveal the struggle in their soliloquies. Doctor Faustus' soliloquies make personal and human the objectified struggle between the Good and the Bad Angels for the conquest of his soul. Cursed with immortality, stretched out between heaven and hell, Faustus the microcosm, in spite of his last agonizing cries, cannot be changed into a mere beast, "a creature wanting soul," nor yet have his soul changed into little water drops, as a Lucretian might desire. Indeed, Faustus in this famous final soliloquy refers by name to Pythagoras, the founder of the microcosm theory of the nature of man. Marlowe draws directly upon it.

Outcroppings of it appear in the character of Tamburlaine, who has shoulders such as might bear Atlas's burden and eyes that "bear encompassed / A heaven of heavenly bodies in their spheres" (Part I, II.i.15–16). He reflects on the fact that Nature framed man of the four warring elements, of which all things are formed, and also gave him an aspiring mind "always moving as the restless spheres" (Part I, II.vii.18–25). In other places Marlowe assumes the reader's familiarity with the figure.[13]

As one would expect, Shakespeare suggests it even more frequently. One of its fullest expressions is in the Syracusan Dromio's description of Nell the kitchen wench who is "spherical, like a globe" and upon whose body may be found represented all countries of the world, even America and the Indies (*Comedy of Errors*, III.ii.115–42). The idea occurs to Warwick in his famous soliloquy as he lies waiting for death: he compares his body to the cedar, his eyes to the sun, and the wrinkles of his brow to kingly sepulchres (*III Henry VI*, V.ii. 11–28). More explicit is Suffolk's remark about Queen Margaret when he is banished from her side: "For where thou art, there is the world itself / With every several pleasure in the world." More to the point is the philosophical Richard II. In the last scene but one of his play he tries but fails in his effort to compare his prison to a world. Then he says,

> Yet I'll hammer it out.
> My brain I'll prove the female to my soul,
> My soul the father; and these two beget
> A generation of still-breeding thoughts;
> And these same thoughts people this little world,
> In humours like the people of this world,
> For no thought is contented.
>
> (V.v.5–11)

And a little later his world becomes a stage on which "Thus play I in one person many people / And none contented." Falstaff's famous dissertation upon sherry includes a comparison of man to a commonwealth, a lesser cosmos. "Sherris," he says, "illumineth the face, which, as a beacon, gives warning to all the rest of this little kingdom, man, to arm; and then the vital commoners and inland petty spirits muster me all to their captain, the heart; who, great and puff'd up with this retinue, doth any deed of courage" (*II Henry IV*, IV.iii.117–23). One is reminded that the title page of Hobbes's *Leviathan* pictures the body politic, wherein one man bears the person of all. Larger than the state is Antony, however. Indeed, it is the earth that is the little world, he the larger, in Cleopatra's recital of her dream of his greatness:

> His face was as the heav'ns, and therein stuck
> A sun and moon, which kept their course and lighted
> The little O, the earth.
>
> (V.ii.79–81)

But in Shakespeare, as in others, the analogy between man and the world is usually drawn by suggestion or by implication, as if every reader or hearer would readily make the necessary connection. One such example occurs in Hamlet's long speech to Rosencrantz and Guildenstern about the nature of the world first, and then of man. Having lost his mirth and foregone all his customary exercise, he has found that

> this goodly frame, the earth, seems to me a sterile promontory; this most excellent canopy, the air, look you, this brave o'er-firmament, this majestical roof fretted with golden fire—why it appeareth no other thing than a foul and pestilent congregation of vapours. What a piece of work is man! how noble in reason! how infinite in faculties! in form and moving how express and admirable! in action how like an angel! in apprehension how like a god! the beauty of the world, the paragon of animals. And yet to me what is this quintessence of dust? (II.ii.310–22)

The two goodly frames are now the same, stale and sterile. The analogy here present in the poet's mind is basic to Hamlet's comments, and not only here but throughout the play. It was likewise present, especially present, to his mind when he wrote *King Lear:* the parallels between nature's acts and man's reveal it.

More direct than Shakespeare is Cyril Tourneur, who in *The Atheist's Tragedy* (1611) has Charlemont declare his rule over himself:

> I'ue lost a Signiorie,
> That was confin'd within a piece of earth;
> A Wart vpon the body of the world,
> But now I am Emp'rour of a world.
> This little world of Man. My passions are
> My Subiects.
>
>   (III.iii.43–48) [14]

And no more explicit statement of the condition of man the microcosm can be found, and perhaps none more to the point, than that in Thomas Nabbes's *Microcosmus: A Morall Mask* (1637). In it the morality play and the masque come together, as they logically should; in it, late as it appears, the protagonist is a microcosm. Named Physander, he is referred to as "the masterpiece / Of Natures workmanship, thou little world." [15] He is modeled upon Adam, the representative of all mankind; his mate, Bellamina, upon Eve.

But further listing of instances is not called for. Obviously the dramatists were not only aware of the concept; they consciously and deliberately made good and common use of it, especially in the delineation of their protagonists. It is a basic assumption in their art, not requiring full or careful analysis in the development of the characters. It functions chiefly in the larger plan of their plays. And it is this larger plan with which we are concerned, the larger pattern in which the action of the individual, the microcosm, reaches outward through the community, the state, and the earth to the heavens beyond.

This larger pattern begins to emerge even in such early semi-history plays as Bale's *King John,* where Imperial Majesty and Verity encompass the action and where the guidance of the characters of England and Scriptures enables John to save the state as well as his own soul. It appears somewhat more fully developed later in Thomas Preston's *Cambises, King of Persia,* where justice is destroyed and the succession broken by the King's headstrong will to vice (represented by Ambidexter) and where the action is carried out or instigated by such allegorical figures as Shame, Cruelty, Execution, Commons' Cry, or by Venus and Cupid. But the spheres of action come more clearly into focus with the appearance of the histories, mythological plays, romances, and early tragedies.

The design may be observed even in Lyly's plays.[16] *Campaspe* represents a sort of digression in the life of Alexander, an interlude. The conqueror turns briefly from the affairs of empire and war to those of love and philosophy, and then turns back. His love for Campaspe interferes for a time with his duties to the state, turning him, as Clytus tells us, from war to softness and ease; but he goes to Diogenes and finds the philosopher altogether opposed to love. Discovering the lady's love for the painter, he magnanimously gives her up. His duty to the state and his regard for the affections of men keep him from untuning the string of degree. He learns that he "cannot subdue the affections of men, though he can conquer their countries." Thus the outside force of philosophy is operative, and order in the state is preserved. Similarly Lyly seems to see his art in its cosmic setting in *Sapho and Phao.* The gods Venus and Cupid frame the action with their plotting and themselves become entangled in their own schemes. With them Sybilla, the prophetess, helps control the action from the outside. Venus changes the plain Phao into a handsome youth who falls in love with the lovely Sapho of Sicily (Elizabeth of England), but Venus herself then falls in love with Phao and manages by means of arrows got from Vulcan to break up the loves of Phao and Sapho. At the same time, Cupid ironically destroys any love Phao may have had for her. If one realizes the rather obvious allegory—the love of Phao for Sapho as that of the Duc d'Alençon for Elizabeth—one the more readily recognizes the middle sphere, the area of state and international affairs. The personal relationship of the two, thus contrived by the

Goddess of Love, involves the state and brings about other complications. But the fanciful character and courtly subject matter of Lyly's plays do not separate the several spheres of action so well as the characters and subject matter of later plays.[17]

George Peele's plays, for example, indicate them much more clearly. In his *Arraignment of Paris*, even, Ate in lowest hell speaks the prologue, and we learn that the whole action derives from "Th' unpartial daughters of necessity." [18] The main or central plot consists of Paris's being bribed to give the golden ball to Helen, his desertion of Oenone, and his consequent arraignment before the court of Jupiter. The action ranges outward from the protagonist's personal affairs to public or state affairs (in this case Jupiter's world empire), and thence to eternal justice as represented by the Fates. Indeed the final song is sung by the Fates as they give up to Queen Elizabeth their distaff, spindle, and knife and as Diana gives her the golden ball. Parallel to this central plot with its three realms is the secondary plot involving much the same pattern in which the simple shepherd Colin dies for love of proud Thestylis, upon whom justice is visited by Venus: Thestylis is made to love a churl who will not love her.

Quite in contrast to this mythological-allegorical play is the same author's *Edward I*, a series of vast historical pageants designed in part to explain certain British place-names and traditions. But in it the areas of action appear, set the one within the other, and somewhat more fully developed. Personal pride and individual desire come into conflict with public good, and supernatural power intervenes to assert eternal justice. Returning from the Crusades, King Edward "Longshanks" has captured a foreign wife, later the beloved of Mortimer and the mistress of a friar by whom she has a child. The Queen's wantonness brings about national and international difficulties, and Edward has to suppress uprisings in Wales and repulse attacks from Scotland. Outside these actions are the supernatural: the murderous, jealous, lecherous Queen is swallowed up by the earth on Charing Green, later to be returned from underground and die repentant, confessing her crimes to her long-suffering husband. The sins of the individual run counter to the good of the state, and the encompassing supernatural power intervenes to bring about justice.

A third sort of play is his *Old Wives' Tale*, romances and fairy tales set in a smith's cottage; yet the encompassing frames of action are apparent, though provided in a way different from that in the other plays. Here is the play-within-the-play, and the play within constitutes a set of parallel plots. Clunch and Madge, the smith and his old wife, with the three servants lost in the wood, form the outside shell or the audience's sphere. They are more than a chorus: they look into a mirror, as it were, where Frolic and Fantastic, spell-bound and regretful when the end comes, will see in Madge's tale a parallel to their own story. The story they see as play turns upon the conflict of the forces of good and evil, between the good deeds worked by Eumenides, the wandering knight, who by burying Jack's bones gained the guidance of Jack's Ghost, and the evil machinations of Sacra-pant, who has stolen away the daughter of the King of Thessaly and by bringing her to England has disrupted the affairs of kingdoms. Although state and public affairs are not of chief interest, they are basic. Delia, her brothers, and her suitors are princes and rulers of the realm of Thessaly; and Erestus and his betrothed are of the nobility. The main action of the play within involves the restoration of the kingdom of Thessaly to normal conditions, as well as the righting of personal wrongs, all of which action is tied together by Erestus's riddles. And the setting of this romantic story is ringed about by the supernatural realm of Jack in conflict with the daemonic realm of Sacrapant. And outside these, as mentioned already, is the play of Madge and Clunch and the three lost in the wood—in a sort, still another realm of action.[19]

More conventionally indicated and more readily observed are the encompassing actions in the same writer's *David and Bethsabe*. In it the lust of the king disrupts the affairs of state, and only with the restoration of eternal justice is order restored to Israel. King David's desire for Bethsabe and the consequent deaths of her husband and child untune the strings of degree and order, break the moral law, and bring about the revolt and death of Absalon as atonement for the sin of the father. The atonement accomplished, the settlement of the succession upon Solomon takes place and with it the re-establishment of national harmony. The selfish desires of David have run counter to the good of his kingdom, and the outside force which works the death of Absalon brings peace and order; the personal, the national, and the spiritual frames of action thus become apparent. Whether by deliberate choice and careful planning, whether by following custom merely and the natural scheme of things, Peele shaped his plays according to the basic pattern: from the immediate and the personal the action ranges outward to the eternal and the infinite.

The Spanish Tragedy (ca. 1589), though it owes much to Seneca, still reveals the care with which Kyd followed the pattern.[20] The family affairs of Hieronimo, the love affair and the death of his son Horatio, stand at the center of the action. Surrounding Hieronimo (a microcosm in which a soul-drama is played out) and his family affairs and sadly interfering with them are the affairs of the court of Spain. The affairs of Spain are involved with the affairs of Portugal, even with those of England, in the settlement of the international situation following the war. Outside the international sphere and directing the cosmic action is the allegorical figure of Revenge, and standing with him is the Ghost of Andrea, watching. It was Andrea's death that started the action, was the first cause. Instigated and controlled by Revenge from the realm of spirit, the whole action may be said to move from the outer circle inward through state affairs actually to the family of Hieronimo, Horatio, and Bel-Imperia. By such movement universality is gained. A technical aspect of the pattern, one of the commonest, comes to the fore in this play: the play-within-the-play. It is frequently discussed by critics, but not recognized as a part of a broader concept of the nature of drama.[21] The Ghost of Andrea and Revenge as

Induction, Prologue, Chorus, and Epilogue with their dumb show constitute one play; they watch another play going on inside the courts of Spain and Portugal; and within this play proper Hieronimo presents the play of Soliman which brings about the catastrophe. From the supernatural world of the Ghost we view the action in the natural world which comes to a most unnatural period in what was supposed to be a world of make-believe but turns out to be only too real.

Though the encompassing forces or areas of action may be easily discovered in all the plays of Robert Greene,[22] they appear most obviously and yet most differently in *Friar Bacon and Friar Bungay* (ca. 1589), *A Looking Glass for London and England* (1590?), and *James IV* (ca. 1591). In the first of these the passion of Prince Edward for Fair Margaret cannot be allowed to interfere with the affairs of state, nor yet the love of Lacy, the Earl of Lincoln, for the yeoman's daughter, to bring discord into the social order. Outside these private loves—and the hunting, the county fairs, and the amusements at Oxford—are the affairs of the kingdom; outside the affairs of the kingdom are the international arrangements for the marriage of Edward to Elinor of Castile and even the international contest of magicians; and outside these encompassing areas is the supernatural represented by Bacon, whose disclosures affect much of the action.

A Looking Glass for London and England is managed quite differently. It is a kind of late morality play in which an angel places the prophet Oseas "over" the stage in a throne to instigate action and also to apply the lessons drawn from ancient Nineveh to contemporary London. But inside his mirror is another prophet, Jonas, who, finding that he cannot escape God's command given through the mouth of his prophet Oseas and the voice of the angel, effects the conversion and repentance of the people of Nineveh from the lowliest clown to the usurer and upward to the wicked King Rasni and his paramour. The drunkenness, lust, and cruelty of Rasni and his paramour, paralleled by the same evils among all classes, bring the state to the brink of disaster. It is saved by Jonas's preaching, and his action is instigated and compelled by the prophet Oseas and the angel. Opposing him are the evil priests and devils who guide Rasni. Thus the conflict of the supernatural world is projected into the natural. The conflicts within Nineveh are extended to other states, moreover, in that Rasni's paramour, Aluida Queen of Paphalgonia, makes love to the King of Cilicia. The conflicts wrought by sin within the soul of the individual, the microcosm, lead to conflicts and corruption among individuals and those to the conflicts and disruptions of the affairs of nations. Outside, the powers of good successfully overcome those of evil in the struggle for the control of men and states.

Similarly in *James IV*. The King's passion for Ida disrupts the government of Scotland and brings on war with England, for James is married to the daughter of the King of England. He listens to the evil counsel of Ateukin (a kind of Mephistopheles) and his servants rather than to his own good counselors, the Bishop of St. Andrewes, Lord Morton, and Douglas. The forces of good and evil are drawn up in conflict. It is only through what seems to be divine intervention, the marriage of Ida before the King can reach her, that the King and his kingdom are saved from ruin. After this he is converted and repents, and justice prevails in both personal and national affairs. But outside King James's inner struggles, outside his domestic conflicts, outside the conflicts within his kingdom, outside the international disturbance is the realm of the metaphysical and supernatural: Bohan, the Scottish philosopher, coming from the tomb, presents the whole play to Oberon, King of Fairyland. These two stand outside as in another world, the one producing the play for the other as a moral for monarchs. Greene gives variety to the pattern.

So does the writer of the pastoral-romantic comedy called *Mucedorus* (1598?).[23] He sets the action of his play in a different metaphysical area—a flyting. The contest is between Envy and Comedy, who present the play. Comedy wins the flyting. Within it Mucedorus, disguised as a shepherd, wins the hand of the daughter of the King of Aragon and then reveals himself as the Prince of Valencia. In so doing he has crossed the King's promise to give his daughter Amadine to the cowardly Segasto. Coming home from the wars, he finds that a brave shepherd has rescued his daughter from a bear, while her lover the gentleman has run away, and now his daughter is in love with the shepherd. Thus an affair of state is created. But ultimately Mucedorus' father, the King of Valencia, appears, identities are disclosed, and all are properly restored. The private loves, the interruption of the even course of state affairs, the international complications are all here, and all are used as a means of proving that Comedy will prevail, or that order and happiness are assured.

The pattern becomes more effective in the plays of Marlowe. Even in *Tamburlaine* (ca. 1587) it emerges. The protagonist, assuredly a microcosm, the would-be emperor of the earth, moved at the center of the play by his cosmic ambition, develops a domestic conflict: his love for Zenocrate runs counter to his ambition to conquer her father's empire, and his affection for his sons runs counter to his family pride in their military honor. His love for his lady brings mercy to her father, and his pride in honor brings death to his son. Outside his family are the kingdoms of the world which Tamburlaine subdues. In the end he is essentially the conqueror of the world, but in the end his achievement has not secured satisfaction in or enjoyment of his high place: at his death heaven and earth do meet, we are told; but after all, Tamburlaine is no god, only God's scourge. The powers beyond this temporal world, the world he has so ruthlessly conquered, are always present to him, and he never allows his hearers to forget them. They direct his drama on the stage of the world.

In *Doctor Faustus* (ca. 1588) the concentric spheres of action are much better defined. At the center is Faustus, the microcosm. His intimates are the scholars, Wagner his servant, and Valdes and Cornelius, the faithless students of magic. Their relationships with him concern the welfare of his soul and the satisfaction of his desires. But outside the domestic affairs are the affairs of state—of Germany, the empire, the Christian world of the papacy. Besides, one might add, there are the doings of the clowns and the servants paralleling those of the nobles, the princes, and the prelates. But beyond these are the spiritual powers struggling for the control of the soul of the learned man, both those of light and those of darkness. The play represents the cosmos.

It represents it no less clearly than does *The Jew of Malta* (ca. 1589). Barabas has not only his private fortune but his daughter and the domestic affairs with which she makes him concerned. Outside these private and family affairs are those of the city-state of Malta, with which his personal and family affairs come in conflict. Outside Malta and encompassing it is the Turkish League, and entangled with the League is the power of Spain. The affairs of the wealthy Jew range outward from his home to the fringes of the civilized world. But outside and beyond sits Machiavelli, a spirit come from Italy to watch, if not to direct the play, which is actually a demonstration among all races and religions of his diabolical invention.

Anthony Munday reveals an understanding of this pattern in all the plays we know are his, but perhaps it is most easily recognized in his *John a Kent and John a Cumber* (1594).[24] The love story of Mirian and Sidanen and their four noble suitors form the central and personal as opposed to state conflicts; but since the suitors come from Scotland, North and South Wales, and England, national and international conflicts arise. Controlling the action and devising the conflicts, not unlike a Machiavelli, is John a Kent, the magician derived from the ancient Vice.

The domestic tragedy, *A Warning for Fair Women* (1599),[25] reveals the anonymous dramatist's feeling for the pattern. Not content merely with dramatizing an exciting murder story out of current events, the playwright must provide an Induction, in which Hystorie, Comedie, and Tragedie discuss the kind of play to be presented, and Tragedie is allowed to present it. This she does by means of dumb shows between the acts, which encompass the central play and explain it: Murder, Lust, the Furies, and Chastity, for example, open Act II; and later a masque of Mercy, Justice, and Diligence shows that a moral order will prevail. These are set forth by Tragedie to enable the audience to see at once the universal meaning of the particular events. Indeed, a morality play here surrounds contemporary history, and the presenter makes the brief chronicle an abstract of the time.

Thus far I have been concerned with the emergence of the encompassing actions or areas of action in the semi-moralities, the histories, historico-heroic-tragedies, and romantic comedies. But what, it may be asked, of the "regular" comedies brought in from ancient Rome and contemporary Italy? Some were outright translations, as Gascoigne's *Supposes;* some were imitations, as *Ralph Roister Doister;* some were played in the original Latin, as *Miles Gloriosus*, by the boys of Westminster School; and some were adaptations, as *The Comedy of Errors.* Now Roman comedy was not so designed as to show the world as a stage, or take into account the areas of action within areas or actions within actions required by such design, and the plays which imitated it slavishly show no such design. But as Schelling observes,[26] not one of the pre-Elizabethan productions of "regular" comedy, either an original play or an adaptation or an imitation of Roman or Italian comedy, was in the repertoire of any troupe of professional players, nor did the professional troupes produce them often, if indeed at all, at any time in the Elizabethan period in anything like pure form. Ben Jonson, the most successful writer of classical comedy, was more often a critic than an imitator. Like Shakespeare before him, he soon found classical strictures much too confining for his genius, as we shall see later. Just now we must be concerned with Shakespeare.

And Shakespeare's adaptation of Plautus' *Menaechmi, The Comedy of Errors*, it should be noted, was written for performance at Gray's Inn, not for the public playhouses. The learned lawyers would appreciate the work. But even for such an audience the poet would not be restricted by his source. Precisely those additions and changes he made in it reveal, though not extensively, the encompassing frames or forces of action. Not only are the sets of twins doubled, but the enveloping action is deliberately added: the parents of the twins with the characters of Ægon, Æmelia, Solinus, Luciana, the Merchants, and Luce enable the dramatist to frame the interior farce taken from Plautus within a larger romantic plot. The inside mix-up of the two Antipholuses is surrounded by the national conflict between Ephesus and Syracuse. The domestic disturbances are further complicated by the commercial dealings of the two brothers with the merchants and the goldsmith who surround them. Less well defined, but very definitely present, is the world of the spirit: the forces of falsehood and deceit, if not of outright evil, are represented by Pinch, the mountebank with his conjuring; and the benevolent forces of right by the Abbess, who is responsible for the emergence of the truth which enables the Duke of Ephesus to mete out proper judgments and restore order. Here one may reasonably argue for our pattern: the domestic mix-up surrounded by the commercial affairs, these two encompassed by the affairs of states, and these three operating, though less obviously, within the ancient struggle between the forces of good and evil.

In *The Two Gentlemen of Verona* the romantic characteristics are more apparent than they are in *The Comedy of Errors*. To his source Shakespeare adds a second pair of lovers, and he encloses doings of the lovers within the doings of the state, the latter represented chiefly by the Duke of Milan. Not only does the Duke dispense justice at the end, having learned the truth through the work of Valentine, but grants mercy as well— forgiveness for the outlaws. More closely connected with the action than many another of his kind, he is nevertheless a sort of onlooker, judge, and director of the action. And one should not forget that deep inside, and not a mere digressive entertainment, is Launce's one-man play with his shoes, staff, hat, and dog as characters, any more than one should forget Proteus and his little soul drama (II.iv.192–214). Outside all is the benevolent forest, a frame of force, where the complications and injustices of courts and cities are simplified and corrected. And the entrance to the forest, at least for some of the characters, is by way of the abbey and the direction of a friar.

Though in *The Taming of the Shrew* Shakespeare still owes a Roman debt, his play is no mere Plautine comedy. He contrives a complex central plot out of romance and farce and sets it within another plot, an encompassing play, not a simple induction, representing reality as opposed to make-believe. But as M. Jacquot has observed, the whole is based upon the life-is-a-dream motif: Sly's new life as a lord is itself a dream. And whereas the outer play, the apparent reality, fades into a sleep, the make-believe of the inner action becomes the apparent reality. The betrothals and marriages of Baptista's two daughters and Hortensio's getting his rich widow make up a play presented by a band of actors come to a Lord's house and by the Lord ordered for the entertainment of a drunken tinker, an outcast of an alehouse. The Lord stands on the outside as the prime mover of the action, the deity of his little cosmos, who plans the whole for his own "pastime" and "sport." His is the laughter of the gods. Next is the audience of the play, Sly and his "lady," who furnish the immediate encompassing action within the Lord's control. The inner play has its own actions within actions: the Petruchio-Katherina plot in a sense encompasses, at least controls, the story of Bianca and her several suitors, for Bianca cannot be married until her shrewish older sister is married. Tangential to these two is the vague and undeveloped affair of Hortensio and his widow. And within each of the two major divisions of this plot are other dramatic contrivances, little plays—Petruchio's schemes to overcome Katherine and the disguises and character interchanges of Bianca's suitors—giving further depth to the action. The role of Baptista, moreover, is to the inside play what the role of the Lord is to the outside, for it is his unquestioned ruling on the marriage of his daughters which brings about and controls the action. The Lord, the prime mover, stands outside, simulating the spiritual world; next come Sly and his lady; next the entertainment furnished for him with Baptista controlling its two main actions, one of which encompasses the other; and within each of these is a set of dramatic contrivances—a total of some six actions-within-actions, a set of spheres like the spheres of the cosmic system. In spite of the fact that the actions here are personal and domestic, as was fitting to comedy according to classical critical theory, the little life was rounded not only with a sleep and a spirit world but with the world of public affairs. Outside the homes of Baptista and Petruchio and constantly present in the background as if threatening to appear are the dukes of Padua, Pisa, and Verona representing the public interest in the action.

Two or three more examples will suffice as illustrations for the rest of Shakespeare's comedies. The encompassing scheme is not explicit in *The Merchant of Venice* (1598), though it is implicit in the structure. The Duke and his laws lie outside the private conflicts of the play, and the private become involved with the commercial affairs of Venice. Beyond these is the realm of Justice and Mercy, into which Portia moves from her personal area of action. This same struggle between Justice and Mercy is played out also on the stage of Shylock's soul. Its realm is the spiritual. In it Portia trusts, and upon it she has come to rely since the testing of the casket scenes.

Nor is the scheme obtrusive in *Much Ado*. A war well on the outside brings together nobles from Florence and Arragon at Messina, an international group; and Messina's state business surrounds the personal affairs of the main plots, the loves of Hero and Claudio and of Beatrice and Benedick. The resolution is effected by Friar Francis, a spiritual power, whose intuition leads to a plan, and by the innocent bumblings of Dogberry and his Watch. World and state affairs enclose the love affairs, and the love affairs are happily settled by a spiritual force, which in reality moves outside all. Within the state, Leonato as governor must act as magistrate, the instrument of the spiritual force, Astraea's vicar.

Like those of *Much Ado,* but more explicit, are the encompassing spheres of *A Midsummer Night's Dream* (1595). If

Theseus and Hippolyta open the play, Titania, Oberon and Puck close it. The national and, indeed, international story of the ruler of Athens and his Amazonian bride surrounds the private loves of the two sets of suitors and the entertainment of the rude mechanicals; but all these are surrounded by the "shadows," the fairies, who, if they have confused the lovers and the tradesmen and thus Theseus, will make amends by blessing the brides' beds. In the last scene it becomes clear that the plot of Theseus and Hippolyta holds within it the plot of the four lovers, within both of these is the plot of the tradesmen who present a play, and outside all are the fairies. *La vida es sueño.*[27]

Vincentio, Duke of Vienna in *Measure for Measure* (1604?), steps outside the action and assumes the role of prime mover, or director, of the world comedy. Leaving the affairs of state in the hands of his deputy Angelo, he disguises himself as a friar so as to observe what will take place and then step back into the action when necessary to assert justice or correct error. But the personal affairs of some of his subjects come at once into conflict with the laws and customs of the state, and the judgment of the substitute ruler is required. Outside the civil and personal matters of the action is the war with Hungary mentioned at the outset. Private deeds and family affairs become the concern of the state, and the state affairs are vaguely surrounded by international affairs, and all of these are encompassed by the all-powerful director on the outside in the garb of a friar. He brings about the resolution of the action through his great mercy, the most divine attribute.

Similarly in the last of Shakespeare's comedies, Prospero in *The Tempest* is prime mover, director, judge, and controller of the action. At the same time he is central to it, for it is out of his soul-drama that the whole conflict springs. In one sense his being is the stage of the entire action. Yet he is surrounded by the spirit world which he conjures up at will; surrounding him also is the audience at the Globe, to whom he speaks the epilogue, asking them to release him—even as he released Ariel. Central to his contrivings is the love of Ferdinand and Miranda, and enveloping it, the national and international plots involving Prospero and his brother and the burlesque revolt of Caliban and his companions as well. Prospero provides a masque, moreover, for further perspective. Here spheres surround spheres, frames of action are set within frames, from the inner workings of Prospero's soul to the love plot, to the usurped government of Milan and the international complications wrought out on the uninhabited island, to the spirit world beyond and its insubstantial pageants. Made explicit in Prospero's speeches, all are set, the one within the other, so as to suggest the infinity of a perfect or complete perspective and fade into the ultimate dream. As time went on, it seems that Shakespeare's use of the pattern in his comedies became more and more complex and facile, if not more obvious.

His chronicle plays likewise reveal encompassing areas of action, though in a somewhat different way. The emphasis in the chronicle plays is, of course, much more upon pageantry, vast movement, and characters of high place than in comedy. Since they must follow at least the larger outlines of English history and tradition, they are not so free as the fiction of comedy to set action within action, to make explicit the supernatural or fantastic, or to allow a monarch to become prime mover or director of the cosmic events. The encompassing frames of action are somewhat less well defined, more likely to merge the one with the other, than in comedy. But they are no less functional in the chronicles. In fact the private or family, the national or state, and the international spheres are basic to the chronicles no less than to the comedies; and since they are all concerned with kingship, they all involve the monarch's relation to the church and to God. A brief account will illustrate.

King John (ca. 1590), perhaps Shakespeare's earliest chronicle play, reveals the encompassing frames in a rather unusual way. The first act is almost wholly taken up with a family affair, the paternity of Philip Faulconbridge, brought for adjudication to the King and thus involved with the state; the second, almost wholly with John's claim to the throne as opposed to Prince

Arthur's, a civil matter extended to the international realm and involved with the possession of Angiers; and much of the third, with the intervention of the papacy through the legate, Cardinal Pandulph, a power surrounding all the others. John, moreover, considers himself "God's wrathful agent," His secular vicar; and though he sees no spiritual power made manifest, he and others are sharply and constantly aware of the presence of heavenly powers, upon whom they frequently call. The action becomes increasingly involved as it moves from the family to the state to the international to the world to the spiritual areas. The denouement is effected by the Church, the representative of the spiritual power on earth, but comes ironically after John's death.

Less apparent in the three parts of *Henry VI*, the encompassing areas are nevertheless inherent in the action. And the action is brought about by the conflict of private with national interests, and the national with international interests. Outside and surrounding these is the Church, and the spirit world appears variously, but chiefly in the witches Joan and Margery Jourdain who frequently consult spirits. The drama within the individual soul, the little world, may be especially observed in Warwick and his reflections at the time of his death and in the various philosophic comments of Henry.

But the microcosmic action, the little drama within the soul, is consciously given us in the character of Richard II, who, as has already been noted, in his play elaborates the metaphor at some length. Likening his brain to the mother and his soul to the father of his "still-breeding thoughts," he holds that "these same thoughts people this little world, / In humours like the people of this world, / For no thought is contented." But his private desires run counter to his public responsibilities, his duties as head of the state, whereas Bolingbroke's are weighted in the opposite direction. These public and national affairs are complicated by their international setting: the Queen is banished to France and trouble ensues. Finally, not explicitly put but always present, is the spiritual realm encompassing all, for as Henry says when he pardons Aumerle, "God shall pardon all."

Similarly Richard III at the center of his play is a microcosm, as his numerous soliloquies so well show: his soul is a stage. This soul-drama, Richard's personal affairs, is surrounded by the drama of the state. In fact, he for a time is able to make the state subservient to his will and his personal desires. The interests of the citizens he bends to his own advantage, surrounding these with his court and the national realm. But in his ruthless rise he drives many into exile, and they rise up, through the aid of divine power, and bring about his violent downfall. The international sphere lies outside England, furnishing Richmond and his followers aid. Outside all lies the force of the curses and prophecies of the Old Queen Margaret and the ghosts of those whom Richard has murdered. The ghosts come to bring despair to Richard and courage to Richmond; the spiritual world meets the microcosm, and the center becomes the circumference.

The two parts of *Henry IV* and *Henry V* may best be treated as a unit; thus one may realize more easily the pattern of the encompassing areas. At the center is the drama which works itself out in the soul of Prince Hal. Close to him and immediately surrounding him at the first are Falstaff and his companions, whose sole concern is self-gratification and the law and the public be damned. But the playlet put on at the Boar's Head, a tiny play within the play, foreshadows Hal's break with them. For surrounding them and touching the Prince closely a little later are the affairs of his father's kingdom, the national safety and welfare with which he from the first had realized he must be concerned. Present from the first also, but made explicit in the action of *Henry V*, is the international sphere. And finally, and again made apparent in the final play of the trilogy, is the surrounding sphere of the Infinite. Falstaff's death may very well symbolize the death of the Old Adam in the Prince; yet the knight made a good end and no doubt rests in Arthur's bosom. Finally, the King's speculations incognito among his common soldiers on the night before Agincourt end in his great prayer: his will surrendered, his internal drama becomes identified with the universal.

Frames of actions set within frames are still apparent in the last of the chronicles, *Henry VIII*, written perhaps in collaboration with Fletcher. Had Henry not been king, his family affairs would have caused no national or international disturbances; had Wolsey not been cardinal and chancellor, his personal ambition had brought no notable downfall. But the personal concerns of these two public figures cannot be dissociated from the concerns of the kingdom, nor can the concerns of the kingdom be separated from the all-embracing Church. Between state and personal realms, moreover, stand the citizens and commons reflecting hatred and fear of Wolsey and sympathy for the King. The drama within the microcosm may best be observed in Wolsey; and the downfall of Buckingham is in itself a little tragedy within the play, just as the pageantry of the coronation procession and the scene following Elizabeth's baptism serve as plays within the play. The spiritual realm is made manifest in the vision of the Queen (IV.ii), and it is powerfully confirmed by Cranmer's prayer and prophecy in the last scene. If the initial incident is a tragedy brought about by ruthless ambition, Wolsey's destruction of Buckingham, the final incident is a holy ceremony designed to celebrate the forthcoming reign of a selfless queen and provide for her ultimate apotheosis. The movement, like the movement in *I* and *II Henry IV* and *Henry V*, is from the personal and selfish area to the public, selfless, and then spiritual. So much for the chronicles.

Shakespeare's Roman plays follow much the same practices as one finds in the chronicles, being themselves based upon history and legend. Even in the pagan *Titus Andronicus* (1594?) the love of Lavinia and Bassanius, the lust of Tamora and Aaron the Moor, the anger and cruelty of Titus bring about the conflict in Rome, and the affairs of the state are complicated with the war against the Goths, who suggest the international sphere. Though no supernatural area is indicated here as such, the characters of Tamora, Demetrius, and Chiron are recognized by Titus as the forces of rape, murder, and revenge; and Aaron derives obviously from the allegorical medieval Vice. In *Julius*

Caesar (1599) Cassius, though no Vice, has close kinship with him: the basic action of the play emerges from his prodding Brutus, a microcosm "with himself at war," too quick to believe that Caesar's personal ambition was not for the public good. Hence the government of Rome is shattered and civil war ensues, reaching beyond the city in its conflicts. Outside and in great measure controlling the central action is the spirit world, and conscience is given direct expression in storms, prophecies, omens, and the Ghost of Caesar. In *Troilus and Cressida* (1601–1602) the areas are well defined. The love triangle of Troilus, Cressida, and Diomedes is a parallel to the enveloping love triangle of Menelaus, Helen, and Paris, the cause of all the conflict. The national and the international order is upset by the passions of three people and war results. Outside both the personal and the international complications is, appropriately enough, the realm of the gods, but more significant is the civil and moral order Ulysses discusses so well. Upon this order the pattern of play is founded. Professor Harold Wilson stated it quite clearly, though without recognizing it as a pattern:

> In *Troilus and Cressida*, the tragic effect does not concern the fortunes of any one central figure, his rise and fall; rather it relates to the plight of mankind as represented in the play, of the human society which it pictures. This effect is achieved through the study of two common human situations: a man in love with a woman, two peoples at war. These situations are interrelated as microcosm and macrocosm.[28]

The Poet's description of his book in the opening scene of *Timon of Athens* (1604–1608) not only foreshadows the basic action of the play but indicates also the spheres of action; for he has "shaped out a man / Whom this beneath world doth embrace" but from whom all fall away as Fortune on her hill spurns him. Timon, the little world, in the play proper comes into sharp conflict with his flatterer-friends, then with the senators representing the state, and then with Alcibiades who represents the world outside Athens. The caustic Apemantus represents a sort of metaphysical sphere himself, and the grace he gives (I.ii) at the first banquet and that which Timon gives at the second (III.vi) are sufficient recognition of the realm of the gods which envelops all. In *Coriolanus* (1608) the conflict between a man's personal desire, in this case his desire for the consulship, and his strong character traits, in this case his unwillingness to stoop to the vulgar in order to win votes, brings down destruction on him. The inner drama and the personal thus confront the state. Banished, he joins the Volsces, enemies of his native land, bringing the international forces into play; and his turning to Rome's enemies instigates his mother's actions and brings about his capitulation to the family. As he does so, he thinks of his action as furnishing the gods with laughter: "Behold, the heavens do ope, / The gods look down, and this unnatural scene / They laugh at." His tragedy on the stage of the world furnishes comedy to the bitter gods.

But the gods were kinder to Pericles. At the center of his play lies his constant love for his wife and daughter. It gets him into trouble with Antiochus and later with Cleon. Family affairs are soon entangled with national events and national events with international: Tyre involved with Antioch, Mytilene, Tharsus, Ephesus. Outside the home, the state, and the neighboring states, however, stands the supernatural sphere of Diana, who at her temple restores Thaisa to her Pericles.

In the tragedies proper considerable variation exists among the patterns of enveloping areas of action. In my description of the nature of these earlier I used as examples *Romeo and Juliet* and *Hamlet*, the one following pretty much the system found in the romantic comedies, with the Duke as arbiter within the cosmic context, and the other following more nearly the pattern discovered in the chronicle play, though with much bolder and clearer lines. Among the tragedies *Othello* perhaps shows least definition of the encompassing spheres. It is just saved from being a domestic tragedy by the high military position of the protagonist. The emphasis falls upon his marriage to Desdemona, the development of his jealousy for her through the contrivances of the villain, and his final murder of her and of himself, as he discovers the truth. His public deeds enter in, and he has done the state some service, but these have been kept almost wholly separate from his domestic affairs. His marriage does bring him to trial before the Senate of Venice, but he is exonerated; and he is sent on his expedition to Cyprus. In this way the international area of conflict is brought in. But it has not much to do with the fearful occasions in the Castle at Cyprus. Of course the soul-struggle within Othello is a play in itself, also; but little emerges expressly to signify the supernatural or the spiritual forces operative on the world-stage. It is assumed in the background, heaven is frequently on the lips of the characters, and Othello speaks of his fear of damnation. Yet no ghost appears, no visions, no omens or portents, no witches or angels, no fairies, no magic, no aberration in Nature.

Such is not true of *King Lear* (1605–1606). Lear at the center is the microcosm, and the whole of the conflict is but the extension of the drama in his soul. Here is a fusion of the concentric areas of action perhaps not hitherto achieved by Shakespeare. Lear's pride, his disappointment in Cordelia, affects his judgment as a king; likewise the family affairs of Gloucester are drawn within the orbit of the sphere of the state. In that she was married to France and went abroad to return with an army, Cordelia brings the action within the international orbit. Outside these earthly areas are the heavens and their intervention into the affairs of men and states—in spite of Edmund's assertion of man's independence of them. The struggle before the hovel on the heath objectifies the power of the heavens and makes manifest in itself the cosmic fusion. It was never done so effectively before, nor has it been done so powerfully since.

It certainly was not so well accomplished in *Macbeth*, where the pattern is less complex. The personal ambitions of the protagonist, set to work by the untrustworthy witches and their riddles and sharpened by Lady Macbeth's own ambition, bring catastrophe to Scotland and move the action ultimately to the fringes of England and Norway. The inner world of the man's soul, his relations with his spouse, his disruption of the kingdom and its relation with neighboring kingdoms, and his foolish reliance upon the powers of darkness which surround every man bring into play the several areas of action. Perhaps the supernatural powers, including the Ghost of Banquo and the vision of the kings, are simply the dramatic realizations of the dark powers within Macbeth's soul. If so, then both within and without, the supernatural is made operative in man's cosmic drama.

At the risk of some repetition I have examined more than enough plays to indicate Shakespeare's use of the general pattern. I have deliberately done so in the hope that I might indicate also the variations and refinements he made in its use. Even more importantly, I hope I have shed some light upon the structure of individual plays. Personal and domestic affairs dominate regular comedies, such as *The Merry Wives,* though other areas of action are always present, with the supernatural being perhaps least dwelt upon. In the romantic comedies the Duke as director, prime mover, or judge, comes to the fore as God's vicar; and through him the private conflicts are subordinated to the city or state. The chronicles obviously emphasize the national sphere and often its conflict with the enveloping international scene or conflict, and much the same is true of the Roman plays. The action of the great tragedies, however, centers upon the microcosm of the protagonist as his internal conflict moves outward through the domestic area to the national and international to the supernatural; and coming full circle, his inner struggle often becomes identified with the cosmic, the infinite, and the ineffable.

To recognize the pattern of the encompassing spheres of force or action in Shakespeare's plays is for many readers to recall them in the work of his contemporaries and successors. It is likewise for some to recall the gradual decline of their appearance. A sampling among the works of his contemporaries and successors, however, is called for to illustrate and to shed some light upon their practices.

A professed follower of Plautus and Terence, Ben Jonson in

comedy would hardly be expected to employ the native structure of enveloping areas of action. And yet in *The Case Is Altered* (1597?) the love affairs involve the government of Milan and the government of Milan is involved in a war with France, where Count Ferneze, settling disputes and handing out justice at the end, becomes the vicar of the spiritual power. Except for the supernatural, the spheres are even better recognized in *Volpone* (1607). At the center are the Fox and the Fly, the one obsessed with greed and lust and an inordinate pride in his power to satisfy them, the other a master of schemes and stratagems with a pride in their practice exceeding his avarice. Their private and domestic gulling and cheating of fools ultimately is brought to the attention of the Senate, and justice is meted out to them. Outside the state and representing the international sphere are Sir Politic Would-be, his wife, and Peregrine. If the spiritual realm is not made explicit, it is no less operative here—as in all of Jonson's comedies—in the formal reassertion of the moral order at the end: "heaven could not long let such crimes be hid." But it is made quite explicit in *The Devil Is an Ass* (1616), a veritable morality play, in which Satan, Pug, and the Vice (Iniquity) surround the action as supernatural force to set off the events; all their deeds are designed to produce evil but all are turned ironically to good. The personal avarice of Fitzdottrel finally brings him to public attention and to the courts; and disguised as a Spanish lady, Wittipol even suggests an international sphere of interest.

However well these plays may suggest the pattern, Jonson best and most frequently demonstrates it in a quite different way—in his use of inductions, prologues, and choruses. He is always aware of his audience as an encompassing force; and, like Shakespeare in *The Taming of the Shrew*, of the world as a place of make-believe, all life as a play.[29] This concept is especially notable in *Everyman out of His Humour, Cynthia's Revels, The Poetaster, Bartholomew Fair, The Staple of News,* and *The Magnetic Lady.* He shows himself also to be very much aware that his play is set in its own little world in *Bartholomew*

Fair and in *The New Inn,* for the Fair is obviously a microcosm and the Host of the Inn tells the audience pointedly that he considers the world a stage and his inn a little world where he sits to watch and laugh at the comedy. The Induction to *The Staple of News* (1625) forms a play outside the play, wherein Tattle, Mirth, Expectation, and Censure sit on stage and comment on the action played out. Within the play proper Pennyboy Canter, standing to the side of the action from the first, sets all in order at the end. Every character is allegorical, or approaches the allegorical; their names indicate something more than the usual humors. The play is really a morality—as is *The Devil Is an Ass* (1616).[30] Like Plautus before him and the writers of the late moralities and interludes as well, Jonson keeps in touch with his audience, but he employs a less direct method than they. Not infrequently he sets his play proper within another play and then relates the encompassing play to yet another—the world of reality. Well aware of the frames or spheres of action, he manages to adapt even his classical comedies to the pattern in his own effective way.

His two Roman tragedies follow the pattern more obviously. At the center of *Sejanus* (1603) a warped soul, out of which "A race of wicked acts / Shall flow . . . , and o'erspread / The world's wide face . . . ," is driven by lust and ambition to wrest the power from the Emperor. The character of the single man threatens the welfare of the empire. But he desecrates the statue of Fortuna in the chapel of his home following a religious service. As a result he is brought unsuspectingly to trial before the Senate in the Temple of Apollo and is destroyed. As the last lines tell us, the power of the gods brings low the insolent man. Likewise, the supernatural is a telling force in *Catiline* (1611). The action is instigated by the Senecan Ghost of Scylla which enters into the spirit of Catiline. Catiline's intent is sealed in a sacramental oath taken with his aides at a solemn ritual near the beginning of the play. Such sacrilegious action is an outward and visible sign of his licentious and dissolute character, within which another play is going on. His suspected insurrection against the state brings Cicero and the Senate down upon him. The Allobroges, representing the international area, are service-able in the action. Jonson admired the Roman drama; he did not write plays strictly according to its rules or practices.

Edward Sharpham's *The Fleir* (1616) [31] is an obvious imita-tion of *Measure for Measure*. The banished Duke disguised as Fleir controls the action much as a god sitting outside. The do-mestic and private affairs of Piso, Nan, Susan, the Knight, Sparke, and Ruffell run counter to the law. Ultimately a trial is necessary. At it justice is effected, and Fleir reveals himself as the disguised Duke. In *Cupid's Whirligig* (1607) Sharpham varies the pattern a little. Cupid, acting as presenter, says at the outset that "though you do not all times eye me, / Yet know at all times I am by yee." Representing the spiritual power behind the action, he comes forward at the end to furnish the conclusion. His agent Wages directs the action of the four lovers at the cen-ter of the play. And just outside their immediate mix-ups stands Old Lord Nonsuch, "my lord Justice," called upon to settle the marital troubles of Master and Mistress Correction. Thus in these two plays of Sharpham two easily recognized treatments of the spheres of encompassing actions emerge.

Not only does John Marston set one action within the frame of another in the ten plays he wrote or had a hand in, but he shows himself to have done so consciously and deliberately, not-ing public powers in conflict with private interests. In *Antonio and Mellida* (1599),[32] for example, Piero, Doge of Venice, calls attention to two frames: "Nor shall the carpet-boy *Antonio* / Match with my daughter, sweet cheekt *Melida*. / No the pub-lic power makes my faction strong." To whom Feliche answers, "Ill, when publick power strengtheneth private wrong." The love of these two is crossed by state interests, and the strife with Genoa indicates the international area. The surrounding heavens are threatening. The boastful Piero is warned that "the ground trembleth" and that the smoke from such an earthquake as his pride can break his neck and make him wish he had "allowed Jehovah a share" in his success. An Induction relates the action directly to the audience.

If the supernatural is not physically represented upon the stage in *Antonio and Mellida*, it is in *Antonio's Revenge*, the sequel. The Senecan Ghost of Andrugio appears to Antonio, calls for revenge, and warns Maria against Piero. A dumb show (V.i) is explained by the Ghost: Nemesis overtakes Piero. Within the supernatural is the international sphere, represented by Venice and Genoa; within Venice the rebellion of the "states" (the three estates) takes place; and at the very center complicating the whole are the love of Antonio and Melida, the hate of Andrugio and Piero, and the friendship of the courtiers.

In *The Malcontent* (1604), a tragi-comedy, the supernatural power is not given a supernatural agent; rather, it is put into the hands of Malevole, who, like Prospero, employs it to regain his rule and teach a usurper a lesson. A microcosm, "Th' elements struggle within him; his own soul is at variance within herself" (I.ii. 34–36). The play has a well-remembered Induction, moreover, with Will Sly, Sinklow, Lowin, and Burbage acting the parts. The author makes clear his awareness of the spheres of audience, players, and play proper. Within the play, the private action involves the lust of Mendoze and Aurelia, revealed and declared to Pietro by the bitter Malevole. This declaration is occasioned by the exile of Malevole, who makes it so as to get back his position as Duke of Genoa. Outside is the power of Florence, threatened by Aurelia. And the whole mix-up is resolved by the semi-allegorical masque, wherein Mercury (played by Malevole) asserts justice, calling himself "god of ghosts" who has come from the "gloomy shades that spread the lower coasts." [33]

An interesting variation in the employment of the spheres of action occurs in *The Parasitaster, or The Fawn* (1604–1606), a "spectacle of life, and publique manners," as the author tells us, a pageant of the court and a morality with numerous allegorical characters surrounding the courtly and private lives of others. The personal concerns and family affairs of the individuals at

court must not interfere with their duties to the state. As Duci-
bel says, Tiberio must not "neglect / The honour of this faith,
just care of state." That is, he is required to put the state marriage of his father ahead of his own love for the lady. The force
of the moral and spiritual realm, however, prevails in the end:
Cupid's Parliament wipes out all the trickery, lying, and intrigue.

Almost typical is *The Insatiate Countess* (ca. 1610). At the
center are the love affairs of Rogero, Claridiana, and Mendoza;
surrounding them and their private concerns, as if they were in
a box within a box, is the state, and outside the state another en-
closing box, the international—Pavia, Medina, and Venice. Outside these is the unlimited area of the spirit, suggested here by
the Church as represented by the Cardinal and the Friar and involving justice.

As time went on, it would seem that Marston the moralist
came more and more to emphasize the conventional pattern of
actions within actions, or spheres of action within spheres.
Whether from the doctrine of decorum or from a natural feeling for the fitness of things or from the current practice of other
dramatists, he seldom does more than suggest the spiritual or supernatural powers in his lighter comedies, though the moral
forces are always present: ultimate justice must be asserted, and
the Duke or the King or the Queen step in to see it done. In the
heavier romantic and tragi-comedies and in the tragedies the
spiritual and supernatural are given roles as *personae*.

Tourneur uses the pattern in his two notable tragedies. In the
first, *The Revenger's Tragedy* (1607), the kinship with the morality play is made evident in the very names of the characters,
such as Vindice, Castiza, Lussorioso, and Ambitioso, as well as in
the theme: though vengeance, which is God's justice, may be
achieved by a man, a man acts only as an agent of God in its accomplishment and may well suffer for taking it into his own
hands. Explicitly, the supernatural sphere rumbles with thunder
at the end of the Revenger's masque, indicating the applause of
the gods. The irregularities in Nature are brought about by in-

justice within the state, and the injustice within the state by the lust and murder committed by the Duke and his family. The scheme is made even more evident in *The Atheist's Tragedy* (1611?), the whole point of which is the disproof of the Atheist's contention that no spiritual powers exist. Tourneur makes it quite clear, as already indicated, that Charlemont at the center of the action, as well as the Atheist, is a microcosm. D'Amville's lust for power, wealth, and progeny to succeed him drives him to plot against the barony. Like King David, he will send a man, his own nephew, to the front lines of battle and also murder his own brother so as to remove people who stand in his way. Outside the spheres of family and state appears the Ghost of Montferrers, D'Amville's brother, representing in person the supernatural which encloses all and supporting the Doctor's proof that a power above nature controls all creation. The masques at the end, enclosed by the rest of the action, resolve the plot.

Since George Chapman was a notable classicist, one would not expect his plays to conform to our pattern but rather to the "rules," and indeed they are less conformative than those of his contemporaries. Yet even in many of his comedies one finds evidence of the enveloping areas of action. In his earliest, *The Blind Beggar of Alexandria* (1596), the depravity of a group of courtiers brings about national and international conflicts, and a supernatural power opens the earth so that the Count can be swallowed up. A great lord in disguise, the Blind Beggar directs the action. Similarly the King in *The Humorous Day's Mirth* (1597), if not director of the action, at any rate steps in to put all to rights as final moral agent; and Fortuna is recognized by some at court as Queen of the World. A masque toward the end serves the denouement. Perhaps *The Widow's Tears* (1603–1609) furnishes the best example among his comedies of Chapman's practice. The play begins with an address to the goddess Fortuna, in which Thrasalio rejects that lady and, as one might expect a Chapman hero to do, changes his allegiance to Confidence (Self-Reliance). The metaphysical sphere and allegorical metier are here established in a more sophisticated manner than usual. The Governor appears at the end to judge and to settle differences. Somewhat the same schemes are followed in *The Gentlemen Usher* and in *Monsieur D'Olive*. Except where he directly depends upon Roman or Italian models in his comedies Chapman makes use of the general pattern.[34]

In tragedy he also makes use of it, though perhaps less obviously or directly than his contemporaries. In *Bussy D'Ambois* (1604) Bussy's struggling soul and his personal ambitions run into conflict with the customs of the court and then with the state and the social order as a whole. From the spirit world Bussy conjures up Behemoth, who explains that Guise and Monsieur are Fate's ministers, and from it a friar's ghost instructs Bussy. The areas of conflict are implicit here, if not well defined. They are also implicit in *The Revenge of Bussy*, though it is not easy to recognize an international sphere. The private revenge of Cleremont, instigated by the Ghost of Bussy, runs athwart the interests of the state and the state's responsibilities. In the two plays of *The Conspiracy of Charles Duke of Byron*, however, the international frame of reference is quite apparent, represented by such dignitaries as the Archduke of Austria, the Duke of Savoy, a Frenchman, etc. Within Byron, a man of overweening pride, a *psychomachia* develops. Indeed, the basic conflict of the whole play is his individual struggle as he is confronted with the demands, responsibilities, and compromises of the state and surrounding states. Representing the supernatural world is La Brosse, the astrologer who foretells Byron's downfall. This prophecy so angers Byron that he defies the Fates and goes to the scaffold without the consolation of the clergy, asking the ministering bishop to leave his soul to himself. In *The Tragedy of Chabot* (1613), as Professor Parrott reminds us, the problem is—as it is in all Chapman's tragedies—to determine the extent of the individual's rights against the rights of the state. The play is made up in large part of colorful trial scenes in courts of justice. In it the areas of individual and state are pushed to the fore; the spiritual or metaphysical, all but excluded except as honor dominates the characters. In *Caesar and Pompey* (1613), however, the supernatural forces are present in strength and even furnish comic spectacle. The forces of Caesar and Pompey move in conflict across the Roman world, and at the center stands Cato, the independent and just man, a world in himself. *Alphonsus of Germany*, if any part of it can be attributed to Chapman, is built around Alexander's revenge for his father's death, an action involving Germany at first and then Europe. The masque of *Fortune's Triumph* within the play provides a spiritual frame of reference; and this masque and the banquet scene (III.i), in which make-believe merges with "reality," furnishes an example of action-within-action and the concept of life as a stage play. And yet with Chapman modification and sophistication have taken place in the use of the several areas of action, especially in the emphasis upon the drama within the character.

And as one would expect, Webster's plays also reveal this microcosmic drama within the individual soul. In *The White Devil* the appearance of the Ghost of Bracciano to Flamineo is really a projection of the struggle within Flamineo's own soul, and in this meeting the individual's world and the spirit world come together: the center and the circumference are one. At the center of the action the break-up in the family and the disruption of Rome's affairs are brought on by the infidelities of Bracciano and Vittoria; these in turn involve other city-states, as well as the Church, through the move to Padua and the banishment of Lodovico. In *The Devil's Law Case* (1610?) Romelio's lust conflicts with his business interests; his business interests are complicated by state and then by international relations, since the war with the Turks involves the city-states of both Italy and Spain. Romelio's *psychomachia*, quite like that manifested by such other characters as Flamineo, is projected just before the combat, but the spirit world is not made visible. The Duchess of Malfi is perhaps the finest example of the microcosm, the soul in which the drama is consciously played out. Like Lear *in extremis*, she sees herself as akin to the whole; yet she has no time for merely personal considerations. As she sinks toward despair, deserted of all, persecuted by those to whom she had trustingly turned for help, she is reduced to elementary concerns only. Offered comfort by Bosola, who has betrayed her, she remarks that she has "not leysure to tend so small a business," and later she says she could curse one who wishes her long life, could curse the stars and the three smiling seasons of the year into a Russian winter—the very world "To its first Chaos." It all began with her private, nobody-else's-business action of marrying Antonio. The marriage brought down upon her the hatred of her brothers. Their interests involve her with state and church: one brother is a cardinal who puts off purple for black armor. Though the bickerings of the Italian states are to be heard in the background, they do not rise to such clamorings as to bring international events into prominence. Most prominent are the family quarrel and the spiritual struggle within the souls of the Duchess, Ferdinand, and Bosola. Sophistication has again taken place: the outside force from the spiritual or supernatural sphere has become directly operative within the characters, and except for the hoax visions prepared for the Duchess's torture, is not projected physically upon the stage.

Since Thomas Heywood's industrious dramatic career extended over the period of the climax of the Elizabethan drama and its decline into the Caroline, a review of representative examples from his plays will indicate something of what generally took place. Though as I have already shown, Heywood was well aware of the theatre as a little world and the action of the play as having a cosmic setting, he seems to have paid less heed to the pattern of encompassing areas of action than many of his contemporaries. Rather, he emphasizes, in his early period especially, the drama as a vast pageant of life ranging across the world and down the centuries. In what is perhaps his earliest play, *The Four Prentices of London* (1592?), the presenter and the chorus form an outside action and provide a consecutive narrative for the audience.[35] The thriving business of the four apprentices, really the sons of the "Earl of Buliogne," is interrupted by their patriotic venture on the Crusade; and their various actions take them across the world. The private, civic, national, and international spheres make up the areas of action. But little if anything gives identity to the spiritual area, although religious motive sets off the whole series of adventures. In *II Edward IV* (1594), possibly Heywood's play, however, the Ghost of Friar Anslem personifies the supernatural force. The petty personal desires of Shaw reach outward to disturb the state and destroy the Princes; their destruction troubles the cosmos. Along the way the love of Edward for Jane Shore brings disorder to the kingdom, and the usual quarrels with France furnish the international background. *The Royal King and the Loyal Subject* (1602?) is really a sophisticated morality play. The King, playing God to Martiall's Mankind, tests Martiall through Clinton and Chester (evil angels) and the Prince and the Captain (good angels). In the "Prologue to the Stage" Heywood explains that in this "curious age" authors bring gods themselves down to the stage.

In *A Woman Killed with Kindness* (1603), however, the several actions are restricted to domestic issues. No supernatural or allegorical beings appear, nor does the state have a place in the main plot, though the civil authorities do imprison Mountford of the secondary. Although remorse brings the leading lady to her death, it is never personified as an allegorical figure. Yet *The Rape of Lucrece* (1603–1608), deriving from classical lore, properly makes use of the Oracle in determining the action, and the Gabines in the play at least suggest the powers surrounding Rome, where the main strife is brought on by lust and deceit. In Part I of *If You Know not Me You Know Nobody* (1605) Elizabeth is protected supernaturally: angels in a dumb show drive back her persecutors; yet in Part II, although the power of heaven saves England and Elizabeth from Spain, that power is not projected onto the stage. In the same play it should be noted that Gresham's commercial ventures lead first to involvement with the affairs of the kingdom and then with the affairs of the world. Indeed, the private affairs of the one person ripple out to

the very hand of God and its protective power, though its physical presence is not disclosed. In *Fortune by Land and by Sea*
(ca. 1607), written with Rowley, the personal, national, and international spheres are made quite explicit; and though the supernatural is not directly in evidence, Young Forest comments
that "The heavens when they be pleased may turn the wheel of
Fortune round," and Anne puts her trust in that high power
which "can best rule our state." Although one may hear in the
background of *The Brazen Age* (1613?) and *The Iron Age*
(1613?) the laughter of the gods from *The Golden Age*
(1611?) and *The Silver Age* (1612?), one does not find them in-
truding upon the action of these two vast pageants. In dramatiza-
tions of the Meleager story and the fall of Troy, the spheres of
action of this world, the personal, domestic, national, and international are made explicit, but the realm of the gods is left
vague. Heywood's interest in the domestic scene and his concern
for the common man's place in the scheme of things seemingly
restricted his vision of the whole. This was even more true of his
work after his return to playwriting in 1624. In *The Captives*
(1624), derived from Plautus, the complications are almost
wholly domestic.[36] And *A Challenge for Beauty* (1634–1635),
finally, is a pre-Restoration love-and-honor play restricted to the
court and its intrigue, a far cry from *The Four Prentices of
London* with which Heywood started his career. His area of action has been severely limited; the world is no longer his stage,
nor are the areas of action set one within another.

So it was with others. Though Dekker boldly and clearly
marks out the pattern of society as encompassing areas for action, like Heywood he does not often in the pattern of his plays
provide for the world beyond. If a force at all, it is commonly
represented vicariously. At the center of *The Shoemaker's Holiday* (1599), for example, the love affair of Lacy in the main plot
and that of Rafe in the secondary are set directly within the
framework of the government of the city of London, and that
of London within the kingdom, and both of these are conditioned by the war with France. The King appears as God's

vicar, as it were, settling all differences and tempering justice
with mercy at the end. Perhaps the very realism of such comedy
made the introduction of the supernatural or allegorical *in per-
sonis* a violation of decorum. Yet the supernatural was very
much a part of William Rowley's *The Shoemaker a Gentleman*
(ca. 1608), probably written to compete with Dekker's play.[37]
Although one might expect the supernatural or metaphysical
made concrete through allegorical figures in Dekker's *The Honest Whore* (1604, 1608?), one finds it in neither part. The emphasis falls upon the domestic intrigues; and though these require the Duke's intervention to see justice done in the end, the
work of God's agent, the action extends no farther from the
center.[38] Written in collaboration with Massinger, *The Virgin
Martyr* (1620?), however, does reveal the three major spheres
of action, though the spirit area has been sophisticated. Harpax
and Angelo stand outside the main action as two forces, the evil
and the good angels struggling for the souls of Dorothea and
Theophilus; but these two outside forces are made human and
act as human beings. The first and last scenes, moreover, envelop
the entire action of the play: in the first, Diocletian goes away;
in the last, he returns; and his decisions control the entire action,
as though he represented the *primum mobile*. Though Dekker's
works show him making straightforward use of the pattern as it
applies to much realistic comedy, they show him avoiding the
supernatural or spiritual areas made explicit so often in romantic
comedy and in tragedy.

No better indication of changes in conventions may be
found than the burlesque. Beaumont and Fletcher's *The Knight
of the Burning Pestle* (1607) reveals in its very exaggerations of
them a conscious turning away from the conventions; in so doing it abundantly reveals what they were. Like *The Old Wives'
Tale* and most of Jonson's plays, it shows the author's playful
concern for the audience's relation to the play; for here is a play-
within-a-play, within-a-play, within-an-even-larger-play of the
world of reality: Rafe's play within Jasper's play within the citizens' play within the audience. The Citizen and his Wife are an

audience within an audience. Within the two interior plots are the customary spheres of action. The apprentice's love for the master's daughter and the conflicting suit of Master Humphrey involve what the master thinks is murder and the appearance of what he takes to be a ghost. And Rafe's Ghost's last speech, a burlesque of the opening speech of Andrea's Ghost in *The Spanish Tragedy*, reveals a careful delineation of the supernatural realm. The national realm is best reflected in Rafe's speech as Lord of the May and that delivered to the daughter of the King of Moldavia. The whole venture into Moldavia, a burlesque of Heywood's *Four Prentices of London*, points up the requirement for the international sphere. By recognizing the conventions and burlesquing them, Beaumont prepares for the changes to come.

In his letter "To the Reader" prefixed to his "pastoral tragi-comedy" Fletcher gives his famous definition of tragi-comedy and indicates also that there "must be a representation of familiar people [as well as nobility and royalty], with such kind of trouble as no life be questioned; so that a god is as lawful in this as in a tragedy, as mean people as in a comedy." Thus Pan lurks just outside the action of *The Faithful Shepherdess* (1608–1609), and his priest is much in evidence. Actually this priest is vicar of the god, performing his functions among the shepherds. This same vicarious function is performed by the Duke in *The Fair Maid of the Inn* (1625/26). Standing outside the action proper, he tries to keep the peace, sets up a court and tries the offenders, and conducts the reconciliation at the end. And he is quite conscious of his function, as he tells us:

> Since it hath pleas'd heaven
> To grace us with this miracle, I that am
> Heavens instrument here, determine thus: Alberto
> Be not unthankfull for the blessings showne you,
> Nor you Baptista: discord was yet never
> A welcome sacrifice; therefore rage layd by,
> Embrace as friends, and let pass'd difference
> Be as a dreame forgotten.[39]
>
> (V.iii.274–81)

The Duke then regards himself as heaven's instrument, the direct representative of the spiritual force in the play—as are so many others who never make the point of saying so.

Earlier, however, the decline is apparent, even in tragicomedy. *Philaster* (ca. 1610) owes much to *Hamlet*. Yet in contrast to *Hamlet*, it has no outside supernatural sphere, no ghostly instigator of action. Philaster's love for the usurping king's daughter opposes his personal desire to his public responsibility and obligation. His rival comes from Spain, a foreign land, though no other international complications are apparent. Furthermore, in contrast to *Hamlet*, Bellario's love for Philaster emphasizes the love interest and the personal as opposed to public and ethical considerations. The outer spheres of action are dimming and the inner becoming preoccupied only with the self.[40]

They grow even dimmer in the later plays, though with occasional bright recurrences. Thus they appear with varying degrees of clarity in the plays of Massinger, Middleton, Ford, Nabbes, Shirley, Glapthorne, and the rest. But to find them fully realized becomes the exception rather than the rule. For example, they are explicit in Middleton's later, less evident in his earlier plays, which were comedies. Those most obviously built upon the pattern are his *The Changeling* (1622) (with Rowley as collaborator) and *A Game at Chess* (1624).[41] At the center of the action in *The Changeling* Beatrice-Joanna, heiress of Alicant, promised to Alonzo, becomes infatuated with Alsemero of Valencia. The lovers' triangle becomes involved in national and international affairs, since the lady and her lover are heirs of Spanish principalities. The Ghost of Alonzo reveals the reality of the supernatural, but only as "A mist of conscience" to Joanna and Deflores. Continuity between Acts III and IV is maintained by the device of the dumb show, a sort of play within the play. But the international broils are no more than suggested by the character of Tomasso Piracquo; the government of Alicant is not threatened; the Ghost instigates no action—it merely pricks consciences. On the other hand, *A Game at Chess* is unique. Its structure is obviously intended to illustrate the cosmic pattern. An induction is used, and Error, standing outside the main action, presents this action to Loyola for his edification. Loyola watches it as a sort of moving picture much as Christopher Sly watched, and like Sly he is forgotten in the end. Within the Loyola-Error play set on the world stage (Loyola aims at "universal monarchy") the struggle between Spain and England takes place; within the international intrigues and conflicts are the national intrigues of the English court; and within these are the individual difficulties brought on by private ambitions and schemes. All are interrelated. The chessboard is obviously a little world.

In Massinger's plays the encompassing actions are perhaps best observed in *The Unnatural Combat* (1621–1625?), in *The Roman Actor* (1626), as one might expect, and in *A Very Woman* (1634), though it emerges in some form in all his plays.[42] In *The Unnatural Combat* the purely personal affairs of Theocrine, Beaufort, Jr., Malefort, and his son and daughter, who form the central group, are soon involved with the government of Marseilles. The city is soon confronted with the revolt of Montreville. Outside Marseilles stand the threatening powers of the pirates of Algiers and the Turkish Empire; and outside all hover the ghosts of Malefort, Jr., and his mother, moved from the center of the action to the periphery to assert divine justice, life beyond life, and the unity of all being.

Similarly in *The Roman Actor*, the dramatist makes clear use of the three spheres as well as the technical device of plays within the play. The lust of Domitian disturbs the government of the empire; the selfish interests of the senators cause them to betray their public trust. The wars from which Domitian returns at the opening of the action suggest the world that surrounds even the Roman world. The apparition of Act V and the words of the Soothsayer suggest the realm of the spirit which contains all. Even more significant is the functional use of the three plays within the play. What would seem at first to be mere professional deeds of the actors playing on a stage at once become public. As Professor Arthur Brown has well pointed out,[43] each of these plays contributes to the plot of the main action. They also exemplify, as the mousetrap does in *Hamlet*, the Elizabethan theory of the drama as rhetorical in purpose—to move men.

The same theory of the nature of the arts is emphatically set forth in *A Very Woman*. Story, music, and the pageant are used as therapy to bring the distraught Cardenas to a quiet mind. Indeed within these arts a struggle goes on between the good and evil geniuses for the soul of Cardenas, the very center of the action. Next him Pedro, Antonio, Leonora, and Almira form the group whose primary actions concern their private or domestic lives; next to them and connecting them with the state are Cuculo and Borachio, agents of the Viceroy of Messina; next beyond the state are the pirates and the Turkish Empire; and outside and beyond all these is Paulo, the doctor disguised as a friar, the prime mover of the action, who administers the arts of story, music, and pageant to the distraught Cardenas. The force farthest removed thus becomes the most inward force in the action. The good and the bad geniuses have become sophisticated; they operate within the main characters, but in an obvious manner. Sophisticated, the areas within areas of action are still apparent.

But as time went on and tastes became restricted by court patronage, the scope and subject matter of the plays became likewise restricted. Noticeable even in the early plays of Beaumont and Fletcher, it became more noticeable in those after 1625, especially in the works of the new playwrights. A few examples from the works of Ford, Shirley, and others will indicate the falling off.

Even *Perkin Warbeck* (1622–1632?),[44] possibly Ford's earliest play and a throwback to the chronicle play tradition, reflects the change. Although the love of Katherine and Warbeck and the interest of Huntley are complicated by Warbeck's claims to the throne, the emphasis of the action is curiously thrown, not upon the upheaval of state and its vast consequences, but upon the strange, powerful, and devoted love of the two principals. It involves a near uprising in England, a conflict with Scotland, and repercussions in Burgundy, but little is made of these surrounding forces. And the supernatural or spiritual is not objectified. In *The Broken Heart* (ca. 1627–1631?), on the other hand, the supernatural is made evident by the use of the Oracle, but this use was not so much deliberate as required, since the setting is ancient Sparta. The international area is likewise made evident in that Ithocles returns as a triumphant conqueror from Messene, but the state affairs of Sparta as such do not come to the fore. The emphasis lies not upon the loves of the several in conflict with the interests of the state—but simply upon the mismatings of these couples. The brooding character of Orgilius suggests the play within the soul, the *psychomachia*.

In *'Tis Pity She's a Whore* (1629–1633) it is more than suggestive: Giovanni describes his sister in terms of the microcosm: "View well her face, and in that little round / You may observe a world of variety; / . . . Hear her but speak, and you will swear the spheres / Make music to the citizens of heaven." (II.v.) His own struggle against his passion for his sister is an inward drama. But it cannot be contained within; and breaking out to affect his sister, it pulls into its orbit the other frustrated lovers and other court intrigues. It is true that these affairs are surrounded by the state affairs of Parma, but little is made of them; and it is true that the international frame of the action is suggested by the presence of the Papal Nuncio and by Philotus' going to a convent at Cremona, but it is no more than suggested. Likewise a spiritual setting beyond these may be suggested by the Friar and the Cardinal, but it is not given a supernatural framework. The device of the wedding masque, set within and a functional part of the plot, furnishes surprise and gives depth to the action. The framing forces of action are present or are suggested, but in this play, as in Ford's other plays, the emphasis is upon the central circle of individual personalities and their personal concerns. And with *Love's Sacrifice* (1632?) the pattern has all but disappeared. The characters are all of the court, but their acts do not really involve the state or the international areas. The intrigue of the Vice (or a descendant of the Vice) D'Avolos and the court intrigues form the action; upon them falls the emphasis. The Church is involved in the Abbot's acts at the end, and the inevitable masque is used to rid the action of the roué who had got three foolish virgins with child. The lust, jealousy, anger, and remorse do not reach beyond the personal concerns of individual characters. Though the encompassing shells for action may be recognized in Ford's plays, they are but shells; and in contrast with his predecessors, his world has become a shrunken place.

Three examples from Shirley's plays will illustrate a more pronounced falling off.[45] The plot of *The Traitor* (1631) does involve the state, but it has no international frame of reference; Lust and the Furies do stand outside the main plot representing the allegorical and spirit realm, but their function is slight. As in Ford, the action focuses only upon the personal interests of the characters. In *The Lady of Pleasure* (1635), a comedy of manners, Sir Thomas Bornwell against his will takes his socially ambitious wife to London, where he pretends to lose his fortune. His pretended loss brings his wife back to her senses—and to the country. But neither city, state, nor realm beyond the seas is disturbed by this action; nor is any judge required to settle the squabbles at the end, no ghost to warn, nor allegorical character to give moral meaning. The action of *The Cardinal* (1641) takes place at the court against a background of war, but the dramatist has lost sight of the relation of his domestic tragedy to the state —which should by rights be much perturbed by the tragedy— or to the world at large or to Divine Providence. The love triangle of Rosaura, D'Alvarez, and Colombo dominates all and brings with it the purely personal revenge of the Cardinal for the death of his nephew. No ghosts, no visions, no priestly ministrations, no king of will and judgment to bring justice back to earth.

But the older patterns were not suddenly or utterly lost sight of. They persisted in the masques especially, as one might expect, and especially in the "moral masques." [46] Thomas Nabbes's *Microcosmus* (1637), as I have already pointed out, retains the basic features of the medieval morality play. His town play of

intrigue, *The Bride, A Comedy* (1638), set among London merchants, is hardly the sort of play in which one would expect to
find even remnants of the old framework; yet Nabbes consciously employs it. The merchants have commerce with foreign
merchants, and the French Kicksaw with them suggests an international area. Vice Raven is obviously of the morality tradition,
and opposing him is Theophilus, who calls himself "justice executioner." Manipulating and directing from outside is Goodlove,
Theophilus's father. We are told, moreover, that Justice operates in the nature of things. Nabbes did not discard the pattern.

Nor did John Day, especially in his version of *The Knave in
Grain, New Vampt* (1638?).[47] The Machiavellian Julio binds
the three plots together. A world to himself, he proposes to take
care of himself alone. He will be guided by his own interests and
controlled by no power beyond this world. Yet his interests
touch interests of others and set off a conflict with the Senate
and the court of Venice. Beyond Venice are the shepherds'
peaceful countryside and beyond them the vague place of exile
of Franciscus and Cornelia, the international area. The Duke outside as divine vicar steps in at the end to assert eternal justice.

———◆———

MY PURPOSE in considering so many examples has not been
merely to prove the existence of the structural pattern of encompassing spheres or areas or forces of action in the Elizabethan drama; it has been also to indicate the development,
growth, and decline of the concept as basic to the shape of the
Elizabethan play. Quite as important, moreover, I hope the discussions of the individual plays will have been in themselves interesting and enlightening. These frames of force or areas of action, roughly paralleling the hierarchy in the social and spiritual
orders, are set within frames like Chinese boxes or like the
spheres of the Ptolemaic system, one within the other. They
suggest the cosmic shape and unity. Not always well defined,
they are sometimes discernible in outline only, as potential rather
than active areas for dramatic use. As time goes on and as, in the

Jacobean and Caroline plays, the action tends to become more circumscribed, the spheres of force or areas of action tend to become sophisticated or to lose their identity altogether. But this is not true of all the plays; in some they persisted and their function with them.

They move the action of the Elizabethan play outward from the center and central characters to involve the city or the state, the world, and even the heavens beyond. At times, in comedy especially, the outside sphere, often represented by the prince or the duke, is recognized as the setting of the moral order in which the vicar of Divine Justice presides. Furthermore, the play or the masque within the play or the induction or sometimes the chorus reveals this same tendency to provide the proper relationships among the several actions or plots. These are "devices," to be sure, and may be thought of as apart from the more organic patterns required by the "fiction" of the play. However that may be, they reveal the same concept of its structure, and they in themselves often provide the concentric functional spheres. They set up a set relationships between the players and the audience and the fiction being represented. The plays are made up of this set of relationships as well as of the relationships inside the fiction—the forces or spheres or areas or frames set one within another. The action ranges outward one way or the other from the individual soul as microcosmic center to whatever is beyond the farthest star—as it were, from the little girl at Grover's Corners to the mind of God, if we may borrow the minister's way of addressing letters as reported wonderingly by Rebecca in Thornton Wilder's *Our Town*.

THREE

The Pageant of the World

§ֺ IN DISCUSSING the masque presented to Ferdinand and Miranda in *The Tempest*, Robert J. Nelson observes that Prospero stages not only this play-within-a-play but all that takes place on the island and that if in this scheme of things some of the players thus become audience, the audience in the very theatre itself may likewise become players to a yet more ultimate audience. The convolutions of plays may become infinite, and "The world-stage concept is the very essence of the play-within-a-play concept." [1] Nelson is here recognizing in the one play the pattern I have pointed out in the preceding chapter as belonging to many. In it I have regarded the play-within-the-play and the masque as well as dumb shows, choruses, and inductions as expressions of the basic phenomenon of the concentric spheres of the play as a whole: in some cases their elaborate development and in others their critical function in the plot require that position. More logically, however, they belong to the scene, for they are really not so much plays within plays as scenes within scenes and might justifiably have asked a place in this chapter. Yet perhaps enough attention has been given these devices already. Whatever space we can afford the discussion of scenes should now be devoted to those other characteristics illustrative of the shaping force of the concept of the world as a stage.

At this point it is well to remember that the Elizabethan

theatre whether public or private made no use of a proscenium curtain, and perhaps not a great deal of an inner curtain. Scenes were "disclosed," it is true, but such disclosures were parts of larger scenes; they were scenes-within-scenes, parts indeed of a continuum. A group of characters, or one character, walk out upon an open stage as if on their way somewhere; they stop, or are stopped by other characters, and converse or execute other action and then move on. During their stay upon the stage, they may observe yet another action, overhear yet another scene. Though the observed scene may sometimes be closed off by a curtain, as a sort of parenthesis within the basic scene, the basic scene of which the other is a part represents a continuum, the illusion of which is deepened by the fact that the actors have to walk off the stage and must continue their actions elsewhere. What the audience sees is really always a parenthesis cut out of infinity, a condition emphasized by the requirements of the Elizabethan as opposed to the modern stage. In one sense every scene is set within another, a part of the eternal continuum. Such concept makes logical the appearance of a single person to act a scene alone and allow the audience to overhear his soul-struggle or his soliloquy, his conversation with himself by which he may explain his actions, or the conversation between a couple of citizens or soldiers who stand a little apart from the main action and comment on it, or the episodic "mirror scenes" which do not so much further plot as reveal meaning or motivation.[2] These are actually only parts of the larger onward-moving pageant of the ages, just as the more spectacular processional or ceremonial scenes more obviously are. The cosmic pageant was basic to the cycles, out of which grew in large part the Elizabethan popular drama. Secularized and greatly enriched by the ceremonies and formalized character of public life, the military and the court life especially, the pomp and circumstance of pageantry were just as basic to the chronicle and history plays—and to the high tragedies as well. They are a little less obvious in romantic and tragi-comedy and still less in domestic tragedy and comedy, though seldom entirely absent. And as time went on and the plots, places, and characters became restricted in complexity and number, they likewise were restricted. The scenes of the Elizabethan play, or rather the one vast scene wherein others are set, and still others within them, reveal the world as a stage "wherein all things are appointed to play their pageants." Surely enough has been said of the scene-within-scene concept, so obvious to any reader; surely not enough of the pageantry. It is with the processions, then, the formal entrances and exits, the ceremonies and ceremonious actions, and the rituals that we are now concerned.

The Renaissance no less than the Middle Ages made much of processions, ceremonies, rituals, and pictorial effects. In both periods men found their places in these passing shows, each conscious of having a role in the cosmic drama that moved from Creation to the Day of Doom. This consciousness provided a condition naturally favorable to the understanding and the production of drama. It also quite naturally required that the familiar expressions of this pageantry be produced upon the stage. From the processions inside the cathedral to those outside on Corpus Christi Day, from the election of a pope to the christening of a child, from the coronation of a king to the king's creation of a knight, from the elaborate tournaments on the Field of the Cloth of Gold to the Lord Mayor's shows, from the audience in the presence chamber or the conduct of the royal court in a state chamber to the trials in the magistrate's court of law, from the triumph of a conqueror to the lowly "formation" of the constable and the watch, from the royal banquet to the alderman's dinner, from a wedding reception in the country gentleman's home to the dance of his servants in the courtyard, from the funeral procession to the procession of prisoners, from the formal welcome of a monarch to a monarch's formal commission of his ambassador, from the herald's formal appearance to the king's oration before battle—ritual, ceremony, and formality were required.

They furnished the playwright and his public the grand illusion of the insubstantial pageant of the world and of time. The magnificent Cottonian Manuscript, Julius E IV, in the British

Museum contains, for example, fifty-three illustrations of the pageants of Richard of Beauchamp, Earl of Warwick. These were merely some of the pageants in which a single earl was featured. Among them are such drawings as that of the creation of "Erle Richard" as Knight of the Garter, the coronation of "Dame Jane, Duchess of Breteyn," the Earl's taking leave of the French court, and the crowning of the King of France. All are ceremonies, and all are such ceremonies as one frequently finds in Elizabethan plays.

Since George Peele was a writer of pageants and at one "time had all the oversight of the pageants," one would expect him to furnish examples of pageant-like and ceremonious scenes. Of the twenty-five scenes in his *Edward I* (1584), twenty either open with formal processions or have such entries within the scene. For example, after the ceremonious entry of the nobility and the Queen Mother at the opening of the play, and after the Queen Mother's formal speech, Edward himself with all his train heralded by trumpets, makes the grand entrance as the conquering hero. The procession is carefully described in the stage directions, and the author asks that the train shall include "as many as may be." At the opening of Scene iii, nine lords of Scotland with their nine pages enter, as well as King Edward, Queen Elinor, the Queen Mother, with the King and Queen under a canopy. Scene xiii is a procession following "the christening and marriage," the two rituals perhaps being presented in dumb show. In his *Battle of Alcazar* (ca. 1589) all fifteen scenes open with formal entries or processions, most of them military of course, or else court scenes such as III.i. In *David and Bethsabe* (1594?) ten of the entrances are decidedly formal and ceremonious. Seven are military, one is the ritualistic lament of King David, barefoot and "with some loose covering over his head," one involves a formal oration, and one is the coronation of Absalom. *The Old Wives' Tale* (1591–1594), even, though it involves no military or monarchs, has considerable ceremony and pageantry, such as the rituals, the riddles, and the songs of the harvest men.

So rich in so much that is typical of Elizabethan drama, Kyd's *Spanish Tragedy* is not less rich in pageantry and cere-

monial scenes than other plays. At least thirteen entrances, and
by implication as many exits, are formal, many of them processions. Among these are two processions of prisoners, one procession to a banquet, one to a play, one a dumb show, and the
rest either military or formal court scenes. One entrance brings
Pedringano as prisoner to Hieronimo's court of justice, both the
prisoner's procession and the court of justice being formal and
ceremonious.

It is nothing new to observe that both parts of Marlowe's
Tamburlaine are made up chiefly of a series of pageants,[3] but
their number and variety have not perhaps been fully realized.
Of the eighteen scenes of Part I, twelve are outright processions:
a group of people, usually officers and soldiers, march on stage in
military formation at the opening and in formation march off at
the end. In Scene i, indeed, two formal groups appear; the second involves the coronation of Cosroe. Later, another involves
Tamburlaine's coronation: he dramatically takes the crown
from the dead Cosroe and with some ceremony crowns himself
on the field of battle. In one scene Cosroe makes a formal battle
oration; in another the Soldan of Egypt holds court. In still another Tamburlaine, on a formal state occasion, has Bajazet
brought on in a cage and then made his footstool to the throne.
In Part II at least fifteen of the scenes are processions. In each a
group of characters come on stage in strict formation, conduct
the action of the scene, and move off as they came on. Besides
these, various ceremonies take place, such as the treaty made between Sigismund and Orcanes, in which formal oaths are sworn
upon swords; such as the prayer, in which Orcanes prays both
to Christ and to Mahomet to punish Sigismund; or such as the
prayer Sigismund utters at his death (II.iii). The crowning of
Callepine (with Callepine's great oration, III.i), that of Almeda,
and that of Amyras furnish still three other spectacular ceremonies. Even more spectacular is the funeral procession: the hearse
of Zenocrate being carried in state opens III.ii. The play consists largely of a series of processions and ceremonies; its
dramatic appeal depends upon the heightened emotions they
bring.

Much the same is true, though not so readily realized, of the middle sections of *Doctor Faustus*, where great variety is accomplished. The ritual of Faustus' calling up Mephistophilis (I.iii) is matched by the ceremony of the compact he makes with Lucifer and Mephistophilis (II.i), and the masque of the Seven Deadly Sins is matched both by the magical tableau of Alexander's fight with Darius (IV.ii) and that of Helen's appearance (V.i). A group of devils bring fine apparel to Faustus and dance for him in burlesque ceremony (II.i); a great papal procession appears (III.i), in which cardinals, bishops, monks, and friars bearing crosiers and singing as they move, precede the Pope himself and the King of Hungary; later a splendid papal banquet is brought on, with the processions before and after it (III.ii); still later (IV.ii) at the court of Charles a grand procession precedes the conference between Faustus and the Emperor and the tableau showing the court of Alexander and Darius; and still another follows as the court moves off. Similarly the Duke of Anholt and his entourage come on in formal procession and, after the horse-play, go off in the same formation (IV.vii). Doubtless the entrance of Benvolio, Martino, Frederick, and soldiers (IV.iii) is in military formation, as well as their exits; wherever soldiers appear, we can be fairly certain they move in formation, and Frederick here indicates as much when he leads them off.

The Massacre at Paris is no less processional and ritualistic. At least half of its twenty-three scenes open with processions, and the play is concluded with a funeral procession: the body of the King is borne off-stage in state. A splendid procession follows the coronation of the King (xiii); less splendid, but more effective emotionally, is the procession of Protestants who kneel to pray before they are massacred (xi). Similar figures and instances might be cited for *Edward II* and *The Jew of Malta*, as any reader knows. Marlowe made much of court processions in state, funeral processions, processions of prisoners, ecclesiastical processions, military formations, oaths, curses, prayers, incantations, abdications, banquets, masques, formal announcements, leavetakings, and contracts. Lifting the action above the commonplace, the rituals, ceremonies, and processions begin to repeat themselves, to become stock scenes or aspects of scenes.

And as might be expected, these were especially numerous in the early chronicle plays, histories, and tragedies. An excellent indication of this use of pageantry and ceremony is supplied by Ernest L. Rhodes's recent study of the plays presented at the Rose Theatre. He finds that the movement of the action in more than three-fourths of the scenes staged at the Rose were either sweeping movements across the stage parallel to the back, or else slanting movements from the ends of the stage toward one or more of the openings at the back, "as formal movements of groups. Of the 861 scenes in the plays we know were presented at the Rose, 655 (or more than three-fourths) were of a formal or ceremonious kind." [4] The actors came on in strict formation according to rank or position or special arrangement; they usually left the stage in the same manner.

If pageantry and ceremony were characteristics of the plays given by Henslowe's players at the Rose, they were equally characteristic of those given by Paul's Boys, wherever they played, and those given by the Children of the Queen's Revels at Blackfriars—if we may judge by the plays of Marston. The mention of Marston should as well suggest pageantry—processions, ceremonies, music, ritual, and *tableaux vivants*—as satire. And Marston was careful to set forth in his stage directions the elaborate nature of these devices. In *Antonio and Mellida* (1599) and in its sequel *Antonio's Revenge* the audience was immediately struck by the military formations and the entrances of princes to their courts in state. In Act I alone of *Antonio and Mellida* six entrances require a flourish of cornets as a procession enters, and the exits are quite as formal. Indeed *Antonio's Revenge* is little more than a grand pageant itself, though a bloody one. In this and all his plays Marston is fond of calling for torches or tapers to lead his processions: "Enter two mourners with Torches, two with streamers: *Castalio & Forobosco*, with torches: a Heralde bearing *Andrugio's* helme & sword: the coffin: *Maria* supported by *Lucio* and *Alberto*. . . ." This description of the funeral procession (II.i) goes on for five more lines. It forms one of at least a dozen such formal processions. *The Malcontent* (1604) is hardly less crowded with them. I mention only a few: The Duke enters his perfumed presence chamber in state (I.ii); Ferneze ushers in Aurelia with Emelia and Maquerelle bearing her train (I.vi); a procession of state follows Mendoza's formal enthronement (V.iii); and a complicated procession is formed as Prepasso and Bilioso are led on by two pages with lights, as Ferrard with Mendoze are led on by two other pages, and as the Duke meets Maria (V.iv). Each furnishes suspense as well as color, impressive episodes to captivate an audience. In *Sophonisba* (1606) the Prologue is itself a double procession, two sets of torches leading it. In the play proper twenty such entrances and as many exits occur. One ceremony involves the preparation of Sophonisba for her bridal bed (I.ii); another, the signing of a document in the Senate (II.i); and another, a "sacrifice" performed before an altar by Sophonisba.[5] Perhaps no period of English drama was so rich as that between 1598 and 1610; perhaps no English drama was so rich in ceremony or formalized entrances and exits or *tableaux*, of pageantry in general; and perhaps no English dramatist of this period made his plays richer in these qualities than did Marston.

A brief examination of a few of Shakespeare's plays will illustrate his practice very well. His chronicle plays, as one would expect, are made up in large measure of pageantry and ceremony. In the first scene of *King John* four formal entrances and exits occur, one court presentation of an ambassador, one trial before the King as judge, and the ceremony of knighting Faulconbridge. Some thirty entrances and exits of the play are formal in nature and ceremonious, most of them processions. One scene includes both a deposition and a coronation: King John himself puts off his crown, but Pandulph, the papal emissary, recrowns him. Another is a formal parley between John and the King of France; still another (IV.iii) includes Salisbury's oath as he kneels beside the body of Arthur. Most of the scenes are taken up with processions or other formal and ceremonious occasions, with only a few informal soliloquies or conversations in which characters particularize a deed or comment upon what has happened, such as the scene of Arthur's death. The emphasis of the play, if one will realize the action in terms of its staging, falls upon the exciting pageantry of this world as it passes before the onlookers.

In *I Henry VI* at least twenty-one entrances and exits are formal, the King and his retinue frequently appearing in courtly order to move off in the same fashion. In addition, at least nine ceremonies take place: a funeral procession for Henry V, a proclamation of the Lord Mayor read before the Tower, a setting of the watch by the French, the trial and the fateful choosing of the roses in the garden of the Temple, a trial in Parliament before the King, Talbot's investiture with the earldom of Shrewesbury, the coronation of Henry as King of France, the oath of fealty sworn by the Governor of Paris, and the Dauphin's swearing of fealty to Henry. The play is really little more than a series of processions and ceremonies involving ritual, and they are all the more dramatic for being formal.

Similarly in *II Henry VI*, in which at least twenty-four entrances and exits are formal. These are usually preceded by a trumpet flourish announcing the King. Troops pass over the stage in military formation, or the court is assembled for a state occasion, or a nobleman with his train comes onstage to transact formal business. At least ten ceremonies occur, four of them in I.i—a report to the King of the espousal of Queen Margaret, the King's prayer as he welcomes his Queen, Gloucester's reading of the articles of the treaty and the marriage agreement, and the creation of the Marquess of Suffolk as Duke of Suffolk. All these are connected in a brilliant court scene. The King says at least three prayers during the course of the play; Eleanor (Gloucester's wife) does her ritual of penance walking barefoot in the street; Iden is knighted by the King; Jack Cade burlesques a trial; and a herald enters twice to make a formal summons.

Pageantry and ceremony are no less prominent in *III Henry VI*. At least thirty-six entrances and exits are formal, some quite ceremonious: IV.i, for example, provides in stage directions that four persons shall stand on one side and four on the other for the King to enter between the two columns. Four well-defined ceremonies occur: the mock crowning of the Duke of York before he is killed, the reception of Queen Margaret by the King of France, the prophecy of Henry VI concerning Richmond, and Edward's being proclaimed king upon his return (IV.vii), in which scene the gauntlet is thrown down and the challenge formally offered. Remove from the early chronicle plays their royal pageantry, their processions, rituals, and ceremonies, and little action is left.

More would be left in the later chronicles, but Shakespeare was in them still not greatly restricted in the use of these devices. He seems to have used them less frequently but developed them more fully. The comic parts of *I Henry IV*, for example, reduce the pageantry of that play. Nevertheless, at least fifteen of its entrances and exits are really formal processions. They involve the entrances of high officials and the King to accomplish court business and make state decisions. One of these involves the entrance of Worcester and Vernon as prisoners—the familiar procession of prisoners, so popular throughout the period. Ceremonies are fewer, too. But the parleys and conferences are at least ceremonious, even that in which Hotspur puts down Glendower and scorns the Welsh songs. More formal is the parley between Blunt and Hotspur and that between Worcester and the King before the battle. And the play that Hal and Falstaff put on in the Boar's Head Tavern is really a burlesque of a formal court scene.

In the sequel *II Henry IV*, some twenty-two entrances and exits are formal, and at least four ceremonies occur. One of the entrances is a burlesque (I.ii): Falstaff enters with a page bearing his sword and buckler before him. As for ceremonies, we have two formal parleys, one between Westmorland and Scroop and one between John of Lancaster and Scroop; the Chief Justice's judgment between Dame Quickly and Falstaff; and Hal's return of the crown, kneeling, to his father.

In *Henry V* at least twenty entrances and exits are formal or ceremonious, requiring banners, salutes from wind instruments, and marching in military formation. Some six ceremonies occur: one the formal arrest of Scroop, Cambridge, and Grey; four appearances of the Herald Montjoy in his official capacity; and the famous prayer of the King before the battle.

Even the belated *Henry VIII*, perhaps mostly the work of Fletcher, is full of pageantry and ceremony. At least eighteen entrances and exits are processions, and the ceremonies include not only the arrest of Buckingham made by the sergeant-at-arms, the petition of the Queen kneeling before Henry to ask for the redress of taxes, and the trials of Queen Katherine and Cranmer, but also the great coronation procession at the crowning of Anne and the magnificent last scene following the baptism of the babe Elizabeth in which Cranmer makes his famous prophecy. As time went on procession, pageantry, and ritual fell off even in the chronicle plays; indeed the chronicles as a genre lost out and were not often written or performed after 1603.

Little distinction can be made between the chronicles and the Roman plays and tragedies: formal processions, ceremony, and ritual were maintained in them. Shakespeare used, as best one can reckon, at least twenty formal entrances and exits in *Titus Andronicus*, most of them being military in character and requiring a group to march on and off with "flourishes." Some serve as prelude to ceremony, some as postlude. In I.i, for example, Titus appears in his great triumphant procession with drums and trumpets sounding. His way has been prepared for by a captain, and within the scene is also a procession of prisoners of war, a funeral procession, two burials performed with Roman rites and funeral orations, and at least three other formal orations. It is a magnificent and stirring opening scene. In addition two banquets are staged in this play, three or four other formal orations, two sets of formal oaths, two ceremonies creating emperors, and one announcement made by a herald, always a ritualistic action. Indeed, viewed upon the stage, the play can appear as little more than a series of formal processions and ceremonies.

But no better example can be found than *Antony and Cleopatra*, a veritable pageant of the world, whose protagonist like a colossus bestrides the globe. At least fifty-two of the entrances and exits are formal. Many are military; many bring upon the stage officials, messengers, and ambassadors. And we can be sure that protocol was observed in the order of their goings and comings. Two Romans, for example, come on in the first scene to present the glittering pageant of Cleopatra's court, as she taunts and teases her triple pillar of the world; and the final entrance is that of Caesar "and all his train." Ventidius's procession of triumph in Syria (III.i) is also a funeral procession, Pacorus' body being borne before the general. At fewest ten formal ceremonies enhance the action, some of them slight or small: such is the leave-taking of Caesar and Octavia (III.ii) or the meeting of Antony and Caesar (II.ii); such is the oath taken by the Triumvirs before the banquet; such the ritual of the banquet itself; such Enobarbus' prayer before his death; such the placing of the guard (IV.iii) before Cleopatra's palace; and such the formal delivery of Antony's sword by Decretas to Caesar. Dressing herself in her royal robe and placing her crown upon her head before she kisses Iras and applies the asp to her breast, the Queen makes of her death a very ritual, conscious to the last that she is acting a role in the world-drama. The whole play, indeed, is a grand pageant set on the world-stage.[6]

Even in *Hamlet*, with no battles to be presented, the pageantry and ceremony make up a surprising amount of the action, and they are perhaps dramatically more effective here than elsewhere in Shakespeare's plays. At least twenty-two formal entries and exits are required, and at least seven ceremonies or ceremonials. The very first scene is a ceremony, the changing of the guard; the second is the grand court procession in which protocol was carefully observed, the formal conduct of court business, and the formal procession from the room of state. Ambassadors are dispatched. Laertes' leave-taking is ceremonious, to say the least; the oath exacted of Hamlet by the Ghost is a ritual; the King's attempted prayer is ritual; so are the funeral proces-

sion and burial of Ophelia; the challenge delivered to Hamlet by
Osric is ceremony; and the fencing match between Hamlet and
Laertes is conducted according to the code. Finally the triumphant military funeral procession at the end, with Hamlet's
body being carried off, is high ceremony. Besides these, Fortinbras' forces marching in military order across the stage and the
procession of the court to see the play furnish effective pageantry by which emotional intensity is built up and climactic action prepared for. As presented upon the flexible Elizabethan
stage, the play as a whole can be regarded as a single procession,
set between a nervous changing of the guard and an orderly
changing of the government of Denmark, a significant happening
within the great continuum in which all events are moved.[7]

In the comedies, especially those derived from the Roman
tradition, one does not expect pageantry or ceremony. Yet the
amount is surprising, whether the play is derived from the classical or the romantic tradition. Even in *The Comedy of Errors*
pageantry and ceremony are not lacking, though they are lacking in its source, *Menaechmi*. And it was just the characters and
actions requiring pageantry which Shakespeare added to his
source: the Duke of Ephesus, his officers, attendants, and addi-
tional merchants. At least half a dozen entrances and exits require "formation," four of them being the Duke with his attendants. The first entrance of the play is a procession to the Duke's
court room, where he formally pronounces judgment upon
Ægeon; so is his entrance in V.i with Ægeon and the officers,
really a procession of prisoners, as well as his exit after presiding
at the play's denouement, a trial scene in which he brings about a
correction of justice. The entrance to III.i is probably formal, as
Antipholus of Ephesus brings the merchants to his home to dinner. The central action is encompassed by procession and ceremony, both entirely lacking in the source.

If somewhat lacking in the play derived directly from Plautus, pageantry and ceremony are abundant in a play merely derived from the Plautine tradition, *The Taming of the Shrew*. In
Scene i of the Induction, for example, four formal entrances and

exits take place, in the play proper at least sixteen more. They include processions to two meals. The banquet scene at the end is a ceremonious occasion, and the wager made in the scene is a formal matter. The supper at Petruchio's country house is a burlesque of ceremony (IV.i). Indeed much of the formality is pure burlesque.

With the romantic comedies, as one would expect, the pageantry and ceremony are abundant, though of a somewhat different kind from that of the chronicles and tragedies. In *The Merchant of Venice* one may find at least a dozen formal entrances and exits, such as the entry of the Duke for the trial scene and his exit with attendants at its end. The trial itself, the longest scene of the play, is formal and ceremonious as court trials must be. The casket scenes are ritualistic, all three of them. So is Portia's giving the ring to Bassanio (III.ii), and so is Launcelot's asking his father's blessing (II.ii), though burlesque. *Much Ado About Nothing* is especially rich in these qualities. The opening scene is a procession before Leonato's orchard, with the formal greeting of the courtiers including the greeting of Don Pedro and his entourage. The opening of Act II is similar, with the formal procession of the ladies and gentlemen and the masque and dance which follow it. Dogberry's setting of the watch, though burlesque, is still a formal ceremony, as is his arrest of the conspirators, Conrad and Borachio. Likewise the wedding and the procession leading to it are ritual and pageantry. In IV.ii and again in V.i come the processions and examination of prisoners, in the last a burlesque trial. The scene in the church before the supposed tomb of Hero in which Claudio makes amends and expiation is a ritual; so is the betrothal in the final scene, to which the ladies have come masked and in procession. In *All's Well that Ends Well* at least twelve entrances and exits, mostly made by the King and his train, should be staged formally. Several ceremonies take place: a formal leave-taking (that of the lords before going to Florence, II.i), two formal contracts (II.i.193–205 and II.iii.184–90), and Bertram's betrothal to Helena. Pageantry and ceremony are so extensively used in *Winter's Tale* and in *The Tempest* that to mention these plays is sufficient to recall them; in the latter the poet deliberately calls attention to the insubstantiality of the pageant which is the world.

In addition to the stock kinds of pageants, rituals, and ceremonies used by his predecessors, Shakespeare exploited investitures and creations of noblemen, dubbing of knights, oaths of fealty, orations, wagers, rituals of penance, arrests, settings of the watch, parleys, betrothals, weddings, and trials. The action of his chronicles indeed consists mostly of a series of processions and pageants involving much ceremony; that of his Roman plays and tragedies was heightened by these same devices; and in his comedies events were raised to occasions by their use, even when they were burlesqued. Since they are formalized and thus generalized, they become by their very nature universal actions, significant always to the whole.

In spite of the fact that Ben Jonson prided himself upon his knowledge of the classics, drew much upon the Latin dramatists (so he would have us believe), and seemed to look with little favor upon the native tradition, he nevertheless followed this tradition in the use of ceremony and pageantry when he left off criticism and came to write his plays. One has only to recall his numerous trial scenes, with their necessary formality and ceremony, to realize the fact. In *Everyman Out of His Humour*, *The Alchemist*, *Epicoene*, and *The Magnetic Lady*, to be sure, one finds little to call pageantry, unless the parading of numerous disguises be pageantry; and in *Everyman in His Humour*, aside from Brainworm's arrest of Stephen and Downright, a half-dozen entrances and exits, and the trial scene of the last act, little is formal or ceremonious. But the later plays are rich enough. *The Case is Altered* has as many as a dozen formal entrances and exits, a procession of prisoners, and a formal parley. In *Cynthia's Revels* few formal processions are staged, but much pageantry and ceremony: Echo's song (I.i), for example, a ritual, is a service for Narcissus's death; such is Crites' prayer to Arete (V.ii);

such the formal reading of the licensing of Asotus (V.ii); and such the two masques at the close of the long extravaganza.

Volpone is remarkable for its pageantry, though it is somewhat different from the pageantry found in tragedy and romantic comedy. A dozen entrances and exits are formal, some being outright processions. Mosca's introduction of each of the gulls in the first scene is ceremonious, if burlesque. The mountebank scene (II.i) is mostly formal, especially Nano's song and Volpone's entrance and great oration. Each of the famous trial scenes (IV.ii and V.vi) takes place in the Scruteneo and requires a colorful procession and the ceremony of seating the court of law; the exits would also have to be formal. The stage directions for each of these entrances to the court are almost identical, correctly so. The first in Gifford's edition reads thus: "*Enter* Avocatori *and take their seats*, BONARIO, CELIA, Notario, Commandadori, Saffi, *and other Officers of justice.*" [8]

Bartholomew Fair, a little world in itself, is rich in ritual and ceremony, though hardly the sort one associates with chronicles and romances: the presentation of the whole Fair in Act II is actually the presentation of the pageant of the world, with booths set out for the fools and the gulls. At least a dozen such formalized entrances as this take place: "*Re-enter* LEATHERHEAD, *with* BRISTLER, HAGGISE, *and other* Officers." (III.i.) These officers then arrest Busy and take him off stage in the familiar procession of prisoners. And in the next scene following (IV.i) these same officials with others enter, again in something resembling military formation. One may easily multiply such instances from others of Jonson's plays, the opening of III.ii in *The New Inn*, for example. For all his love of Latin comedy, with the exception of four or five of his own comedies, Jonson followed rather the practices of his contemporaries—though in his own distinctive way—in the use of ceremony and pageantry. Except as burlesque, pomp does not intrude; across his stage, rather, move processions of gulls, imposters, mountebanks, and charlatans. Many of his characters are not what they seem; many must play a part within a part, a role within a role.

On the other hand, pomp and ceremony are fully exploited in his Roman plays. Two of the most elaborate spectacles of Elizabethan drama occur in *Sejanus*. A procession and ritual are presented in Sejanus's home (V.iv): "*Enter* Praecones, Flamen, Tubicines, SEJANUS, TERENTIUS, SATRIUS, NATTA. *etc.*" [9] Following this entrance comes the ritual elaborately described by Jonson, in which the Flamen takes honey on his finger and, tasting it, gives it to all the others. The altar is sprinkled with milk and censed. Even more splendid than this is the procession into the Temple of Apollo (V.x), where Tiberius makes his oration. Similarly, in *Catiline* some twenty-six formalized entrances and exits are made, many of them processions. Catiline's sinister oath-taking with the conspirators and Cicero's great oration before the Senate furnish superb ritual and ceremonious occasions by which the drama is intensified. In both plays the pageantry is magnificent, and Jonson makes effective use of it.

Since several of Chapman's comedies were derived directly from Roman comedy and since most of them, especially the later ones, were written for the Children and produced at Blackfriars, one would not expect much pageantry in them. Yet even the plays for the Children are not without it, and the earlier comedies, produced at the Rose, are rich in it. Chapman opens seven of the ten scenes of *The Blind Beggar of Alexander* (1596), for example, with processions. To open the play the Queen sweeps on stage with her attendants, and to open the second scene the King marches in court procession with the proper functionaries to hold court and receive a herald with proper ceremony. At the end of this scene Samathis and her maids enter with a "banquet." Opening with a formal procession, the fourth scene (act divisions are not marked) is a court scene, into which enters still another procession. Procession follows procession throughout. In the humors comedy, *A Humorous Day's Mirth* (1597), likewise produced at the Rose, one finds such stage directions as this: "*Enter the* King *and all the* Lords *with the trumpets.*" And the play ends with a masque in which two attendants enter with torches, "Moren *then my* Host *and his* Son *then his* Maid *dressed as* Queen of Fortune" (Scene xiv). The stage direction is precise as to the order to be observed.

Protocol is likewise strictly observed in Chapman's *The Gentleman Usher* (1602?), written for the Children at Blackfriars. The opening direction is typical, in which "Bassiolo [goes] *bare before.*" Five entrances in the first three scenes are strictly processional, and at the end of the play Strozzo makes a formal oration. *The Widow's Tears* (1603) begins with an oration, Tharsalio's address to the Goddess Fortuna; and Chapman carefully indicates the proper order as he directs Eudora to be escorted to the stage, with "Argus, *bearhead, with whom another usher,* Lycus, *joins.* . . ." The entrance of the audience to the masque is similarly marked as a pageant. On the whole Chapman's comedies have more pageantry than most comedies of the time.

And if his comedies contain it, his tragedies are full of it. In spite of the Senecan influence, which one would usually regard as a restraint upon pageantry, *Bussy D'Ambois* (1604) is full of effective processions and ritual. At least eleven entrances are carefully marked as formal, requiring the characters to come on stage in strict order, and the ritual of calling up Behemoth (IV.ii) is a sensational one. In *The Revenge of Bussy* (1610) at least ten entrances, to say nothing of the exits, require the king or the nobility or marching soldiers or attending ushers to move in formation and observe strict protocol. The two Byron plays, *The Conspiracy* and *The Tragedy*, called by Swinburne "a small epic in ten books," are rich in both processions and ceremony. In the first, at fewest seven entrances are formal; in the latter, at fewest a dozen, including the moving spectacle of Byron in a prisoner's procession, with the Bishop and guards being taken to the scaffold. In *The Tragedy of Byron* at least six ceremonies heighten the emotion of the audience, such as the presentation of the Dauphin, the arrest, trial, and sentencing of Byron. In *The Tragedy of Chabot* (1613), at fewest ten entrances are elaborately formal and as many exits. These include the processions to the courts of law, with the "Chancellor *attended, the* Protocol-General *whispering in his ear, two* Judges *follow-ing. . . .*" The scenes include two court trials, one court pardon, and the pronouncing of a formal sentence. Centered at the court of the King of France, this play is really a series of formalities staged with much pomp and circumstance.[10] Throughout his career Chapman shows himself acutely aware of the pageant afforded by the world's events and of his obligation to present it in his theater.

Though one might not expect him to be, Dekker is also aware of it and intent, especially in his earlier plays, upon presenting it. *Old Fortunatus* (1599), mostly a set of masques and fantasies, depends almost entirely upon procession and ceremony for its appeal. At least a dozen entrances require formal processions, and as many exits. And the ceremonies are almost as numerous. The Prologue at Court requires of its two old men a prayer for the Queen; Old Fortunatus kneels (II.ii) to the Goddess Fortuna; and Andelocia kneels to pray to Arete (IV.i). The masque-like processions, such as that of Fortune and the allegorical characters surrounding her in the same scene, are just as ritualistic in their actions.

As many as twenty-one formal entrances and exits occur in *The Shoemaker's Holiday* (1599), Dekker being careful to indicate some of them in the dialogue as well as in the stage directions. Eyre makes at least two ceremonial requests of the King. At the end of I.i a military group passes over the stage in proper formation: "*Sound drumme, enter* Lord Maior, Lincolne, Lacy, Askew, Dodger, *and souldiers, They passe ouer the stage,* Rafe *falles in amongst them,* Firke *and the rest cry Farewel, &c. and so Exeunt.*" At the end of II.iii is a fine example of a formal exit which would not be noted except for the dialogue. Margery, having heard that she is now an alderman's wife, must go about properly attended. In gay burlesque she says to the bubbling Firke: "ha, ha, prithe peace, thou mak'st my worshippe laugh, but let that passe: come Ile go in, *Hodge* prethee goe before me, *Firke* follow me." And Firke replies, "*Firke* doth follow, *Hodge*

passe out in state." Later (III.ii) Firke as usher leads "her worshippe" on stage. At the opening of the final scene (V.v) with a
"*flourish or two*" the King and his nobles, Eyre, Margery, Rose,
Lacy, and the rest come on stage, Lacy and Rose kneeling ceremoniously for the King's pardon. Lacy is knighted in formal
ceremony in this scene; Eyre on bended knee invites his monarch to the Shoemakers' banquet; and all march out at the end in
formal procession. The play makes more, and more effective, use
of pageantry and ceremony than is at first apparent.[11]

If we take *The Noble Spanish Soldier* (1631) as indicative of
what was happening toward the end of Dekker's career—and
our period—we discover that the processions became fewer but
more elaborate, or at least more fully described in the stage directions. Act I, Scene i opens with this royal procession: "*Enter
in magnificent state, to the sound of lowd musicke, the King and
Queene, as from Church, attended by the Cardinall, Count*
Malateste, Daenia, . . ." etc. The description continues for
seven lines, but the procession of attendants is soon dismissed
(having no functional part in the plot), and the King is left
alone with the Cardinal. The opening of the next scene is a ceremony set apparently in Onaelia's apartment: "*A Table set out
cover'd with blacke: two waxen Tapers: the Kings Picture at
one end.* . . ." Onaelia walks weeping before a crucifix, and a
song is sung in the background, a question and answer song in
two voices. Some ten other entrances and exits are formal or
processional. The Cardinal, as his "good Angell," kneels ceremoniously to the King, trying to persuade him against murder
(IV.ii). Then "*A Banquet is set out, Cornets sounding:* . . ." at
the opening of V.iv. This elaborate scene culminates in the disastrous drinking of the toasts. In the later plays such as this,
scenes are fewer, directions are fuller, and apparently properties
are used in greater number or are at least more fully described.
Though the chance for pageant and ceremony is made less in the
later plays, especially by the reduction of the number of scenes
(only fourteen scenes in this play), their presentation was apparently more elaborate. Dekker was fond of using them.

So was his sometime collaborator, John Webster. In *The Devil's Law Case* (1610?) perhaps more of ceremony than of procession occurs. In I.ii Leonora kneels as she pronounces a formal curse upon Jolenta, if Jolenta should ever marry Contarino; in II.iii a Capuchin with the two "Belmen" asks that Romelio and Leonora "Sigh a soft Requiem, and let fall a Bead" for the supposedly dead Ercole and Contarino, whereupon Romelio makes a formal meditation upon them, and his mother says her beads. The trial scene is quite formal (IV.ii): Crispiano and the other judge lead the procession and the court sits with ceremony. The opening of V.iv is referred to as a "dumb Pageant." In it Leonora enters *"with two Coffins borne by her servants, and two Winding-sheets stuck with flowers. . . ."* And the combat in V.v is a ritual as well as a pageant, in which "The Lists are set up," the judges enter and take their seats, and a herald appears and makes the call to combat. Preoccupation with the sensational is apparent.

The White Devil (1609–1612) is rich in ceremony and procession, and the two are inseparable. At the opening of I.ii, for example, Vittoria with several attendants and in procession ceremoniously welcomes Bracciano. Within this scene Cornelia, Vittoria's mother, pronounces her curse upon her wayward daughter. The Cardinal at the opening of Act II leads a procession with Francisco. Within the very next scene two pageant-like mirror scenes present the audience with a pantomime of the death of Camillo and then another of the death of Isabella, each sensationally revealing off-stage action. The most important ceremonies and pageants, however, make up the intensely dramatic scenes of Act III. As it opens, Francisco, Montecelso, and the Chancellor and Register enter the antechamber of the Papal consistory as prelude to the trial. Into the scene Flamineo and Marcello are marched under guard, the familiar prisoners' procession. The ambassadors singly pass over the stage ceremoniously on their way to the courtroom. The whole scene is calculated to build up suspense in anticipation of the trial scene in the papal courtroom. Far more elaborate is the opening of the trial itself

(III.ii). It is headed: "THE ARRAIGNMENT OF VIT-
TORIA. *Enter* FRANCISCO, MONTECELSO, *the six lieger
Ambassadors*, BRACCIANO, VITTORIA, ZANCHE, FLA-
MINEO, MARCELLO, *Lawyer, and a guard*." Being sentenced,
Vittoria and Zanche are marched off by the guard. At the open-
ing of IV.iii is a meeting in procession of Lodowick, Gaspero, the
six ambassadors, and Francisco. But the most magnificent is
Montecelso's state procession following his election as Pope
(IV.iii), in which he takes occasion to pronounce his papal bless-
ing. The opening of Act V is a passage over the stage of Bracci-
ano, Flamineo, and several others. And the opening of V.iii is a
"fight at barriers: first single pairs, then three to three," in which
Bracciano through the treachery of Lodovico is killed. What was
to have been a ceremony and a pageant following the marriage of
Vittoria turns out a ritual of death for the bridegroom.

In *The Duchess of Malfi* Webster makes less frequent use of
procession and ceremony; yet what he does use is most effective.
A half-dozen entrances and as many exits require formal or processional movement; as many as a dozen will certainly allow it,
such as the entrance to III.iii. But more apparent and more effective are the ceremonies and rituals. Perhaps the most moving of
these is the irregular and non-canonical marriage of Antonio and
the Duchess (I.i), a ritual as poignant as it is simple; perhaps the
most splendid and fearsome is the divestment of the Cardinal of
his ecclesiastical attire and his military investiture before the
shrine of Loretto, a ceremony requiring a grand procession. Besides these, Bosola's formal meditation upon the prodigies of Nature (II.i), the dance of the madmen, and Antonio's echo scene
(V.iii) are at least ritualistic in origin. Webster uses pageantry
and ceremony elaborately, sometimes sensationally, poignantly,
and generally very effectively, though somewhat less frequently
than his predecessors.[12]

The prolific Thomas Heywood emphasizes the practices of
his contemporaries, especially in his earlier career. To mention
his "Four Ages" presented in five plays is to mention a vast series
of dumb shows, pageants, *tableaux vivants*, processions, and

ceremonies. In *The Golden Age* at least fifteen entrances are processions; in *The Silver Age* at least twelve; in *The Iron Age* thirty, with seven in Act I alone; in *The Brazen Age* at least eighteen; and, obviously with public acclaim, twenty in *The Second Part of the Iron Age*. Typical of these is the stage direction for the opening of II.i in *The Golden Age: "Enter with music, before* Diana *and* Calisto, *six satyrs; after them all their Nymphs, garlands on their heads, and javelins in their hands, their bows and quivers. The Satyrs sing."* In *The Silver Age* "Jupiter *appears in his glory under a rainbow, to whom they all kneel."* Following the Calydonian boar hunt in *The Brazen Age* (Act II) the boar's head is carried in to the feast with much ceremony; in Act IV (scenes are unmarked) *"all the gods appeare aboue and laugh"*; in Act V two priests make sacrifice at an altar. In each of these plays at least one banquet is set forth. Procession and ceremony are especially appropriate to the heroic characters and their equally heroic deeds.

They are also appropriate to *Love's Mistress* (1634), a series of moralized masques on the Cupid and Psyche story. Utterly different in subject and characters from these, *The Fair Maid of the West* (I and II, 1610?, 1630?) and *A Maidenhead Well Lost* (1625–1634?) are yet made up mostly of pageantry.[13] And although he protests in his Prologue to *The English Traveller* (ca. 1627) that in it he calls for no drum, trumpet, dumb show, combat, song, dance, or masque, Heywood cannot resist a banquet and at least ten formalized entrances. Though his pageantry is less, here it is more directly functional than in his earlier plays.

Necessarily he modified it in such domestic plays as *A Woman Killed with Kindness* (1603) and *The Wise Woman of Hogsdon* (ca. 1604); and yet in the former, though not of courtly splendor, it is of manor house abundance. The play opens with a procession of gentle folk to the dance, and its second scene with the same for the servants. As they prepare for dinner at Frankford's house, the servants (III.ii) "march in order, and retire in battle array." Besides the dances in this play, are the ritual of the card game (III.ii), the wager (I.i), the duel

(I.iii), the dinner in the background (III.ii), the arrest of Sir Charles (I.iii), and the ceremonious death (re-married with a kiss) of Mrs. Frankford (V.vi). Frankford's judgment is a formal ceremony (IV.vi), such as the sentence pronounced by a judge ("Woman, hear thy judgment"), and at least ten entrances and exits require formal staging. Most notable here: many of the scenes are carefully presented as action "in transit," the characters entering, either singly or in groups, as if emerging from action offstage (as Frankford from the dinner, brushing crumbs from his clothes), speaking their lines, and moving off to indicated action off stage. *The Wise Woman*, even though of Plautine tradition, requires a half-dozen formal entrances and exits, a dice game (I.i), a ceremonious betrothal (I.ii), and a dinner given back-stage with servants marching to and fro across stage to serve it. Heywood made extravagant use of pageantry; even in comedy he found place for it. Frequently it was the procession that held his play together.

Middleton used it less than Heywood did, but perhaps to better dramatic purpose. Little is to be found, for example, in *A Fair Quarrel* (1615?–1617) (written in collaboration with William Rowley), perhaps no more than six entrances being processional; little for the kind of play in *The Changeling* (1622), also written with Rowley; and least of all in *Anything for a Quiet Life* (ca. 1621). Yet at least seven entrances and as many exits in *The Changeling* are formal; three petitions are presented on bended knee, including DeFlores' request of Beatrice to be allowed to kill Alonzo and Beatrice's request of DeFlores not to press his contract with her; and an elaborate *tableau vivant* is given, in which Beatrice's wedding procession takes place. But Middleton makes greatest use of pageantry in such plays as *Blurt, Master Constable* (1601–1602), *The Phoenix* (1603–1604), *The Old Law*, *The Mayor of Quinborough* (1616–1620), and *The Spanish Gipsie* (1623). In *The Old Law* (perhaps in some form dating back to 1599) at least twenty entrances and exits are processions, one of special interest: "*Enter* Simonides *and* Courtiers, *sword and mace carried before them.*"

Following this direction comes the trial scene; and besides it, there is a fencing match and a dance. The triumphant procession of the conqueror opens *Blurt, Master Constable*; later come a procession of prisoners, an oration, a banquet, and a masque. Even in *Women Beware Women* twelve entrances and twelve exits are formal; and not only is a banquet staged, but a procession to it, where formal toasts are drunk; later a masque is given. Similarly in *A Chaste Maid in Cheapside* (1611) Middleton burlesques a procession (II.iv): "*Before* Allwit's *House, Enter* Midwife *with the child,* Lady Kix, *and other* Gossips *who exeunt; then* Maudlin, Puritans, *and other* Gossips." Two funeral processions enter simultaneously, one from one side and one from the other (V.iv), the biers being set down "the one right over against the other." Though the play is not rich in pageantry, *A Trick to Catch the Old One* (1604–1606?) calls for several farcically formalized entrances of Witgood's creditors, Witgood's being marched on and off by the sergeants (IV.iii) as a prisoner, and the Courtesan's renunciation with Witgood's formal confession in the last scene. Since Middleton writes mostly about the middle and lower classes, his plays naturally afford less opportunity for processions and formal ceremonies than those of most of the other playwrights; hence these devices are not so prominent in his plays. Yet he uses them effectively, especially for burlesque.

To examine the pageantry in the plays of Beaumont and Fletcher is to repeat with little variety what has already been repeated. They put into their plays the same sort of processions and ceremonies their predecessors used. Sometimes they elaborate these more than their predecessors and contemporaries did, as in the fully developed masque in I.ii of *The Maid's Tragedy* (1611) or the elaborated rituals of the Priest of Pan in *The Faithful Shepherdess* (1608–1609), especially that in I.ii and that in V.v. This apparent preoccupation with the device as an end in itself, rather than a direct means of moving the action along, may indicate a falling off in their concept of the larger structure of the play. Such falling off may also be indicated by the fact that the number of scenes in their plays is usually fewer than in those of their predecessors.[14] Yet in *Bonduca* (1609–1614), a chronicle, Fletcher requires twenty-two formal entrances, including processions, and at least twenty such exits. The two dramatists make much use of the formal entrance, such as the procession of the conquering hero (note that of I.i in *A King and No King*, 1611); their monarchs hold court and conduct formal affairs of state in their "Presence Chambers" (note especially the opening scene of *Philaster*, 1610), or hold a trial and mete out justice in them (note the final scene of *Philaster*); they bring upon the stage many character groups in formal fashion; they use much ritual (such as that in *The Faithful Shepherdess*, in which the Priest of Pan sprinkles the shepherds with water and purges them of any unchastity, and in the final scene, penance having been wrought, blesses the shepherds and all sing a hymn addressed to the woods and bowers); they used the masque, the banquet, and such ceremonies as the separation of Evadne and Amintor in *The Maid's Tragedy*; and they often used the funeral procession and a procession of prisoners (such as one finds in *Bonduca*, or burlesqued in *The Knight of the Burning Pestle*, 1607). Fletcher especially liked these devices.

If any falling off in the use of pageantry took place toward the end of our period, the plays of Philip Massinger fail to show it. Indeed, they show an increase. In none of his plays is it lacking; in most of them it is abundant. In *The Virgin Martyr* (1620?), written in collaboration with Dekker, he makes striking use of ritual and ceremony. As a sort of scene within I.i, a religious ceremony is presented: "*Enter a Priest with the Image of Iupiter, Caliste, Christeta.*" Later (III.ii) this same ritual is ironically broken up by the power of the saintly Dorothea. In I.i also the conquering hero, Diocletian, comes on in procession with three kings as prisoners. And in IV.iii a prisoner is marched on and off to her execution: "*Enter a guard bringing in Dorothea, a headsman before her, followed by Theophilus, Sapritius, Harpax.*" At the end of the play the apotheosis of Theophilus is effected by means of his vision of the martyred Dorothea and the other martyrs presented in a grand *tableau*. In Massinger's late, if not his latest, play *The Bashful Lover* (1636) fifteen or more entrances require formal presentation and at least ten exits. In it also is a fine triumphal procession with Lorenzo and Matilda being drawn by soldiers upon the stage in a chariot; in it are several ceremonials, such as Galeazzo's kneeling to offer his love at a proper distance to Matilda (I.i), or the Ambassador's presenting a petition to the court upon his knee (V.iii). Much of it is found even in *A New Way to Pay Old Debts* (1621–1622?), the plot of which does not lend itself to pageantry any more than does that of *A Trick to Catch the Old One* (1604–1606?) to which it is often compared. For example, I.ii opens with a procession of Lady Allworth's servants, and I.iii with a formal entrance of Overreach and his train to meet Lady Allworth. Wellborn's entrance dressed in a rich habit with Tapwell presenting him his bill on bended knee (IV.ii) is ceremony; and in V.i the bridal procession moves on stage to the accompaniment of appropriate music. Much more is here than in *A Trick to Catch the Old One*; and dropped to a lower key, adapted to comedy from chronicle or tragedy or romance, it is effectively used.[15] In eighteen of Massinger's plays, none is without at least a dozen formal entrances, processions, ceremonies, or other formal occasions.

Nor did Ford make less use of these devices. Apparently he found them especially adapted to the creation of the sort of sensationalism he desired. Quite naturally he turned to them in the writing of his belated chronicle *Perkin Warbeck* (1622–1632?), in which more than twenty processions and formalized entrances and exits occur. Among these is a procession of ladies who come into the gallery (II.i), one of King James of Scotland moving into the presence chamber (II.i), a procession of prisoners, one of King Henry at the Tower of London refusing to see Stanley (II.ii), who is brought in as prisoner and marched off to the scaffold. *Love's Sacrifice* (1632?), with fewer processions than the chronicle, is filled with ceremonies: the ritual at the tomb (V.iii), the Duke's formal oath (IV.i), the ritualistic chess game with its *double entendre* (II.iii), the dumb show passing over the stage (III.iii), the ritual of the stabbing of Ferentes in the dance (III.iv), the banishing of Mauruccio and Morona (IV.i), and the sensational oration of the Duke at the tomb in the final scene. Some of the dozen formal entrances (with their exits) in *The Broken Heart* (1627–1631?) involve ritual and ceremony: Calantha crowns with a chaplet the returning hero, Ithocles (I.ii); a tableau opens III.ii; Ithocles presents a ring to Calantha in ceremony (IV.i); Amyclas contracts Ithocles and Calantha (IV.iii); Calantha continues her ritualistic and sensational dance as the succession of messengers bring their fatal news; and she as the Broken Heart marries the lifeless trunk in the final ceremony. Ceremony and pageantry here especially intensify the sensationalism and intrude upon the basic action, as if they were ends in themselves. Thus Ford's work indicates a late development.[16]

If we can take Shirley's plays as indicative of the main trend in the decade before the closing of the theatres, we can be sure a great falling off took place in the use of pageantry and ceremony, at least in the plays written for the public stage. Shirley scarcely put them in his plays at all.[17] His comedies anticipate practices of the Restoration dramatists; and even though such a play as his *The Cardinal* (1641) is associated in our minds with the tragedies Webster and Ford produced, it is decidedly lacking in processions, ceremony, and ritual. In it the King enters half a dozen times attended by his lords, and makes possibly two or three formal exits. Shirley takes no opportunity to bring in Colombo in a triumphal procession, as his predecessors would have done, in III.i. Even Colombo's council of war (II.i), a formal affair, involves no procession. The fatal masque (III.ii) furnishes most of the play's pageantry. What would have been staged as an arrest and a prisoner's procession in other men's plays is not in this indicated as such; no stage direction to this effect is given. The King, speaking to the guard, simply says, "To the castle with him—." In *The Witty Fair One* as early as 1628 no pageantry is used. Little might be expected, of course, in that the play is a town comedy dealing with the lower classes; yet, though Sir George Richley with Brains and others may enter formally, they are not required to do so—except perhaps on one occasion. If Massinger had been writing this play, he would have used several formal entrances and exits and several processions. In *Hyde Park* (1632) perhaps half a dozen entrances ask for formal presentation, but *The Lady of Pleasure* (1635) requires none. Shirley, looking forward to a new era, felt little need for pageantry in the plays he wrote for the public theatre.

———•·•———

SIR EDMUND CHAMBERS observed in his *Elizabethan Stage* (1923) that "The tradition of pageantry [in English life] had its roots deep in the Middle Ages. But it made its appeal also to the Renaissance, of which nothing was more characteristic than the passion for colour and all the splendid external vesture of things. . . . The Tudor kings and queens," he says, "came and went about their public affairs in a constant atmosphere of make-believe, with a sibyl lurking in every courtyard and gateway. . . ." [18] And if the kings and queens, then their courts with the nobles and gentry and, to a lesser extent, the citizens and lower classes. As we have noticed in Chapter I, the whole of society moved as the world's pageant, each person having his place in it, his part to play. The playwrights demonstrate the tradition, whether deliberately or not, by their constant and varied use of the materials and devices of pageantry, however conventionalized these devices and materials became. They consist of formal entrances and exits, various types of processions or formal movements of characters, often military in design, and of ceremonies or ceremonious actions, or ritual. Overlapping may take place, of course, and disagreement as to whether a given entrance, exit, or action requires formalized presentation. But by and large, the requirement is clear, whether the author wrote it into his stage direction or not.

The most frequently repeated kinds of formal entrances and exits, the most conventionalized, were these: the procession of a monarch (a king or prince or a duke or other nobleman) into his "presence room" or room of "state," the triumphal procession of a conquering hero with attendants and often with his prisoners, the formal filing into a courtroom of law or a senate or other council chamber, the formal procession into a dinner or banquet or dance or masque or play, the entrance and exit of a contingent of soldiers on the march, the procession of servants with their dishes into a banquet room, a movement of constables or watchmen in formation, a funeral procession, a bridal procession, the entrance or exit of any leader with his attendants or any small group or even a single person with an usher, and many "passings over the stage."

Closely allied to these, and frequently a part of them are the formal ceremonies, ceremonious acts, or rituals. Often the two merge. For example, the funeral procession may be stopped and funeral orations spoken as part of the ceremony, or a procession may be stopped for a *tableau vivant* or mirror scene, or a masque or dumb show may require a procession across the stage. Such devices may fill in precedent action for the audience. Related to these are the numerous temple scenes with their accustomed rituals, the rituals at tombs, and the scenes in senate chambers with formal orations. Always a means for providing dramatic intensity are the numerous trial scenes, requiring formality and ceremony, and often used to effect the denouement. These are the most frequently introduced ceremonies, ceremonious actions, or rituals: banquets, toasts, petitions delivered or requests made formally (usually on bended knee), oaths, meetings and leave-takings, coronations, enthronements, delivery of challenges, delivery of messages (often by a herald), formal banishings, the change of the guard or setting of the watch, arrests, trials, the official court sessions of a prince, contracts, betrothals, formal orations, prayers, wagers, confessions, games (chess, cards, dice), masques, dances, religious rituals, conjurings and incantations, and duels. All these (and surely others) occur with some frequency. They are conventional, and they are by nature dramatic, for they provide form, suspense, and the means for an action; they enable a decision or a turn or break in an otherwise monotonous continuum.

In *Antony and Cleopatra* Octavius Caesar is not a particularly dramatic personage. He has not the imagination to see himself as having a role in the world drama, as being a triple pillar of the world. He has little sense of the formality required for action on such a stage. On the other hand, Cleopatra must plan a ritual for her death and die in a ceremony. If upon Caesar's leaving her, she had merely applied the asps, as Caesar in like circumstance would probably have done, we had got no drama out of the scene. The individual act must be lifted to larger, more general significance. These formal, ceremonious, ritualistic materials, celebrating as they do repeated, customary, and formalized human actions, give universality to the art in which they appear.

·FOUR·

The Places of Action in Elizabethan Plays

§ᴧ Mᴜʟᴛɪᴘʟᴇ sᴄᴇɴᴇs or changes of place within the play were apparently almost unknown to the Ancients.[1] The scene of Greek tragedy was usually well confined to the front of a building of some sort, a palace, a temple, a council hall, a dwelling, or a hut, though the play might be enacted before the cave of the Cyclops; and though a change from this basic exterior might be effected to represent an interior, it seems to have been seldom and then awkwardly done. Equally awkward was the introduction of the realm of the gods by the use of the machine. Likewise the action of late Greek and of Roman comedy was usually confined to the street before or between two dwellings, though the front of a farmhouse or a cave or a public square might be designated. The change of scene within the play was not called for. Granted that the classical dramatists recognized the three great areas for action and their relationship with each other—the interior and domestic, the exterior and public, and the unseen and spiritual—, they chose to focus the action upon the second or middle area and set each play in one place only.

With the rise of the drama anew in the Middle Ages the three areas were quite as well recognized and far more frequently and deliberately represented on the stage or by the stage. The localization of action was at first quite as well known, even if not stated explicitly, for the events presented and the place of their happening were known by all who saw the mystery plays. The birth in the stable of Bethlehem, the crucifixion on Golgotha, or the resurrection from Joseph of Aramathea's tomb in Jerusalem needed no markings either on stage or in the text. The Corpus Christi pageants indicated well enough the places of their representation. The Wakefield Master could with complete confidence in the understanding of his audience place a contemporary shepherd's hut on a Yorkshire moor, as it were, next door to the sacred *crèche*. The difference lay in the whole. Even in trilogy, Greek tragedies were discrete. The pageants, on the other hand, though separated the one from the other in scene, were linked together to form a whole play, whose complete stage was the world and whose time was all time. The series reached from Eden to Eternity, from Creation till the last syllable of recorded time has brought the dissolution of the great globe itself. Neither heaven nor hell was excluded from the scene, and time future as well as time present was rifled to furnish the required pageant. The history of the race was set forth in memorable scenes.

This history was presented in a quite different way in the morality plays, especially the earlier ones. In them it became the account of the universal pattern of salvation, the history of the individual Mankind as opposed to the race. The scene thus became cosmic in a very different way. No particular place was required; none under such circumstances was logically possible. Since every man became Everyman, one man, every place became one place, Everywhere. So it was that Everyman, Mankind, *Humanum Genus*, and the rest played Everywhere, on the stage of the world indeed. To particularize their state would be to destroy their scene. Even such a set as that of *The Castle of Perseverance*, since it is allegorical, is of cosmic design: we all live in this castle. Later the secular moralities, even, were set in a scene no less broad, as were such interludes as *The Four Elements*.

The Elizabethan playwrights, making use of their direct heritage, might follow the practice of multiple scenes as did the writers of the cycles and also the practice of the universalized or non-indicated scene of the writers of the moralities. From the cycles they probably inherited the idea of history as basic subject matter. They probably saw in it, as Miss E. Catherine Dunn thinks the cyclic dramatists saw, "the unfolding of God's plan for his people." [2] Just so they found in the narrative verse tragedies, whose subjects were from history, models of popular morality and turned them into series of pageants to tell the life and death of kings. And whether historical or not, the pageantry of history pervaded their tragedies; it also furnished the scheme for much of romantic comedy; and by its variety and movement it enriched the domestic comedy and farce brought from ancient Rome. However much Sidney and the new critics of his day might object to moving the action of a play from one place to another in defiance of the Ancients, the playwrights mostly regarded him not; [3] they knew better. Following the writers of the moralities they might leave the place of action entirely indefinite, suggesting in neither direction nor dialogue any place for it, or merely vaguely indicating it as a plain or a wood or an open space. From whichever heritage, the Elizabethan faced the same paradox the medieval dramatist faced: his theatre at once contained the world and was contained in it. Perhaps, however, this is nothing more than one expression of the paradox of all drama—or indeed all art.

And perhaps it was this very paradox that enabled the Elizabethan playwright to express so well the universal within the particular and the particular within the universal which give his art its supreme worth. He stood between the universal of the past age and the partial and particular of the new, a happy place for the artist to stand. And his management of place and scene, especially their variety, reveals his conscious attempt to make his drama suggest the whole world if not the cosmos. A look at the variety and kind of scenes in some of the Elizabethan dramatists' plays will serve, I believe, to reveal one of their methods of universalizing their art. And it derives, whether directly or not, from their frequently expressed commonplace that the world is a stage.

Granted that specific localities for the action are not always forthcoming either from stage direction or from dialogue, granted that editors may not always agree upon the exact place for a given scene, granted that dramatists were deliberately vague about place but interested chiefly in an open space for action, their intentions are usually fairly clear, and most readers can agree upon the place of most scenes. They can usually tell whether a scene is an exterior or an interior, or whether its place is clearly understood or only vaguely suggested. Whether "you have Asia of one side, and Afric of the other," frequently the actor "when he cometh in, must ever begin with telling where he is," especially in the early plays. In John Bale's *King John* (ca. 1535) we know only that the scenes are vaguely England and Rome; it is too much the morality play to require more specific places for the action, such as rooms of state. On the other hand, Johan Johan is careful to mention "this, my house" in his first speech in John Heywood's domestic interlude, *Johan Johan, Tyb, and Sir Johan* (ca. 1533). But by 1567 John Pickering in his *History of Horestes*, even though imposing much morality structure upon his classical story, has indicated exteriors, with battle fields and city gates, and interiors, with rooms of state suggested. And by 1569 one finds in *King Cambises* the presence chamber or room of state, as well as other palace rooms, a banqueting hall, then a park or orchard or garden, and then a street. Thus the conventional places for the action of many plays are established, to be repeated in one play after another until the closing of the theatres.

With Lyly, however much he presents classical story, his scenes are varied. Although the whole of *Campaspe* takes place in Athens, as R. W. Bond observes, "no economy can reduce the number of scenes below four." They include a "suburb," a palace, the market place, and Apelles' shop or studio. *Sapho and Phao* (1584), out of Greek legend, reminds us also of Greek staging; but whereas the Greeks would use only one place for the entire play, Lyly uses several. The several scenes are at the ferry, before Sybilla's cave, in Sapho's palace, and before the forge. And *Gallathea* reminds us in its settings of plays to come, of *A Midsummer Night's Dream* and *As You Like It*, for its action takes place in the enchanted wood of Diana and her nymphs on the outskirts of a forest "not far from the estuary of the Humber, with a large oak in the background." The place is particularized, its importance to the action emphasized.

Likewise the setting of George Peele's *Arraignment of Paris* (1584), also out of Greek mythology, requires a forest setting. The arraignment takes place in Diana's bower. But it also takes place within Queen Elizabeth's great hall, where in the final scene the Queen herself has a part in the action. Peele's predilection for setting scene within scene becomes more pronounced and more complicated in *The Old Wives' Tale* (1591–1594), in which the scene moves from the wood into Clunch's cottage. Once inside, a variety of places are presented, such as the cross, the well, the area before Sacrapant's study, the inside of the study, and a dinner within a tavern. But Peele is not often detailed enough or specific enough to leave his reader quite certain of the exact setting of a scene. In the twenty-five scenes of *Edward I* (1593?), for example, it is often difficult to determine where they take place. That is, we may know that a particular scene takes place in Carnarvon Castle, but whether it is in the courtyard or in the Presence Chamber we cannot be sure. And yet we can make sure that one scene takes place before a potter's dwelling, another before a tent, another on a battlefield, another at Charing Cross, another in the forest, and yet another before a city's or a castle's wall (though we cannot be quite sure what city or castle). Much the same sort of practice is followed in *David and Bethsabe* (1594?) and in *The Battle of Alcazar* (ca. 1589), both like *Edward I* made up of series of extravagant processions and pageants. Mostly they require only an open space for the accommodation of the procession; where it takes place is not very important. The object is to suggest vastness and to move the scenes across the face of the earth.

Much the same is true of the scenes of Robert Greene's plays. His *History of Alphonsus King of Aragon* (ca. 1587) spreads its action well across the world, with scenes in Aragon, Naples, Constantinople, and vaguely suggested places in the Near East. And the places of action include the battlefields, the presence chambers, or courts of kings, a "grove," and a temple of Mahomet. The *History of Orlando Furioso* (1591) is, if anything, even more extensive in its scene, as may be illustrated by the monarchs and nobility appearing in it. They include not only the emperor of Africa and the Soldan of Egypt, but also the kings of Cuba, Mexico, and the "isles"—and the Twelve Peers of France. Many of the places of the action are vaguely suggested, some being indeterminate. Act I, Scene ii takes place before the gates of Rodamant's Castle, another in a forest, where Orlando hangs verses on trees, another in the wood near the Castle of Marsilius, and another on a battlefield. In *George a Greene, Pinner of Wakefield* (1593), thought to be Greene's play, however, the scenes are restricted to Britain, though some of them can be no better specified than "near Bradford" or "at Wakefield," both exteriors certainly, and one perhaps a street. Yet the King's Court in London is well enough indicated for one scene, Sherwood Forest for another, the area before George's "cell" or "cottage" for a third, and that before castles for two more. In *Friar Bacon and Friar Bungay* (ca. 1589) place is more precisely indicated, and again the places are confined to England, though foreign potentates and scholars have parts. The King holds court both at Hampton Court and at London, and the Prince holds council in what must be a tavern at Framlingham. Other scenes take place in Bacon's study, at Harleston Fair, on a street in Oxford, in a room at the Keeper's lodge, on a street in Fressingfield, and in some sort of large room at Oxford. One scene involves a mirror to show what is happening off stage, the duel between Serlesby and Lambert. Gradually the places of action are being better indicated.

In Marlowe's plays, though the places of action are sometimes not set forth explicitly, one can usually tell a good deal about them. In *Tamburlaine*, Part I (ca. 1587), some sixteen scenes range from the familiar army camp to a road, a hill, four battlefields, two palace scenes, the walls of Damascus, and some sort of holy place, a mosque perhaps. In *Doctor Faustus* (ca. 1588) they range from Faustus' study to other rooms within his house, to a grove outside and a field, to an inn yard and a room inside the inn, to the Pope's palace, the Emperor's palace, and an area before Faustus' door. The indications of the places of action in *The Jew of Malta* (ca. 1589) are quite vague. Yet one can infer from what evidence there is that much action took place in the street and before Barabas's house, some of it in his counting house, some in the court chamber of Ferneze, some in the market place where the slaves are sold, and some in Bellamira's house. None reaches beyond Malta. *Edward II* (ca. 1592), however, like the chronicles generally, not only ranges well over England, but into France also, and suggests action in Ireland. Scenes are set in a street in Westminster, in open country, in various rooms in various castles, in the Temple and in the Royal Palace at Westminster.

In his *Spanish Tragedy* (ca. 1589) Thomas Kyd brings the Ghost of Andrea from hell with Revenge to sit to one side and "see the mystery." And its scenes are fairly well located, or can be fairly well deduced. Action takes place at both the court chamber of Spain and that of Portugal, at the banquet hall of the Spanish court and in a room at Don Cyprian's house, in Hieronimo's garden and in a park, in several streets and in a court of justice.

By Shakespeare's time the pattern was becoming conventionalized, and places for the separate scenes were often well enough indicated in the dialogue or in an occasional stage direction to let the attentive onlooker or reader know where the action was. The places, moreover, were not restricted in a single play either to exteriors or interiors. Quite the contrary. Both were employed almost invariably in every play. And almost as invariably one finds a combination of exterior-interior scenes, such as were anticipated in the Greek and Roman settings for the action of a whole play: an area before a city wall or gate from which action could emerge. Later, as we shall see, scenes became fewer and exterior scenes less frequent. Shakespeare's practice will illustrate the three types and also the great variety within the play.

First among his exteriors are the numerous garden, park, and orchard scenes. The parks, such at that in *Love's Labour's Lost*, are hardly rural scenes, but places where pavilions are set up, games played, and dancing done. Likewise, the gardens and orchards represent nature methodized, where ladies and gentlemen disport themselves or take their ease or meditate and philosophize. Not so in the equally numerous forest scenes. Though the forest may furnish a kindly retreat from the harsh realities of the city, as in *As You Like It*, it may also be a place for mix-ups as in *A Midsummer Night's Dream*. Such are the rough country scenes like that before Belarius' cave in *Cymbeline* or that before Prospero's cell, or those on heaths, or plains, or open country. In at least seventeen of Shakespeare's plays we find garden, park, and orchard scenes, not counting repetitions within a play. Perhaps some of the "fields" should be listed among these, though most fields are associated with battle scenes, and among the lonely seacoast scenes and desert country near the sea, such as one finds in *Winter's Tale*. The whole of *Love's Labour's Lost*, according to most editors, takes place in the King's park, though nothing in the first several scenes precludes their being played in the palace halls. However this may be, public exteriors are more numerous. I refer to streets, roads, "public places," seaports, forums, inn yards, courtyards of castles, and all such. Many of these are vaguely suggested in the dialogue and as vaguely marked by the editors. The many battle scenes belong among these. As I reckon them, following the divisions of modern editors, at least forty-two scenes take place on battlefields in thirteen of Shakespeare's plays. Associated with these are the many camp scenes, almost indistinguishable from them. And to round out our lives there are the graveyard scenes, such as those in *Romeo and Juliet, Hamlet,* and *Much Ado.* Most are places of bustle and exchange, places for emphasis on physical activity. Groups and masses of men gather in them for challenges, quarrels, squabbles, fights, marchings and countermarchings, processions, meetings, assignations, the delivery of messages, warnings, judgments, and so on. Shakespeare and his contemporaries enjoyed the flexibility afforded them in the public exteriors.

Allied to these and used for many of the same purposes are what I shall call the threshold scenes, the scenes "before" something, which I have mentioned as resembling the places for the action of the Greek and Roman plays. But whereas all the plays of the Greeks and Romans were staged "before" something, the Elizabethans were not so restricted; and whereas the "ante" scenes in the classical drama were limited to about half a dozen, the Elizabethans placed their actions before any number of openings: not only before the city wall or gate, but before a house, a hovel, a palace, a cave, a cell, a castle, a shrine, a tent, a prison, a temple, a monastery, or a church. Thus the Elizabethan gained great latitude in his action. The Tower of London, often used, like the walls of a city, allows two levels for action; so does Brabantio's window in *Othello;* so does Cleopatra's monument at Alexandria. A street before a shop permits action in both exterior and interior, and great speeches are spoken from the walls of a castle or city. In a storm before a hovel on a heath four men's minds are torn to fragments, their souls stripped bare, and their beings reduced to their essential nakedness; and then into the hovel they go. Following a tempest on a savage island before a magician's cell a happy resolution and a just restitution are effected, and out of the cell two happy lovers come. In such scenes one looks from the exterior into the interior, as one so often does when viewing a medieval or Renaissance painting or illumination: the heavens, the earth, and then the covered place.

If the exteriors and thresholds furnish flexibility, the interiors furnish variety. As with the two former, so with the latter type of scene: it frequently furnishes neutral acting space, no special kind of interior being of any help in the presentation of the scene. As time went on, the interiors became more numerous. Many of them merely call for a room in a house or a palace or a castle or a tavern, any kind of room. But it is important for the onlooker to know whose house or palace or castle it is, or what its name is. For example, the first scene of *I Henry IV* is perhaps a council chamber in the King's palace in London, where Henry meets his barons; so is Scene iii, Act I. But the place is only vaguely indicated. Act III, Scene i of *II Henry IV* is merely set in some undesignated room in the Palace at Westminster, into which the sleepless King comes in his nightgown, whereas IV.iv is doubtless properly designated as the Jerusalem Chamber. I count five vaguely indicated interiors in *Henry V* alone, two in *Coriolanus* (in which play five scenes can be no better specified than "A public place"), and at least seven in *King Lear*. Nevertheless a great many of the interiors are more than casually suggested, place and kind being designated by the text. As already shown, numerous scenes of Elizabethan drama take place in rooms of state, court or presence chambers, where the king assembles his court to conduct the business of his realm. Among the best known of these in Shakespeare is the second scene in *Hamlet*, where King Claudius disposes of the business of state. As indicated above, such scenes are formal, ceremonious, dignified, and colorful. In them embassies are received and dispatched, declarations made, debates conducted, trials managed, and judgments rendered. Next to the scenes played in rooms of state are the numerous scenes played in the council chamber of the monarch or the duke or lord of a castle. Less formal, these are still used for the conduct of official business. *Hamlet* II.ii seems to be set in such a room, where Claudius receives Rosencrantz and Guildenstern. Numerous actions also take place in the hall of a castle, or in the gallery; and Shakespeare as well as the other dramatists often placed his action in a banquet hall, or else placed a banquet just offstage in the palace hall. It was a favorite kind of scene. One of these, it will be remembered, took place aboard Pompey's ship in *Antony and Cleopatra*, though it turned out to be a drinking party—as was often the case with banquets. Such scenes furnish opportunity for much spectacle, as well as the chance to put upon the stage one of the customary activities of humankind. They are still popular with play-wrights. The closet or cabinet, too, was a place of action, private action, such as Gertrude's most private chamber in Elsinore. And scenes are not infrequently played in a bedroom, the bed very probably being regularly pushed out upon the stage to in-dicate the place and provide the necessary property. One recalls the final scene of *Othello* as a notable example. Thus other uni-versal activities of humankind are provided for or suggested by the places of action.

Less conventional interiors are also employed by Shakespeare and his contemporaries. The Roman Senate and the Capitol are especially remembered from *Julius Caesar, Coriolanus,* and from Jonson's *Catiline.* The Venetian Council Chamber in *Othello* is the same kind of place. The Parliament House similarly fur-nished the proper place for official government acts and debates in the chronicle plays. Churches are likewise called for, such as in the brilliant opening scene of *I Henry VI,* or the Abbey of Bury St. Edmunds in III.i of *II Henry VI,* or the church in *Much Ado,* or the chapel of *Winter's Tale,* or the Temple of Diana in *Pericles,* or the magnificent Temple of Apollo in the final scene of Jonson's *Sejanus.* In this way still another cus-tomary if not universal activity of humankind is furnished a place. Associated with these in function are the friars' cells, such as Friar Laurence's in *Romeo and Juliet* and in many another play of the period. A few scenes take place in monasteries and nunneries, such as those in *Measure for Measure.* One of Shake-speare's scenes seems to be played in a witches' cavern (*Mac-beth,* IV.i); some few are played aboard ship, such as those in *Pericles* and the celebrated ones in *Antony and Cleopatra* and *The Tempest.* More common are the prison scenes, three in *Measure for Measure,* for example, and one in *Much Ado.* Tavern scenes abound, as they do in Heywood's and Middle-ton's plays. One scarcely need be reminded of the great ones in *I* and *II Henry IV*. In *Pericles*, moreover, two scenes take place in a brothel at Mytilene.

Shakespeare's interiors range, as those of his contemporaries do, though his somewhat more widely than most, from rooms of state and an abbey church to a brothel, from a king's council chamber to a tavern, from an abbey in Milan to a prison in Vienna, from a bedchamber to a hall or gallery in a castle, from a closet to a banquet hall. The exteriors range just as widely— from gardens, parks, and orchards to lonely heaths and sea-shores, to busy and brawling streets, from wild caves in Wales to the Forest of Arden, to the garden of the Temple in London, to the platform before the castle at Elsinore, and to the graveyard nearby. The threshold or combination scenes furnish a like vari-ety. If we consider the entire corpus of Shakespeare's plays, we realize that almost every kind of place one can think of on the face of the globe, except perhaps a mountain top, is used for ac-tion; and of course the Globe theatre furnished just the kind of stage needed for such range of scenes, such variety of places.

Similarly, as we look within the individual play, we find the variety equally remarkable and Shakespeare's design even more apparent. The choice of localities for scenes shows conscious effort, as it did for his predecessors and contemporaries, to sug-gest a microcosm for each play and thus to indicate by place, within the restrictions imposed by plot, a certain degree of uni-versality. His effort is apparent from his earliest plays onward.

In his most Plautine *Comedy of Errors*, for example, one dis-covers a variety of scene altogether lacking in the *Menaechmi*, its source, just as one discovers more variety of plot and much more pageantry. Whereas in the original the whole action takes place in a street before the houses of Menaechmus and Erotium, in Shakespeare's handling it takes place within the Duke's palace, within the house of Antipholus of Ephesus, before his house, then in the market place, in some public place merely (IV.i), in a street, and in front of a priory. The very scenes themselves suggest the orders of society: the ruler, the merchants and tradesmen, and the church—the home of the administrator of the law and public affairs, the home of the merchant, the streets and public places for everybody, and the home of the representative of the spiritual body. What is more, Shakespeare's addition to his source suggests the outside area beyond the city of the play. No scenes are enacted in Syracuse, but that city is always present to the mind of the reader and the playgoer. The action moves implicitly outward beyond the home of Antipholus of Ephesus, to the palace of the ruler, to the city itself, and then to the world beyond. Classical restrictions are removed, and the pattern and variety of scenes suggest the world as stage.

Two Gentlemen of Verona, another play with Roman affinities, reveals a like expansion, a greater one; for into it romance intrudes, and the scenes are not restricted to one city. The action moves from Verona to Milan and thence to a forest outside that city; and the places of action vary from private rooms in Antonio's house and the dukes' palaces to public rooms in their palaces; from a mere open space and a street to a private garden, to a scene under the walls of Milan's palace; from a brief scene apparently in an abbey to the forest, where the action is concluded. As in *The Comedy of Errors*, domestic and public interiors and exteriors are indicated, as well as combinations of interiors and exteriors. The forest scene brings in the lawless men and irregular nature, both more kind and just than the more methodized and civilized. And it is through the abbey that Sylvia escapes to the ultimate kindness and justice of the forest.

In the later, especially the romantic, comedies the same practices prevail—only still further expanded. The actions of *A Midsummer Night's Dream* are staged within the room of state of Theseus's palace, within the humble home of Peter Quince, and then in various parts of the forest, generally a fairyland and spirit realm. Those of *Much Ado* are staged in various rooms of Leonato's house (both private and public rooms), in his orchard, his garden, a place before his threshold, a street, a prison, and a church; those in *As You Like It*, in various rooms in the Duke's palace, before Oliver's house, and in various places in the Forest of Arden. The places for action in *The Merchant of Venice* are brilliant and varied, those of Portia's house at Belmont especially; and they are set not only in her house but in her garden, in the streets of Venice, in a room in Shylock's house, and in a court of justice. Even the farcical *Taming of the Shrew* provides, besides the threshold scenes before the alehouse on the heath and the bedroom of the Lord's house in the Induction, threshold scenes before Baptista's house and before Lucentio's house, rooms in Baptista's, Lucentio's and Petrucio's houses, some for dining and some for instruction, and scenes in a public road and the street, as well as one no better indicated than a "public place."

Among the later comedies *Cymbeline* furnishes great variety. It moves in some twenty-seven scenes across ancient Britain to Rome and back again. The action takes place in the wild Welsh countryside, in and before a cave, on battlefields, in public places in Rome, in rooms of the private home of Philario, and in various rooms of Cymbeline's palace, including Imogen's bedchamber. A similar variety is to be observed in the seventeen scenes of *Measure for Measure:* an apartment in the Duke's palace, a street, a monastery, a nunnery, a hall in Angelo's house, a room in a prison (three scenes in this room), a room in Angelo's house, a street before the prison, a street near the city gate, fields outside the town, and the city gate. This variety is in severe contrast to *The Tempest,* in which only three "sets" are required for the nine scenes. But even here it should be noted that the civilized and ordered world represented by the scenes before Prospero's cell, with the presentation of the masque, is contrasted with the disordered, confused, and barbaric world of the scenes on "the other part" of the island, and that both these are encompassed by the magical sea of the shipwreck and Ariel's domain.

To turn from the comedies to the histories, especially from the late comedies to the early histories, is to turn from a lesser to a larger form and to an outright attempt on the part of the dramatist to put upon the stage the pageantry of national and world events. The places of the action were frequently chosen, or left vague indeed, so as to magnify the pageantry of the action and thus reveal something of the vast or the universal plan of history.

As in other types of Elizabethan plays, scenes were left unlocal-
ized and seemingly were used, for their locality had no importance, to conduct a necessary piece of business and get on with
the story. Yet most of the time the place can be designated and
named. And the number and variety of places given or suggested
tend to produce the effect of the passage of men across the stage
of the world itself.

Examples are numerous. To pick at random, *Richard III* has
twenty-five scenes, if we accept the usual division. Of these, five
are played in the streets of London, six in the King's palace in
London, one in front of it, one in a room of Lord Darby's house,
one before Lord Hastings' house, two before and two inside the
Tower of London, one at Bayard's castle and one at Pomfret
Castle, one in a camp, one on Salisbury Plain, and three on Bosworth Field. Of course the dramatist must choose his scenes
from history; he is to a degree controlled. And yet a pattern is
apparent. The earlier actions are confined to the King's palace
and the streets of London; the central scenes are extended to the
Tower and to the castles of noblemen; and the later ones, to
camps, open plains, and battlefields. The movement is outward
from interior to exterior, from the narrow to the wide and the
vast. Almost the same pattern is to be found in *I Henry IV*,
though not in *II Henry IV*, and almost the same in each of the
three parts of *Henry VI*. It is notable also that in the chronicles
churchly scenes are common, an abbey showing in the background or such splendid scenes as the opening of *I Henry VI* in
Westminster Abbey. Shakespeare, following the fashion of his
time, rather generally indicates three types of places in his
chronicles—the private or domestic, the public or state, and (less
obtrusively) the spiritual or ecclesiastical. And those places only
vaguely suggested, or "non-localized," all the more strongly
suggest the cosmic extent of his play.

The point is the more readily realized in *Antony and Cleopatra*, where the pageant of the ancient world sweeps by. The
Folio, our only source for the text, gives neither act nor scene
division, and rightfully so. It is a moving piece. But the places of

action do change—some forty-five times according to modern editors. And by their range and multiplicity they help to create the magnitude of the action and the character of the protagonists. The three-pillared world is indeed represented, suggested, or symbolized by the variety of places in which it appears. The scenes in the rooms of Cleopatra's palace are matched by the scenes in Caesar's house, or by those in Pompey's house or Lepidus' house. The rare banquet scene on board Pompey's galley literally rocked the three pillars of the world; it is balanced by the triumphant procession of Ventidius on a Syrian plain. The various camp scenes at Actium and those before Alexandria in Act IV are preliminaries to the scenes on the battlefields. And finally the poet places his action in the remarkable monument scenes at the end of Acts IV and V, scenes surely not without their symbolic significance. For high lifted up was Antony in his going and his queen also, as it were in their own memorial. And with all the multiplicity of scenes, even more are implied than are put upon the stage: no one will forget Enobarbus' creation of that upon the barge on the Cydnus, though it was never put upon any stage. The action runs far beyond the compass of the here and the now.

Perhaps two observations should be made about the procession of these numerous scenes, one about their variety and one about their geography. The audience is asked to realize in scene the same variety that it realizes in the character of Cleopatra: here are private rooms and public halls, rooms of state and a banquet room aboard a ship, street scenes and a scene beside a city wall, a plain and military camps, and then a monument—both exterior and interior. Public and private places, interiors and exteriors and combinations are called for: the family, the state, and (if we accept the monument as symbolic) the spiritual realms are all suggested. But as time runs out, the geography of the scenes is narrowed. In the last two acts the play does not leave Alexandria. It gradually grows to a point in the monument, being literally reduced to a period. If in the chronicle plays the scenes of action tend to become more and more widespread, in this play

they tend to become less and less so. Yet from the outset the
world is this play's scene, and its creator selected the places of its
action and deliberately arranged them to emphasize this fact and
to show also how the scene grows smaller as the character of
Antony crumbles to a memory of greatness.

In the great tragedies, plays owing more to the *psychomachia* of the moralities than the chronicles owe, the area of action becomes more circumscribed than in the chronicles and
Roman plays, whose greater debt is perhaps to the mystery
plays. In *Hamlet*, for example, the action moves from the foggy
platform before Elsinore, the very edge of the mysterious world
where men and spirits mingle, to the room of state where the
King conducts the kingdom's business. Thence it moves to a
private room in Polonius's house, then variously to smaller and
more private rooms of the palace, to a hall, and then to the boudoir of the Queen. Later it moves outward to a plain with soldiers marching and still later to a churchyard, where the funeral
procession moves. And scenes not represented are yet mentioned
or described: we wonder after we read whether a shipboard action did not take place on stage, or whether the one anticipated
in England might not have, or whether still another did not take
place on the skirts of Norway, where Fortinbras sharked up his
band. The action moves from the bourn whence a traveler *does*
return to places appropriate to intimate, domestic, public, and
national affairs, and by suggestion to the international and ultimately, coming full circle, to the mysterious again, where a soul
may rest. From a meeting with a ghost on the platform before
Elsinore Hamlet moves through the court, the play, the boudoir,
the capture by pirates (reported only), the cemetery, and the
duel to be carried off in triumph to "the stage" (could it be a
platform before Elsinore?), where another meeting may be
expected—between two ghosts now at rest.

In *King Lear* the scenes spread wide over Britain and reach
even beyond to France. Within the country they vary from the
King's presence chamber to the hut on the heath and from
Gloucester's castle to open country, from Albany's castle and

open areas before castle gates or courtyards to a farmhouse and the fields of battle. Generally, as in *Richard III* and other chronicles, the movement is outward from interior to exterior, from the confined to the unconfined areas. And beyond these is a place not represented but so vividly described as to be remembered best—the Cliffs of Dover, one way to the world beyond. Place also here suggests the conditions of men: the highest ranks of humankind and the lowest find their places in this play, the highest reduced to the lowliest place.

The places of action in *Macbeth* range widely too: from a blasted heath in Scotland to the front of Edward's palace in England, from Macbeth's castle at Inverness to Macduff's castle, from the castle at Forres to a cavern on the heath, and from Dunsinane to a battlefield in front of it. From the place of mysterious prophecy where the battle's lost and won the action moves to public and private places, places enough to indicate the national and international scope of the action, and back to a battlefield where again the battle's won and lost, the juggling fiends too long believed "That palter with us in a double sense."

Othello, with emphasis upon the domestic conflict, suggests less explicitly the realm of spirit than the other great tragedies, unless it be the crucial garden scene where the protagonist and the villain, the tempter and the tempted, kneel together to swear murder. We dare think it a suggestion of Eden and the Fall. The place of the play moves from Venice to Cyprus, and the individual scenes resemble more closely those of *Romeo and Juliet* than those of *Macbeth* or *Lear* or *Hamlet*, those of romantic comedy than those of historical tragedy. The action moves from the public street to the public council chamber of the Senate, to the seaport in Cyprus and then to the castle room, the garden and street and finally the bedroom. The general pattern is from the broad and public to the narrow and private, just the reverse of the chronicles, or the other great tragedies; and no monument or ritual is indicated or even a faithful Kent to answer a master's call.

One might continue indefinitely—and repetitiously, if not

tediously. Enough has been said to show that Shakespeare chose the various places of action, the scenes or scene-places, with some attention to their appropriateness or power to suggest action of world-wide and cosmic import. Every one of his plays has exterior scenes, and, with one possible exception, every one has interiors. Each play by its scenes indicates or implies its private, public and spiritual context.

It is perhaps notable that Chapman's Bussy d'Ambois, the free and uncommitted bold man, moves from a first exterior scene, a forest near Paris, to interiors only, where he becomes increasingly circumscribed in space as he becomes increasingly embroiled in the intrigues of the court and the doings of lesser men. Just such restriction is reflected in the plays of Shakespeare's later contemporaries and successors. As time went on, their plays came to suggest less and less the heroic proportions of character and universal import of the action. Not only did they use fewer scenes, but, more important, fewer exteriors. The tendency was to move indoors. And yet this was a general change, practices varied from one playwright to another, and subject matter of course determined much.

Perhaps Marston's work, with its satirical slant—and satire somehow belongs inside—, indicates the change among the contemporaries. Whereas his tragedy, *Antonio and Mellida* (1599), takes place in a courtyard before a palace, a presence chamber within the palace, other rooms in it, and on "the Venice marsh," its sequel, *Antonio's Revenge*, takes place, with the exception of one scene (as best one can deduce from the text), on the inside. The several rooms of the Doge's palace are used, including a banqueting place and a court of justice, the interior of St. Mark's church, and—the exception—a field or heath in the final scene. In *The Malcontent* (1604), although the first act is divided into seven scenes, all seven are probably played in the same room at court, and the five of the second act in a "passageway" of the palace. The first three scenes of Act III are played in a room of the palace; the other two, in a field where a hunt is taking place. The scenes of Acts IV and V are confined to the palace courtyard and the presence chamber. Of its twenty-seven scenes no more than four can be exteriors. In *The Fawn* (1604–1606) apparently only two scenes are exteriors, a road overlooking Urbin and a scene within a scene for a masque requiring a balcony. Most of the rest of the action, if not all, takes place in the presence chamber. The action of *The Dutch Courtesan* (1603–1604) takes place in rooms of private houses (one a ballroom and one a "parlor") and in the streets before these houses or before certain shops, a reminder of the Plautine comedy. In *Sophonisba* (1606), a tragedy, the variety is much greater. The play begins in the palace courtyard at Cirta and ends, as best one can tell, within the palace, though it could be the same courtyard. Otherwise the action ranges from various rooms of the palace to Sophonisba's bedroom, the Senate Chamber, the forest (somewhat enchanted), and to several battlefields. The scenes in *The Insatiate Countess* (1610) are restricted to the street, the Venetian Senate House, the Castle courtyard, and various rooms in the palace. Variety is in a measure retained, the sky has not been entirely lost sight of, but the shift to the inside is apparent.

Ben Jonson, lover of Plautus and Terence though he was, especially in his early plays, nevertheless moves at will from the traditional threshold or street scene inside the house. His audience look into three rooms of Lovewit's house and upon three scenes before it in *The Alchemist*. In *Volpone* they look into the main room in Volpone's house, as well as into passageways and closets in it, into rooms in Corvino's and rooms in Sir Politic's house, into the Senate House, and upon the famous street scenes, especially that set before St. Mark's place (II.ii). In *Bartholomew Fair* the action moves from a room in Littlewit's house to the little world of the Fair, where the audience observes at least three areas of it: the area before several booths and stalls, that before and at the back of Ursula's booth, and the puppet show. *The New Inn*, likewise a microcosm, restricts the action to the Inn, except for one scene in the yard. In *The Case is Altered*, probably Jonson's earliest play, a considerable variety is maintained. Among the several street scenes one, the first, takes place before Juniper's shop, one before Ferneze's house, and two before Jaques de Prie's house. Three take place in the courtyard of Jaques' house, seven inside Ferneze's house, and one, the final scene, in "open country." In *Sejanus*, as already suggested, Jonson furnished as much variety of scene as any other writer of tragedy: a room of state, the Senate House, the facade of the Temple of Apollo and the splendid scene inside it, various private rooms in private homes, a garden, and the street. The proper places for the gods, statesmen, and the commonality are carefully provided. They are similarly provided in *Catiline*. It will be sufficient to mention the title of *Eastward Ho* (1605) (by Jonson, Chapman, and Marston) to recall the street scenes before Goldsmith's Row, those in the Blue Anchor Tavern, in an alehouse, at Cuckold's Haven, in Touchstone's house, the inn yard, and various places in the Counter, a prison. The places are sufficient to suggest the world of the people of London, especially the tradesmen, the apprentices, and the characters of the streets.

Of all the dramatists of the time none was so prodigal of place for the action of his plays as Thomas Heywood. Except in his later works such as *The Captives* (1624) and *The English Traveller* (ca. 1627),[4] the trend toward the interior and the restriction on the number of scenes is not noticeable. Although the immediate scene is seldom localized in the plays of the Four Ages, there is no mistaking the vastness of the area implied for the action of the single play or for the series. Throughout, the various places of the whole Mediterranean area are indicated: Crete, Calydonia, Troy, Argos, etc. Heywood thinks nothing of moving his scene within a single play from a tavern in Plymouth to the splendid courts of oriental princes and back to the forests of Italy; or in another play, from France to England, to the walls of Jerusalem, with Ireland fetched in by way of a dumb show. His practice of putting narrative upon the stage made the multiplicity of places quite necessary. He is often deliberately vague about the place of his scene, as even in *The Captives* or *A Maidenhead Well Lost* (1625–1634?), but he seldom restricts movement from place to place. Even when his geography is circumscribed and limited, as in *A Woman Killed with Kindness,* he furnishes great variety of place. The action moves from the ballroom in Frankford's house to the yard, then to open country where a hawking contest goes on, to the jail, to various other rooms in Frankford's house, to Mountford's house, to a simple outside open space, to a dungeon in York Castle, to a place before Acton's house, to the road, and to the bedroom in the Manor house. The action of *The Fair Maid of the West* takes place in fields, in streets, on shipboard, in several taverns, in a bedroom, and in three splendid rooms of state at the court of Morocco. In *The English Traveller* seven scenes can be identified only as rooms, one as a sort of dining room, four as "threshold" scenes before some sort of house, one as a tavern, one as a street, and one as a garden. More variety exists in *The Rape of Lucrece:* the Senate House, a temple, rooms in Collatine's house, two bedchambers, two interiors of tents (one with a banquet set out), three camps, a space before a tent, then a bridge, and finally open country on the outskirts of Rome. Most of the interests of most classes and occupations of men are suggested by the very location of the scenes in Heywood's plays, and many of these interests within a single play. The variety of scene fits the variety of men appearing in his plays, and Heywood seems to have been deliberate in furnishing the variety.

This is less true of others. Of the sixteen scenes in Webster's *The White Devil* (1609–1612) only four are exteriors, though these are not without variety: streets, a courtyard, an open space before the Vatican. The interiors include the courtroom of the papal consistory, anterooms, and halls as well as private apartments. The five exteriors of *The Duchess of Malfi* (1613–1614) furnish more variety: two of them are on the road to Loretto, one is before the shrine there, one is a moonlit courtyard, and one simply a "public place" in Milan. Likewise the fourteen interiors in it are varied: they include a "fortification," a prison, and a presence chamber as well as the various halls and apartments and the Duchess' bedchamber.

In Dekker's early *Old Fortunatus* (1599) five scenes are exteriors, five are interiors, and one is a combination exterior-interior. And whereas Part I of *The Honest Whore* (1604) has five exteriors, seven interiors, and three combination or threshold scenes, Part II (published in 1630) has only one exterior, two combinations, and ten interiors, a fact which may argue for a later composition of this part than has frequently been deduced from the vague entry in the Stationer's Register. Likewise the nineteen scenes of *The Shoemaker's Holiday* (1599) range widely: from London streets to the garden at the Old Ford, from an area before Simon Eyre's house and shop in Tower Street to a field near the Old Ford, from a room in Eyre's house to one in the Lord Mayor's house, from a shop in Tower Street to the street before St. Faith's Church, and to the great hall of the new Lord Mayor with the banquet set for the King in the background. Of the thirteen scenes in *The Noble Spanish Soldier* (S. R., 1631) not one is an exterior, though some are vague as to place. Two take place in the King's presence chamber, one in a banquet hall, two in a gallery, and the rest in private rooms and apartments in the palace and elsewhere. At most only four sets would be required for their presentation on a modern stage. As time goes on, Dekker's practice reveals the growing tendency to reduce the number of places for action for the single play.

So does that of Beaumont and Fletcher. Among the practices burlesqued in *The Knight of the Burning Pestle* (1607) are the number and ridiculous variety of scenes used in a single play. Its twenty-four scenes include the theatre itself within which, we must not forget, all other scenes take place. These include a hall in the palace of the King of Moldavia, a grocer's shop, rooms in the houses of the Merchant and of Merrythought, streets, Waltham Forest, and scenes before a barber's shop, an inn, and a dwelling. *Philaster* (ca. 1610) has only seventeen scenes played in some nine different places. Four of them are such outright exteriors as the three forest scenes and the one street scene; three are what I have called threshold scenes, such as the two before the palace and the one before Pharamond's apartment; one is a prison; three are scenes in the presence chamber or a room of state; and the rest are rooms and apartments in various parts of the palace. By contrast, in *The Maid's Tragedy* (1611), a play not very different in kind from *Philaster*, there are only twelve scenes, all interiors save one, and it is a threshold scene "Before the Citadel." Variety of place has here all but gone: only a hall in the palace is called for, where a masque is given and where a banquet may be served; the rest are bedrooms or "apartments."

Likewise such variety is for the most part lost in Middleton's and his collaborators' plays. With few exceptions his plays are set in various rooms of private houses, streets, and taverns, with now and then a garden or a shop. Although *A Trick to Catch the Old One* (1604–1606?) moves the area of its action from Leicestershire to London and although it has seventeen scenes, the places of action are restricted to the street (six scenes), to a tavern (one scene), and to rooms in Witgood's, Hoard's, Lucre's, and Dampit's houses. And this general pattern is repeated often. The street and the threshold before Harebrain's house in *A Mad World, My Masters* (1606?) leads only to interior scenes; and numerous though they are, they turn out to be bedchambers and a hall or two. On the other hand, a good deal more variety is achieved in *The Roaring Girl* (ca. 1610) (written with Dekker), though it has only ten scenes. Action takes place in Sir Alexander's house, in a street, in a street before shops, in a shop, in Gray's Inn Fields, and in a garden. But in *The Changeling* (1622), written with William Rowley, the places of action are kept inside. After the characters leave the street before the temple in the opening scene, they are never again seen in the open, but rather, in some thirteen scenes, in a room in Alibius's house (three scenes), various rooms and apartments in Vermandero's castle, passageways, vaults, and "galleries." In *A Game at Chess* (1624) of course the action is carefully restricted in keeping with the allegorical nature of the play to a "Field between the two houses," to a space "Before the Black House," to an apartment in the Black House, and to "A chamber with a large mirror." Of these places for the twelve scenes, most of the action takes place on the first, the common scene. Further localization is not desired, for the intent is to make the action universal in import. But on the whole Middleton tends to restrict both area and place of action—and not altogether because of the type of play he customarily wrote.

Such is not true of Massinger. Not one of his sixteen plays lacks exterior scenes, and most of them have several. It is true that the scene of his plays did not move from one continent to another (even in *The Emperor of the East* he holds the area to Constantinople), but he did manage more variety within the area than did many of his contemporaries. In *The Fatal Dowry* (1616–1619), perhaps his earliest play, at least four scenes are laid in the streets; one is specified as before the court of justice and one as before a prison. Besides rooms in various private houses, he places one scene in a sort of Parliament, another in a court of justice. In *A New Way to Pay Old Debts* (1621–1622?) Massinger places two brilliant scenes before Tapwell's tavern, two in open country, as well as those in Lady Allworth's country house and in Overreach's less attractive place. *The Roman Actor* (1626) manages a scene within the theatre in Rome, one in front of the Capitol, one in the Senate House, and one in the gardens of the palace; the rest are staged in the rooms and halls of the palace. In *The Emperor of the East* (1630), even though Massinger uses only four places for his various scenes, he provides a space before the palace for one. *The Renegado* (1624) requires at least twenty-seven scenes, and fourteen different places are designated, including a bazaar and a street before a bazaar, a "Court" in Donuza's palace as well as a room of state with rich jewels spread out, some three or four other scenes on the street, and so on. And in what is perhaps his last play, *The Bashful Lover* (1636), he indicates the customary room of state of the palace as well as other rooms there, a part of the country before Octavio's cottage, St. Leo's Castle, four scenes in a forest, and another countryside scene. Generally Massinger, who constructs his plays with great care, seems to have restricted the places of his action less than did many of his contemporaries. Though they often live a low life above stairs, in contrast to Middleton's, Massinger's leading characters belong to noble and princely classes; hence they probably require a somewhat wider area and more varied scene for their action.

Such is not the case with later playwrights. In five of Ford's plays there are ninety scenes, twenty-eight of them in *'Tis Pity She's a Whore* (1629?–1633), only twelve in *The Lover's Melancholy* (1628). Of the twenty-eight in *'Tis Pity*, only seven are exteriors (all street scenes), three of them obviously "before" certain houses, including a monastery and the Cardinal's house; and the variety of the interiors, for the number, is not great: two in Bonaventura's cell, two in a hall, perhaps two in bedrooms, one in a banqueting hall (perhaps a withdrawing room), and the rest simply rooms in the houses of various people. *Perkin Warbeck* (1622–1632?), a revival of the chronicle play, however, furnishes the expected variety of scenes in such plays. Their geography is widespread. The action takes place in Westminster (in the Palace, including the presence chamber), Edinburgh, London, at Ayton, before Norham Castle, on the coast of Cornwall, on St. Michael's Mount, and at Salisbury. The three London scenes are in the Tower, those at Edinburgh in an apartment at Huntley's house, and in the presence chamber and other rooms of the palace, and the ones at Ayton and on the coast of Cornwall in camps. In the remaining plays the exteriors consist of six street scenes and two garden or grove scenes. Two out of these five plays are entirely without exterior scenes; and the interiors are more and more restricted to private apartments and bedrooms. The subject matter has become more and more restricted, the plot more and more confined to private and individual concerns; thus the scene of action has become circumscribed, and the world is less and less the stage for human action.

This is particularly true of Shirley. In five of his plays dating from 1628 to 1641 he uses only fifty-six scenes. Of these, only nineteen are exteriors, and six of these nineteen are accounted for by *Hyde Park*, where the exteriors were especially to be expected. In *The Witty Fair One* (1628) the entire first act (perhaps three scenes) takes place in Worthy's garden in London; Act II takes place in a room of Sir Nicholas' house at Croydon and in Worthy's house in London; Act III, in five rooms of various private houses in London, including Violetta's bedroom; Act IV, in five rooms of the same houses and with one scene in the street; Act V, in a street and in a bedroom. The variety is not great; the attempt to suggest an action of nation- or world-wide significance, not in evidence. Out of the twelve scenes of *The Traitor* (1631) one is played in a garden and one in a street; the rest are confined to interiors, one a hall of some size perhaps, the others simply indicated as a "room" in the homes of various people. Of the ten scenes in *The Lady of Pleasure* (1635) not one is an exterior; and every interior is a room in a private home, one a dressing room. Since *The Cardinal* (1641) belongs to the Websterian tradition, one expects a somewhat wider range of action and the suggestion of a significance beyond the Capital of Navarre; and the choice of places of action will allow such significance. Indeed just such scenes as he uses had been conventional since the time of Preston's *King Cambises* (1569). But Shirley used only thirteen scenes, only three of which were exteriors, one a combination scene with Colombo's tent set up before the walls of a frontier city, one a garden, and one an open field outside the city. The other ten are to be played in rooms of the palace and of the Duchess's house. Yet for such a play Webster would have used nineteen or twenty scenes, judging by what he did in the *Duchess of Malfi*, and he would have moved his action from Navarre to Rome, to Loretto, and to Milan, setting it not only in a presence chamber and a bedroom, but in a courtyard of a castle, in a hall or gallery, a fort, a road, a space before a shrine, a prison, and so on. Shirley's restriction is apparent. As with characters, so with scenes. Shirley shows less concern with the wider implications of his art, more with the particular and the sufficiency of the immediate action, than his predecessors. His choice of scenes, their variety and their pattern, does not often symbolize or even suggest a cosmos any more than his characters assume allegorical or symbolic or universalized human proportions. His plays anticipate the restrictions of a later time and a less flexible stage.

Fortunately for us the work of Shakespeare and his contemporaries stands between the two extremes—the non-restricted but unified and allegorical past and the restricted, particularized, and fragmented future. Fortunately the process of restriction and fragmentation was not accomplished before the closing of the theatres in 1642. One aspect of this happy synthesis, this realization of the one in the many, was the variety of scenes and the wide choice of places for action within the play. When taken together they had the power in a single play to suggest something more than a segment of individualized and personal and private human action cut off in space from all other such action; they could suggest a world. And this flexibility of choice helped the dramatists to achieve an effective particularization and a humanizing of their art without sacrificing its universality.

FIVE

The Characters:
Orders and Degrees

§ IN THE PREFACE to his edition of Shakespeare (1765) Dr. Johnson praises Shakespeare because "his drama is the mirrour of life," and in that praise justifies the poet's mixing comic with tragic scenes. He then points out that the plays are "not in the rigorous and critical sense either tragedies or comedies, but compositions of a distinct kind; exhibiting the real state of sublunary nature, which partakes of good and evil, joy and sorrow, mingled with endless variety of proportion and innumerable modes of combination; and expressing the course of the world, in which the loss of one is the gain of another." [1] Thus Johnson suggests implicitly, though he does not recognize in so many words, the basic concept lying behind the structure of Shakespeare's—and if Shakespeare's, his contemporaries'—plays: the play is patterned from the world, its form derived from the currently accepted belief as to what was the order and arrangement of the society of men and spirits.

What Dr. Johnson here writes reminds us no little of what Ascham had written in the *Schoolmaster*, as I quote in Chapter I, that "The whole doctrines of Comedies and Tragedies is a perfite *imitation*, or faire livelie painted picture of the life of everie degree of man." Or it suggests what Pierre Boaistuau had said about plays' having in them artificers as well as kings, dukes, earls, barons, and others; or what Abraham Fleming had said in *The Diamant of Devotion* to the effect that plowmen as well as kings, lords, and artificers stalk the stage.[2] Since the stage represents a little world, the players must represent all degrees of men as they play upon it. The whole social structure, in so far as possible, should be represented.

And it should be so represented in any one play, though of course the emphasis in tragedy would necessarily be upon characters of greater position and dignity than the characters in comedy. Neither tragedy nor history would be limited to the nobility and the monarch and unconcerned with the rest of society, nor would comedy exclude a ruler or a nobleman. More important, as Polonius prided himself on knowing and as Dr. Johnson much later suggested, the types and classifications of plays are far more numerous and complicated than pure and simple comedy and tragedy. Not only these but chronicles, histories, historical tragedies, tragi-comedies, pastorals, romantic comedies, and the myriad combinations require for each type varied combinations of characters. Nor could any single play succeed with five characters and a chorus in suggesting the various orders and degrees of society. They were more likely to have two dozen characters in them and to suggest, by one device or another, as many more. Whatever else the Elizabethan dramatist may have learned from Plautus and Seneca, he did not learn to restrict his plays either to the number of characters they used or to the social strata from which they drew their characters for each type of play. The intervening medieval drama, the mystery and the morality plays especially, gave him another concept of dramatic purpose and another popular practice to follow.

In the cycles he found that the stage—the series of "pageants"—was indeed a representation of the history of the world, reaching in time from the Day of Creation to the Day of Doom and presenting the essential story of the race of men. In the moralities he found a representation of every single man's story, the microcosm's *psychomachia* and struggle for salvation. He was familiar with the realistic and comic insertions into the Biblical account of the race's history with its high and low characters. In the cycles he found the King of Kings revealed in the humblest of circumstances, not to three kings only, but to simple shepherds, and the story of this epiphany was not the less sacred or joyful for being associated with the ancient folktale of the roguish sheep stealer. Miss Muriel Bradbrook has remarked as wisely as wittily that "Falstaff and Mak the sheep stealer are equally irrelevant in one sense, equally necessary in another." [3] Their appearance in their particular plays grows out of the same concept and practice. It is the same as that permitting the comic interlude and the roguish characters of the boy Colle and his quackish master Brundyche in *The Play of the Sacrament*.

But it is in the early combinations of histories with moralities that one finds a fuller representation of the basic pattern of society, with the spiritual and allegorical beings surrounding it. Perhaps none better reveals the combination than Bale's *King John*. In it the historical characters of the Pope, King John, Cardinal Pandulphus, Stephen Langdon, and Swinsett appear; but with the exception of John, they become allegorical and assume the names of Dissimulation (Swinsett), Private Wealth (Pandulphus), Usurped Power (the Pope), etc. Other allegorical characters are Verity, Treason, and Sedition. More important are those representing the social order, the estates: Imperial Majesty, Nobility, Clergy, and Commonality. In such an interlude as Medwall's *Fulgens & Lucres* (1497?) the orders or estates are indicated in their Roman setting: Fulgens (Roman Senator), Publius Cornelius (a Patrician), Gaius Flaminius (a Plebeian), A (a youth), B (a servant). Of course Sir David Lindsay's lengthy *Satyre of the Three Estates* (1552, 1554) is based upon the threefold structure of the state and the proper keeping of order and responsibility. Hardly a historical play, it does involve the struggle of Rex Humanitas as God's vicar to rule well, surrounded as he is with such allegorical characters as Wantonness, Placebo, Solace, Flattery, Deceit, etc. To get him out of state troubles, God sends down Divine Correction who advises that he call a

Parliament of the Three Estates. Thus all society is represented so that justice may be accomplished.

The combinations of the allegorical with the real and the representative, however, are finely exemplified in Pickering's *The History of Horestes* (1567?). In addition to Truth, Fame, and Dewtey, Councell, Nobilitie, Commons, and Nature play their parts; and in addition to Horestes and his court with such nobles as Menelaus, Nestor, Egestus, and Clytemnestra, Vyce, Rusticus, Hodge, Halltersycke, and Hempstryng have roles. Besides these, such characters as a Woman, a Sodyer, a Harrauld, and a messenger act as intermediaries. At about the same time Thomas Preston in his *King Cambises* alloted his characters among the various degrees and employments of men, with the exception of the merchant class (who had not yet become a class apart) and clergy, and had given them allegorical companions. To name a few will indicate the range: Cambises with his brother and his queen, the judge (Sisamnes), the judge's son (Smirdis), three Lords, a courtier (Praxaspes), and a knight; among the commons are the soldiers Huf, Ruf, and Snuf and the bumpkins Rob and Lob; among the allegorical are Vice, Commons Cry, Commons Complaints, Diligence, Cruelty, Execution, etc.; and outside all are Venus and Cupid.

One might continue with the same sort of illustration from other plays like these and of the same general period, but here are enough to indicate how it was that plays of the later dramatists and of the richer period had in them representatives of the many classes and orders. Two properties they inherited: the classical philosophical metaphor of the world as a stage as repeated by the Fathers and the later humanists, and the practice of the writers of mysteries, moralities, and early history plays. In the remainder of this chapter I hope to illustrate at first the richness and breadth of this inheritance and later, in the Jacobean and Caroline period, its loss and gradual narrowing. A common sense caution must be entered here. The dramatists were, of course, always limited by the fictions they chose and by their own invention. One does not expect a king often to appear in broad farce, satirical comedy, or domestic tragedy; and yet the Elizabethan playwright will probably suggest to his audience that the king keeps court not far off stage. And though neither the Weird Sisters nor the direct agents of Satan are likely to find roles in such plays, fairies and goblins very well may find them. Yet even in these, and especially in romantic comedies, a duke may supply the place of the monarch, especially to perform his duty as magistrate. It was, I believe, the Elizabethan dramatists' inheritance of the idea that a play should be made as nearly as possible world-wide in the scope it suggests which put the enormous casts and the great variety of characters upon their stage.

The size of the casts makes evident at once the tendency. Even though the direct imitations and adaptations from the Roman drama indicate the classical practice—*Ralph Roister Doister*, for example, has only thirteen characters, *Gammer Gurton's Needle* ten, and *Gorboduc* only sixteen and the chorus—they usually require more characters than their antecedents. When Shakespeare adapts Plautus' *Menaechmi*, he adds seven speaking characters as well as officers and serving men. And whereas Machiavelli used only eight characters in his *Mandragola*, out of the Roman tradition, Shakespeare in *Love's Labour's Lost*, much influenced by the Roman-Italian comedy, required eighteen and the customary "Lords and Attendants," and in *The Taming of the Shrew* nineteen together with "servants." Plautus' plays average fewer than eleven characters; and even though Terence often doubled his plots, his plays average only about twelve characters. Jonson's more strictly Roman-like comedies, *The Alchemist, Every Man In His Humour, Every Man Out of His Humour, Epicoene*, and *Volpone* average seventeen characters with the attendants and mutes in the background. Whereas *The Alchemist* has only twelve speaking characters, it has a considerable number of neighbors and officers taking part in the background; and *Volpone* requires twenty-three speaking parts with a crowd in the background. The Senecan influence upon the stage plays of the period did not restrict the casts: *Titus Andronicus*, for example, requires about twenty-five speaking characters and as large a contingent of Romans, Goths, Senators, Tribunes, Officers, Soldiers, and Attendants as could be mustered upon the stage.

A simple recital of a few figures may be helpful in showing the remarkable size of the casts in all sorts of plays. I find that the average number of characters, not counting the various mutes and attendants, in eighty plays produced over the period roughly from 1540 to 1640 is twenty-three. These plays include *Ralph Roister Doister, Gorboduc*, and *Two Gentlemen of Verona*, as well as *The Spanish Tragedy, Henry V*, and Shirley's *The Cardinal*. Twelve chronicle plays, most of Shakespeare's, average thirty-three characters; fifteen romantic comedies average twenty-one characters, not including the attendants and mutes; twenty-three tragedies and Roman plays average twenty-six characters, besides the numerous background people —attendants, courtiers, gentlemen, citizens, etc. Twenty-three satiric or "regular" comedies average about nineteen characters, plus the background people. The pattern is pretty plain. The chronicles with their great pageantry and the tragedies and Roman plays, though only roughly classified, use the greatest number of characters. Then come the romantic comedies and last, as one would expect, the more nearly "regular" comedy. It is interesting to notice how Dekker and his collaborators seem to have maintained about the same number of characters in each of their plays. The average number is about twenty-two, but except for two plays, the range in number is from twenty to thirty-three characters. All calculations are, of course, imprecise and subject to modification or correction, for some of the characters indicated as "soldiers" or "citizens" or "gentlemen" or such designation as background persons may have not inconsiderable roles and some of those distinguished by name as among the more active characters may actually have little to say or do.

Just as interesting an observation is that, as time went on, there was a general, though not great, falling off in the size of the *dramatis personae* of the plays. Marston, for example, seems to have focused his action upon fewer characters than most of his contemporaries; and Beaumont and Fletcher, writing either together or separately, use on the whole fewer characters than their earlier contemporaries. In ten of their plays the average number of characters is about seventeen, and this includes mostly tragedies, tragi-comedies, and romantic comedies, in which the number of characters is usually greater than in the domestic or regular comedies. More striking are the figures for Shirley's plays. They average fewer than fifteen characters to the play. Even in *The Cardinal* Shirley employs only fourteen, besides the few attendants and other background characters. His practice apparently indicates a trend.[4] Fewer characters took direct part in the action—and fewer appeared upon the stage in the background: attendants, gentlemen, pages, messengers, torch-bearers, etc., "as many as may be spared."

It was these latter who did much to create the illusion of a little world or cross-section of society being presented to the Elizabethan audience. With the principals to the fore they could furnish the impression of the entire social spectrum passing in review, for the characters of the Elizabethan play shaded from the heroes and heroines, the kings and the dukes, to the less important, to the non-important, or least active, to those who came on merely to fill out the monarch's train or the ranks of the army. In this background were gentlemen and ladies in attendance, heralds, messengers, citizens, soldiers, knights, lawyers, doctors, priests, and numerous other functionaries. In *The Old Wives' Tale*, to pick at random, a friar, harvest men and harvest women, with two Furies and fiddlers are required; in *1 Tamburlaine* "Bassoes, Lords, Citizens, Moors, and Attendants"; in *Macbeth* "Lords, Gentlemen, Officers, Soldiers, Murderers, Messengers, Attendants"; in *As You Like It* "Lords, Pages, and Attendants"; in *Philaster* only the King's train; and in *The Cardinal* no characters of these classes are called for. If Marston keeps the number of his principals reduced, he makes up for this in his background characters: in *Antonio and Mellida*, for example, he has gentlemen about the court, a gentlewoman attendant on Mellida, a page to Andrugio, a painter, a herald, waiting women, pages, and torch-bearers. Enough of such characters as these appeared in almost every play of the period to enable the audience to realize that the principals belonged to a community and a social order with a ruler at its head set in a cosmic system with a spiritual power controlling it. The minor and background figures fade out into anonymity, so that, as in familiar human experience, they lose their identity in the background. And yet their presence is necessary to credible action and to the representation of a world on the stage.

This representation becomes much more apparent when one examines the actual *dramatis personae*. As I have already indicated, the cycles and moralities present or suggest all history or all men, and the hybrid moralities, combining allegorical and historical or individual characters, reveal a conscious awareness of the social structure in their *dramatis personae*. The later plays, especially the histories, chronicles, tragedies, and romantic comedies, illustrate this awareness more fully, and indicate that the dramatists were not merely paying lip-service to an ideal or repeating a popular commonplace when they spoke of the world as a stage and life as a play. A sampling of these *dramatis personae* will be sufficient to establish the point, to illustrate, and to clarify.

Even in the restricted high comedy of Lyly, derived largely from classical legend, evidence of the social spectrum may be found. In *Sapho and Phao* the gods are involved in an action having to do with a princess (Sapho), a courtier, court ladies, a scholar (Pandion), a page, a soothsayer, and the young ferryman (Phao). In his *Campaspe,* the spread is much wider, for at the head of the cast is Alexander the Great, next below him Hephestion and old Clytus, his generals, then eight philosophers, then a painter and his apprentice, the citizens of Athens, servants, etc. Here is a far greater spread of characters than was in his source.

Similarly, in such a fanciful pastoral, classical story, adapted from the medieval narrative tragedy form, as *The Arraignment of Paris,* George Peele managed to bring into the action most of the pantheon, including Cupid and with him the Cyclops, the Fates, the Muses, and varied nymphs. With these he mingled such mortals as Paris, Oenone, Helen, and Thestylis, and several knights, and with these, on the lower level, certain shepherds including Colin, Hobbinol, Diggon, and Thenot. In his *Edward I* (1593?) his characters range from the King to nobles, to a bishop, to Welsh barons, a knight, a harper, a farmer, a friar, and a potter's wife. Even in such an unusual play as *The Old Wives' Tale* (1591–1594) the range is greater than one might think: aside from the Smith and his Old Wife of the outside action, on the inside appear Delia, a king's daughter, and her two brothers, besides Eumenides, the knight, a churchwarden, a sexton, a conjurer, harvest men and harvest women, a soldier, and a ghost. In one way or another the three estates are represented and with their subdivisions. In *David and Bethsabe* (1594?) his characters range downward from David, the king, and his family, to Urias and Bethsabe, to soldiers of lower rank, to shepherds and attendants. An attempt is made to suggest the whole of society, and David is punished in part for untuning the string of "degree" in taking Bethsabe.

All the pageants of Robert Greene demonstrate this same attempt to suggest the whole of society by including in the cast of each representatives of the various orders. Perhaps none better shows the practice than *James IV* (ca. 1591), a play designed as good counsel for the monarch. Oberon of the fairies and Bohan, the ghost of a philosopher, present the play, in which the forces of evil are represented by Ateukin and those of good by the Bishop of St. Andrewes as they struggle for the soul of King James IV of Scotland. Not only does the cast include the two estates already mentioned, the King and his court and the clergy; but very soon we learn of others: here are a lawyer, a merchant, a tailor, a shoemaker, a cutler, and huntsmen. The commonality are well represented in the action. The resolution of the plot is secured by the work of a faithful knight who bribes one "Slipper" to steal the warrant for the death of the Queen. In *A Looking Glass for London and England* (1590?), which Greene did with Lodge, the characters range from Rasni (King of Nineveh) and the Kings of Cilicia, Crete, and Paphlagonia, to "Alcon, a poor man," to a usurer, a lawyer, Oseas (a prophet), Jonas (a prophet), priests of the sun, a master of a ship, magi, merchants, sailors, a good angel, and an evil angel. The two writers feel obliged to present the entire spectrum. And one could point out much the same social spectrum in *Friar Bacon and Friar Bungay*, where the sturdy yeomen are chiefly celebrated, as they are also in *George a Green, Pinner of Wakefield*, though in it the clergy and the supernatural have little part.

Kyd's *The Spanish Tragedy* (ca. 1589), except for the clergy, represents the whole of society.[5] The allegorical character of Revenge presents the play for the Ghost of Andrea, and the cast calls for a king, a viceroy, dukes, the Marshall of Spain, a Spanish general, Portuguese and other noblemen, ambassadors, officers, soldiers, a painter, three citizens, three watchmen, and a hangman. Besides these, numerous attendants are called for and the *dramatis personae* for Hieronimo's play, the cast of which is taken from the cast of the play proper.

Much the same is true of Marlowe's plays. Even in the "tragic glass" of Tamburlaine with emphasis upon military panoply and conquest, representatives appear from most social levels. In addition to the emperors, some fourteen kings, soldans, viceroys, commanders, bashaws, and lords appear, as well as the Queen, the virgins of Damascus, and assorted Turkish concubines; then come moors, common soldiers, physicians, and citizens. Only the clergy are omitted, though they might well have been employed. But they do appear, however much to their discredit, in *The Jew of Malta*, which has the Abbess, the Nun, and the two Friars. Here also appear two merchants, other than Barabas and the two other Jews of that class. No kings in their pomp parade here, but Ferneze, the Governor of Malta, and the son of the Grand Seignior make their bold and colorful entrances, as does the Admiral of Spain with his knights. But we also have Pila-Borsa (the bully), Bellamira (the Courtesan),

Ithamore (the slave), and a carpenter. In *The Massacre of Paris* Marlowe is at special pains to represent every degree and class. Not only does he bring on, as required by his history, Charles IX of France, the Duke of Anjou, their mother Catherine, the Lord High Admiral, Guise and other nobles, but, as not required by his history, Ramus, the philosopher, Taleus, the rhetorician, a Protestant preacher, and a friar. He carefully brings into the action a Captain of the Guard, an English agent, and soldiers, and then schoolmasters, a surgeon, an apothecary, and a cutpurse. He exercises the same care in *Edward II*, a genuine chronicle play in which one expects to find a cross-section of the body politic. Next below Edward II and the royal family are the nobles, such as the Mortimers, Warwick, Lancaster, and Pembroke. The Church is well represented by the Archbishop of Canterbury, the Bishop of Coventry, an abbot, and several monks. The rising nobles and gentry are indicated in Gaveston, the Spencers, Baldock, etc. The commonality, kept in the background except for the murderers, are nevertheless carefully suggested by James, a mower, certain "Poor Men," and the soldiers. To mention *Doctor Faustus* is at once to recall a vast number of people of all degrees and orders and occupations. Rival popes appear, cardinals, the Archbishop of Rheims, and unnamed bishops, monks, and friars to represent (satirically) the Church's magnificence. Charles V and the King of Hungary, and the Dukes of Anholt and Saxony with their courtiers represent magnificently the temporal power. Faustus, the scholars, Valdes and Cornelius, and an old man form the divisions among the men of learning. Wagner, Robin, the Hostess, Dick, the Horse-Courser, etc. suggest the tradesmen class and the clowns. Outside these are the spiritual powers, both good and bad—good and evil angels—Mephistophilis, Lucifer and various devils. And called up as in a mirror are Helen of Troy and Alexander the Great, as well as the pageant of the Seven Deadly Sins. Marlowe makes conscious effort to suggest the cosmic structure in his *dramatis personae*.

So does Shakespeare, especially in the chronicles, the tragedies, and the romantic comedies. It is true that the neoclassical doctrine restricted comedy to characters of the lower classes; it is equally true that the doctrine was well-known among the dramatists and that it was to some degree regarded in practice, especially by those who thought to make their comedy pure and "regular." But it is also true that the Elizabethan playwrights did not often keep separate one species of play from another; they could not easily disregard the reality of the structure of society which allowed no such separation; hence they seldom wrote "regular" or unadulterated comedy or pure farce, even when they took it direct from Plautus. Shakespeare put into his *Comedy of Errors* the Duke of Ephesus and thus gave representation to the first estate; he introduced Æmelia into the plot as an abbess at Ephesus to help untie the knotted action and thus gave representation to the second estate. Aside from Pinch the schoolmaster, the jailers, and officers—good enough Plautine characters—he introduced six others whom Plautus did not use. It is indeed only in *The Taming of the Shrew* and *The Merry Wives of Windsor* that no ruling class is involved, and in the former the Lord who takes in Sly may be regarded as the controlling duke. The latter, said to have been written to order, is the exception to prove the rule. Shakespeare's comedies, of whatever classification, do place greater emphasis upon the action of "low" characters, of course, than his tragedies and his chronicles. Merchants, tradesmen, innkeepers, lower clergy, professional men, clowns, and servants more often find roles, some drawn directly from the stock characters of Plautus.

A few examples from his romantic comedy will illustrate. Even in the early neo-Roman *Two Gentlemen of Verona* (1594?) with its small cast, the social levels are pretty well suggested. At the top are the Duke of Milan, with the two gentlemen and two ladies and their associates. Eglamour and Thurio are of a lower class. The Host at the house where Julia lives represents the citizenry and merchant class. Below him are the clowns, outlaws, and servants, and in the background are the musicians and other attendants. *Much Ado* (1598) calls for a fuller representation of society. The Prince, the Governor, the young lords and ladies of the court stand at the top of the ladder. Below them, suggesting the clergy, are Friar Francis and a Sexton, and then come the low comedy people, Dogberry, Verges and the Watch. A much larger representation appears in *Measure for Measure* (1604). To the court group, with the Duke at the top, are added the citizens, a justice, friars and a nun, a "fantastic," officers, an executioner, a bawd, and various attendants. Here the whole ladder is indicated. Much the same had been true of *The Merchant of Venice* (1598). In it the rich merchant class forms the nucleus of action and is fully represented. Yet the Duke of Venice appears as judge and the colorful princes come to woo Portia. In addition magnificoes, officers, a jailer, a clown, confidants, attendants, and servants have their parts. Though marriages are impending and perhaps a baptism at the end, no priest is called for. These are surely enough to recall the usual character groupings or patterns in Shakespeare's comedies.

The chronicles, histories, and tragedies, if we may classify roughly, by their very nature require a more complete cross-section of society. In them royalty and nobility dominate the action, with courtiers, knights, and gentlemen surrounding them; and yet in all Shakespeare's chronicles but one, *III Henry VI*, the upper clergy have parts. The commons quite properly have their roles in every one of them. In all but two, *Richard II* and *Henry VIII*, citizens or their representatives such as lord mayors have roles. Aside from the numerous functionaries of the court, knights and gentlemen and lords, numerous people of lower rank have their parts. They range from professional men and soldiers to murderers: Ambassadors, heralds, governors or mayors of cities, sheriffs, counselors, justices, and aldermen appear; so do friars, prophets, beadles, conjurers, scriveners, watchmen, shipmasters, butchers, weavers, porters, apprentices, falconers, armorers, tavern keepers, drawers, carriers, grooms, pages, gardeners, clerks, doctors, and even an old shepherd. *Henry V* requires, besides the two kings with their nobility and the ladies of the court, knights and gentry, clergy, captains and common soldiers, the governor (or mayor) of a city and his "citizens" and the hostess of a tavern. In addition such functionaries as two heralds, ambassadors, the Constable of France, a boy, and various messengers are specified in the *dramatis personae*. These are typical.

And much the same pattern, modified to fit the Roman source, may be observed in the Roman plays. Aside from soothsayers and priests, a fair representation of Roman society appears even in the early *Titus Andronicus*. Oddly its cast includes a clown and a nurse with a black child. The outlines of the Roman government are apparent in the Emperor, the senators, the nobles, the tribune of the people, and the military. Much the same groupings are likewise apparent in *Julius Caesar*, though they are more inclusive and more fully represented; for in it appear a soothsayer, two poets, a philosopher, and citizens with their tribunes, as well as the upper groups and the military. The second estate, as it were, and the scholars have a place. *Coriolanus*, though without emperor of course, contains consuls, patricians, and tribunes of the people to indicate the ancient orders of Roman society. In it too are senators, soldiers, and citizens represented by their aediles with control of public works and grain supply, and in it are the lictors, messengers, and other functionaries and servants. *Cymbeline*, likewise, however we may classify it, suggests the pattern. Below the King of Britain and his courtiers in the hierarchy of orders come the Roman senators and other officials, including the tribunes. The soothsayer represents the clergy, as it were, and the physician, the learned class, comes between clergy and commonality. Then in addition to officers and messengers, the cast includes musicians and a jailer.

In *Romeo and Juliet*, following the basic pattern of romantic comedy, the cast represents the whole of the society of Verona. The play requires the Prince at the top as arbiter and judge, protecting the interests of the state. Next below him forming the nucleus of the action are the members of the two noble families. The friars represent the clergy, and the citizens of Verona, the

guards, watchmen, torchbearers, pages, musicians, and an apothecary have unusually active parts. So do the retainers of the two
households.

The four great tragedies, except for *Hamlet,* are lacking in
clergy and necessarily have few parts for the citizenry or merchant or tradesmen class. Their omission must not be taken,
however, for a disregard of their estate or class. They belonged
to the vast commonality. Hence such persons as the players, or
gravediggers, or sailors, of the commonality too, might represent
them; so might the mob who rally to Laertes.[6] Among these
plays, perhaps *Macbeth* represents society least well, perhaps
Othello is most explicit, and perhaps Lear most effectively expresses a concern for those of the lowest orders. Hamlet's remark that "the toe of the peasant comes so near the heel of the
courtier that he galls his kibe" and Lear's confession that he has
taken too little care of the poor naked wretches of this world indicate Shakespeare's awareness of the kinship of all men; they
also indicate his acute sense of the responsibility required by the
several orders and degrees of society, especially that of royalty
and the nobility. The full pattern may best be observed in *Hamlet.* Next below the King, Queen and two princes (Hamlet and
Fortinbras) are the courtiers and gentlemen and the chief coun-
selor (Polonius); the clergy are represented, not to their credit,
by the Priest who comes to bury Ophelia, and Horatio is the
scholar, with whom might be associated as a class the ambassadors; next come the commonality represented by the common
soldiers and their captains, then the sailors, and finally the gravediggers, the clowns. Thus the three estates with some delineation
of degrees within them are indicated. It is the basic social pattern
governing all functions of state and of law. It lent itself even to
church ritual, wherein it gave pattern to all intercessions, as in
the Book of Common Prayer. Surely here is enough to illustrate
Shakespeare's conscious effort, so far as was possible within the
materials he was shaping, to indicate the entire social order—and
with his supernatural characters, the cosmic order—in his plays.

Ben Jonson's effort is less apparent, though no less conscious.

Even in the Roman plays, where the subject matter and the vast number of characters give the impression of an entire society, representatives of the commonality are given little opportunity directly to express themselves. And yet they are present in the background. In *Sejanus* (1603), with all its vast pageantry, much is made of the priestly office (the flamens), and of the heralds (the praecones); Eudemus is physician to Livia—and go-between for Sejanus—but withal a learned man. The orders range from the Emperor Tiberius, to the Senators and patricians, to the priests and tribunes of the people and the various functionaries of the government. The lower orders really have no voice, though their presence is felt. In *Catiline* (1611) the restrictions are less. The Ghost of Scylla acts as presenter of the play, and the highest orders of Roman society are fully represented, the patricians (in Julius Caesar), the consuls, senators, and others. The ambassadors of the Allobroges represent the learned—or should do so, as the witty Sempronia indicates—and the Tribunes, soldiers, and "People" do have their parts. Yet they are kept farther in the background than such characters are kept in the plays of Shakespeare and of Jonson's predecessors. Faithful to his sources, Jonson deliberately restricts himself.

Likewise, he restricts himself in his comedies—especially those derived most directly from the Roman tradition. In *The Case is Altered* (1597?), possibly his earliest play, however, the more conventional pattern prevails: the characters reflect the hierarchy, ranging downward from Count Ferneze and his family to the "learned" pageant poet Antonio Balladino, to the steward of the court, to the seeming beggar Jaques de Prie, to the tradesman, Juniper the cobbler, to Peter Onion (the groom), and to various pages and servants. Royalty do not appear, nor do the clergy, but the spectrum is wide for comedy. In *Every Man in His Humour* (1598), though the Plautine scheme is basic, the range of characters suggests a more complete society than does Plautus. Knowell, his son Edward, George Downright (the country squire), and Justice Clement represent an upper class; next come Kitely and Tom Cash, the merchant group;

next, the military in Bobadill (and his gulls perhaps); and finally, Cob and Tib, the low-life characters, together with servants in the background. Brainworm, the witty servant, stands outside to manipulate. These are indeed the "persons, such as comedy would choose," but they still represent a considerable variety: gentleman and scholar, the law, the merchant, the military, the tradesman or laborer, and the servant. The clergy, not present, are just off stage, for a marriage must soon be performed. In the Induction to *Every Man Out of His Humour* (1599) Jonson has Cordatus state his position regarding the "rules" of comedy. He indicates that, though he respects the Ancients, he thinks the successive generations of poets should make their own contributions to the art, should heighten their own invention. He is admittedly interested more in what every man is like than in what rank of society he belongs to; yet he must give every man his place in that society so as to make his point—that most classes of mankind have their asses and fools. How else could he show the follies and fopperies of the world, of every man? So a considerable representation of the various ranks, as well as the various dispositions, of men is given. At the top is the absurd knight Puntarvolo and his lady, with Fastidious Brisk, the "affecting courtier"; next is Carlo Buffone, the gentleman and "gallant," who teaches Sogliardo how to act like a gentleman, for Sogliardo "will be a gentleman whatsoever it cost me." Next in order come Malicente, the scholar, and Fungoso, the student; then Clove and Orange, two fops, and Shift, a would-be soldier. Lower in the scale are Sordido, the farmer, then the shoemaker, the tailor, the haberdasher, the huntsman, the drawers, the groom, and certain "Rustics." The follies of all estates are represented.

Alan C. Dessen has recently shown that Jonson deliberately presented a cross-section of society even in *The Alchemist* (1610).[7] Subtle, Face, and Doll, descendants of the morality Vice, confront a "panoramic cross section of his [Jonson's] contemporary society," in the characters of Dapper (lawyer and fop), Abel Drugger (merchant), Sir Epicure Mammon (knight), Ananias and Tribulation Wholesome (men of religion), and Kastril (country gentleman). These form a "modified version of the late morality's 'estates.'" The action is not restricted to the stock characters and low life of Plautine comedy nor yet to the particular souls of a given London street, but broadened to represent an entire social order. His regard for the unities in this play did not require Jonson to disregard the social unity; indeed it might be thought of as a fourth unity.

Likewise Jonson is at pains to suggest a little world in *Bartholomew Fair* (1614), though a society of rogues and charlatans. Winwife and Cokes are gentry, and Overdo a justice; Littlewit, a proctor of the ecclesiastical court, represents a second estate; then come the tradesmen such as the baker, Zeal-of-the-Land Busy, the beadle, and the toymen of the Fair; and below them among the commonality are the gamesters, beggars, porters, cutpurse, and tapisters. Gentlemen, professional men, tradesmen, servants, and riff-raff have their places. In *The Devil is an Ass* (1616) the orders range from the knight downward: Sir Paul Eitherside, the gentleman Fabian Fitzdotterel, and Wittipol, the gallant, are followed by the tradesmen, a gentleman usurer, a smith, and others. The social scheme is better observed in *The New Inn* (1629), in which the chief characters are not at all what they seem. The Host is actually Lord Frampul; the Nurse, apparently a one-eyed crone, is actually Lady Frampul; and Frank turns out to be Laetitia, daughter of the Host. We are entertained by the Lords Latimer and Beaufort, who in their intrigue remind us much of Goldsmith's two young gentlemen in a much later play. Lovel is a complete gentleman, soldier, and scholar. Below these lords, ladies and gentlefolk, emerge Sir Glorious Tipto, the *miles gloriosus*, the drawer, Nick Stuff (the tailor) and his wife, Jug (the tapister), the smith, the hostler, and various servants. In *The New Inn* Jonson is deliberately creating a little world.

He does much the same in *The Tale of a Tub* (1633). Finsbury Hundred is indeed a restricted but complete community, involving neither the Duke's palace, nor the King's court, but the home of Lady Tub and the environs of Kentish-town. The characters highest in the social register are, therefore, Lady Tub and her son Squire Tub. With them come Justice Preamble, Canon Hugh (Vicar of St. Pancras), and Diogenes Scriben (a "great writer"). Next below them Tobie Turf (the high constable), Sybil his wife, and Awdry his daughter have their parts, and below them are ranged the cooper, the farrier, the minstrel, and the servants. This little state is made up of the country squire and the community he rules. It is significant that Jonson here, as elsewhere, chooses his characters so as to indicate the entire community: a restricted world, it represents the whole. The events of comedy do not greatly shake the state nor yet the world; they do disturb the even course of community life. Thus restricted, Jonson's vision is not the less effective in suggesting the full and proper structure of society.[8]

Enough evidence has been adduced already for those familiar with Elizabethan drama to clarify and illustrate the point of this chapter: that the dramatists generally attempted to put into each play, whether comedy or tragedy, representatives of a sufficient number of the orders of society to suggest, at least, that the action was representative of the whole. This is not to contend that a mechanical formula was prescribed or followed or that exceptions did not take place. The dramatists usually found out their own way of making their suggestion. And in comedy, especially that deriving most directly from the Roman tradition, assuredly the character range was more circumscribed than in the romantic comedy, tragi-comedy, tragedy, or chronicle plays. It will thus be sufficient henceforth to present a few examples from later dramatists to show continuation, later changes, and the apparent decline of attempts to indicate a microcosm in the individual play.

As one would expect, Chapman the classicist shows least inclination of any to represent the whole of society in his plays. And yet his plays reveal more of a cross-section of it than those of Plautus or Terence or Seneca. However Senecan *Bussy D'Ambois* (1604) may be, Chapman gets into its plot about twenty-five speaking characters, besides the court lords, ladies, pages, and other background people, including the clergy by way of the Friar. More important perhaps, the conflict of the play concerns whether a poor gentleman may by worth rise to position at court and be accepted as one of the nobility. Much the same is true of *The Revenge of Bussy* (1610), *The Conspiracy of Byron* (1608), and *Chabot* (1613?) (possibly revised by Shirley), though in *Chabot* the elaborate trial required an increase in character-spread. In *Caesar and Pompey* (1613?) Chapman, abandoning Seneca for the most part, presents upon the stage not only great heroes, but emperors and demi-gods, then Roman nobles and senators, then a soothsayer (clergy), soldiers, citizens, ushers, and "ruffians."

Even in those comedies chiefly derived from Terence, Chapman does not restrict the range of his characters to his sources. In *All Fools* (1604?), for example, are two knights and their two sons (somewhat higher in rank than the pairs in Terence), two courtiers, "a start-up gentleman," a scrivener, a surgeon, a drawer, and servants. Though at bottom, as Parrott says, these may be stock Roman comedy people, they are adapted to English society and range from the equestrian order downward. In his romantic comedies, though he still makes use of stock Roman characters, Chapman greatly widens the scope of his *dramatis personae*. In *The Gentleman Usher* (1602?) at the top of the social ladder is Duke Alphonso, Prince Vincentio, and Strozzo, a lord. Then, aside from court retainers, a pedant, a doctor, huntsmen, and guards have parts. In the masque the variety is increased by an enchanter, spirits, a nymph, etc. Likewise in *The Widow's Tears* (1603) the range is from the Governor of Cyprus and the widowed countess to a gentleman usher and waiting women, from soldiers and a captain of the watch to a panderess and a courtesan. It is in the introduction of the upper classes, the princes and governors, that Chapman deviates from Plautus and Terence. And however much he may at times restrict the social spectrum and fail to suggest a complete society in a play, he does in each put enough characters upon the stage to make up in some measure for the restriction.

Marston seems not to have felt an obligation to represent the various strata of society, yet he is less restrictive than Chapman. In *Antonio and Mellida* (1599) and in *Antonio's Revenge*, its sequel, a ghost appears from the spirit world. The Dukes of Genoa, Venice, and Milan and their sons top the social structure. They are aided by the gentlemen and the senators of Venice; and these, by a herald and a painter, to a degree suggesting the professions; and all, finally, by the waiting women, torch-bearers, pages, etc. No clergy appear. But in *The Malcontent* (1604), if one accepts Pietro's disguise as a hermit, the clergy are obliquely drawn into the action. Otherwise in this play one finds about the same representatives of the orders and degrees as one found in the Antonio plays: the ducal class, courtiers and syc-ophants, the military in the choleric old marshal, the gentle-man usher, a page, Passarello (a fool), and a panderess. Trades-men are not drawn in. *Sophonisba* (1606) makes use of about the same orders: kings, generals, senators, a surgeon, an enchant-ress, and waiting women. Outside stands the Ghost of Asdrubal. In *What You Will* (1601), a comedy, a much wider representa-tion of society takes part in the action. Highest in rank are the Duke of Venice, Iacomo, Celia, and their kin; next are the courtiers and gentlemen, much satirized; next, the professionals or tradesmen, one a perfumer; and next, such servants as Slip, Noose, and Trip. *The Dutch Courtesan* (1603–1604) is re-stricted to knights, tradesmen (vintners, a goldsmith, etc.), watchmen, and various servants. In *The Parasitaster, or The Fawn* (1604–1605) Marston makes more of an effort to include in his cast someone from every rank. Hercules, the disguised Faunus, Duke of Ferrara, with his son and the Duke of Urbin with his daughter as rulers are surrounded by court people, though not very noble; next are the sickly knight, the "common lover," and the foolish Dondola, with other knaves of the house-hold. But—and this is significant—with these come a priest, a page, a laundress, and attendants to fill out the pattern. A masque within the play furnishes Cupid and such allegorical characters as Drunkenness, Sloth, Pride, Beggary, and Laughter. *The Insatiate Countess* (1610) likewise includes a broad cover-

age of degrees: the three estates, from dukes to courtiers to senators to a cardinal and a friar, to a colonel and his soldiers, to
watchmen, an executioner, torchbearers, and maids, are represented. Having broken away from the tradition of the chronicles
and spectacles, Marston at the first of his career restricted his
casts and limited the range of his *dramatis personae*, but returned to the older practice in his later plays. He never at any
time disregarded the social pattern.

Although we tend to think of him as primarily the dramatist
of London middle-class and apprentice life, Thomas Dekker
perhaps more than any other playwright of the period consist-
ently represented all degrees in each of his plays. Fourteen out
of twenty of them, or plays he had a hand in, present not only
tradesmen, apprentices, clowns, and cutpurses, but kings and
dukes and courtiers. Only three of them are without either king
or duke and place a knight *in locum principis* above the tradesmen, apprentices, gulls, knaves, and suchlike. In contrast, only
three of the plays in which he had a hand include no citizens or
tradesmen; but even in these, such people as a poet, a disguised
doctor, captains of the guard, and clowns have roles.

Even in a fantasy such as *Old Fortunatus* (1599) Dekker
must represent the three estates as well as the spirit world upon
the stage. The chief character is a beggar, and surrounding the
inner action of the play are the goddess Fortuna with Virtue and
Vice in a struggle. Attending upon Fortune are the three Des-
tinies, a priest, and a company of satyrs and nymphs. Royalty
finds itself magnificently displayed in the characters of the
Soldan of Babylon, four kings ruined by Fortune, and King
Athelstane of England, at whose court are both Scottish and
English noblemen. There is also the Prince of Cyprus with his
courtiers. But carefully included in the cast below these are a
Monk, a Tailor, a Carter, and a Shepherd, in addition to the
soldiers.

One usually thinks of *The Shoemaker's Holiday* (1599) as a
play of apprentice life in London, and it is basically that. Yet the
King at the top has a controlling part, and so do the Earls of

Cornwall and Lincoln with the latter's nephew Rowland Lacy. Of the gentlemanly class are Askew, Hammond, perhaps Sir Roger Otley, and Master Scott. Ranged below these are Simon Eyre, his wife, and his shoemakers and the Dutch merchant. In the background are soldiers, huntsmen, other shoemakers, and apprentices.

In *The Honest Whore*, Parts I and II (1604, 1608?) the range is not so great, but it does reach from the Count Hippolito of Milan and the Duke of Milan and his daughter Infelice to the gallants or court "butterflies," to Candido a rich draper and his wife, to Anselmo (a friar), to a poor scholar, to Benedict (a doctor), to Fustigo (a sailor), to a constable, to apprentices, and then to a porter, a sweeper, madmen, and servants. In *Lust's Dominion* (1600?) and *The Noble Spanish Soldier* (1631?), far apart as they are and both done obviously in collaboration with other dramatists, no citizens or tradesmen appear. And yet in the one, besides the King and the Prince of Fez and Barbary with their various noblemen, a Cardinal and two friars, a captain, and soldiers appear; in the other, though no tradesmen have roles, a poet, a captain of the guard, and a soldier do have them. Dekker was not the poet merely of the tradesmen and apprentices.

If one should think of all the characters in the whole corpus of Thomas Heywood's plays as appearing in one vast pageant, one would indeed be astonished at their variety. The people of his plays range downward from the gods of Olympus and the heroes of Greek epic to Eastern potentates and historical monarchs, including Queen Elizabeth; from dukes and nobles of various lands and lords and ladies of various courts to mayors and aldermen, great merchants and lesser tradesmen; from abbots, preachers, and friars to apprentices, tavern-keepers, and bouncing barmaids; from hearty sailors, huntsmen, and witty servants to clowns, courtesans, and whore-masters. But Heywood, well aware of the strictures of neoclassical criticism, did not always represent every man in each play. In fact he is critical of the excesses of the Elizabethans in trying to ransack the universe for characters, saying that

To give content to this most curious Age,
The gods themselves we'have brought downe to the Stage,
And figur'd them in Planets, made even Hell
Deliver up the Furies, by no spell,
(Saving the *Muses* rapture) further, we
Have traffickt by their helpe, no History
We have left unrifled.[9]

And he goes on to mention the fairies and remark that the dramatists have reached out to the *primum mobile* for character and story. Yet he knows that English—and the French, Italian, Spanish, and Dutch—drama differs from the Roman and Athenian, and must differ, especially in its variety. He says in the Prologue to *A Challenge for Beauty:*

For where before great Patriots, Dukes and Kings
Presented for some hie fascinorious things,
Were the Stage-Subiect; now we strive to flie
In their low pitch, who never could soare hie:
For now the common argument intreats,
Of puling Lovers, craftie Bawdes or Cheates.[10]

High tragedy and the heroic subject have given way to the romantic story and perhaps to tragi-comedy. Hence the inclusion of lower persons in the plays. And hence, in spite of his awareness of the "rules" and his sympathy with them, the variety of his practice.

Out of some twenty-three of his plays only five have no king or duke to head the cast, among them *The Wise Woman of Hogsdon,* but allow a knight or gentleman to head it; and only in about four plays does one fail to find low- or middle-class characters, and three of these are from the five plays on the Four Ages of man, where some of the gods indeed resemble London tradesmen. He makes a fair distribution of roles among the various ranks in thirteen of his plays, though it is greater in some than in others. Even in *The Second Part of the Iron Age* (1613), in which a *Götterdämmerung* has set in, a priest of

Apollo, two Trojan citizens, with their wives, a guard, and attendants appear, characters of a class not seen hitherto in the Ages series. More revealing is his adaptation of Plautus' *Rudens* in *The Captives* (1624). Whereas Plautus uses only nine characters, Heywood uses an indeterminate number indicated by "officers," etc. And in Heywood's play they range from the Duke and his Duchess to four merchants and their families, to an abbot and two friars, to a baker, a fisherman, and other "citizens," and to a sheriff, officers, a procurer, and a clown. *I and II Edward IV* (1594–1599?), possibly Heywood's earliest play, is replete with kings and the king-maker (Warwick), lord mayors, the wealthy London Merchant, Shore and his wife, Hob the witty tanner of Tamworth, soldiers and officers—a rather careful representation from the various walks of life. And in the late *Love's Mistress, the Queen's Mask* (1634) Heywood apparently made an effort to range his characters from deities, to kings, to "swains," and to "a Beggar." Few plays bring into their cast a wider variety of mankind than *The Fair Maid of the West*, I (1610?) and II (1630?). The chief character of its two parts is Besse a barmaid. In her exciting voyagings about the world— and she covers most of it—she encounters the King of Fez, his unfaithful queen and other Eastern potentates, the Earl of Essex, numerous dukes and noblemen, the gentry, and merchants of all varieties. She has to do with a "General at sea," a "Lieutenant of the Moors," banditti, the sturdy and loyal tradesmen of London, Clem the clown, and numerous others. Perhaps Heywood made a more conscious effort to present a cross-section of English society in his patriotic *If You Know not Me You Know Nobody* (1605), the two-part pageant-play of Elizabeth's coming into and then retaining her power against evil churchmen, foreign powers, and traitors at home. At the outset her guardian angel saves her from the machinations of the clergy, the Bishop of Winchester and certain friars. In the two parts other monarchs than the Queen have roles, and with them numerous noblemen, high churchmen, and great soldiers and seamen. But her power is strengthened greatly by the solid help of her sturdy merchants, such as Sir Thomas Gresham, whose support in turn depends upon the clerks, apprentices, and peddlers represented in the play. Such plays as *A Woman Killed with Kindness* (1603) and *Fortune by Land and Sea* (ca. 1607) deal primarily with the gentry and the middle classes, knights being the highest in rank. Yet it is surprising how full is the representation of the hierarchy of an ordered society. Besides the knights and gentlemen and their ladies, officers, sheriffs, merchants, sailors, jailers, hunters, falconers, country fellows, carters, tavernkeepers, musicians, and various servants appear. Except for the clergy, a good representation of the various degrees and vocations below that of knighthood is made. Though Heywood knew and respected the strictures of neoclassical decorum upon the kind and number of characters proper to each kind of play, he also knew, as we have already observed,[11] and regarded in his practice, the larger concept of the stage and the play as a representation of the world in little, requiring in each play "as many as may be" to represent as fully as possible "degree, priority, and place."

Thomas Middleton, Chronologer of the City of London, adapter of Terence, and writer of comedies of London life, however much he wrote for the same audience as Heywood, did not at all follow Heywood's practice. Whereas Heywood within a single play moved his scene over the face of the earth and drew his characters from everywhere and every order, Middleton generally restricted his scene and his society. And yet he seems to have started his career by suggesting, at least, the whole of society in a single play. In four of his early plays he retains the general scheme of society from the nobility downward, even though in them he puts the emphasis upon the middle and lower classes; and in three or four toward the end of his career he seems to return to the older scheme. At most, eight of his plays suggest a complete society, ranging from kings or dukes to clowns and laborers; twelve or thirteen out of twenty-one indicate only that part of the social spectrum including and below the rank of gentleman. The clergy seldom appear. In *The Old Law* (1599?), for example, the Duke of Epire and his courtiers head the cast; but they have much less to do than the parish clerk, the lawyers, the bailiff, the tailor, drawer, cook, coachman, executioner, and the clown. So it is with *Blurt, Master Constable* (1601–1602), an imitation of *Much Ado About Nothing:* though the Duke of Venice is present and effects, with Blurt, the denouement, his household—his ladies and gentlemen —in contrast to that of Leonato, Governor of Messina, is decidedly "low" and dissolute. As the title suggests, the chief interest lies in the Constable's effectiveness and in the doings of the beadle, the friar, watchmen, and Imperia, keeper of the bawdyhouse. In *The Mayor of Quinborough* (1616–1620?) the characters do range in degree from the Sons of Constantine and Uther Pendragon to footmen and murderers; but again, the interest centers upon the shrewd tradesmen. British Lords of Devonshire, the Mayor and his clerk, two monks, a tailor, a barber, a feltmonger, a footman, and players mingle with Hengst and Horsa. Heading the cast of *The Phoenix* (1603–1604) is the Duke of Ferrara and Phoenix, his son, and certain nobles, below which are ranged a lawyer and a justice of the peace, a groom, constable, drawer, etc. In *The Witch* (1610–1616) are, for once, no tradesmen, the Duke and his court serving, with servants, as the cast. *The Changeling* (1622) (with William Rowley), a powerful tragedy, lacks the normal character range of such plays. At the top stand the Governor of Alicante and his little court; in the secondary plot are the intriguing gentlemen at the mad house. But the distribution of characters is quite restricted. In *More Dissemblers Besides Women* (ca. 1615) the Duchess of Milan heads the cast and then the Cardinal, prince of the Church; but only the ducal household appears, no tradesmen or rude mechanicals.

In *A Game at Chess* (1624), however, Middleton deliberately and quite consciously represents a little world and a whole society. The characters are chess men, who in themselves represent the three estates and more; and the White Queen's Pawn opens her attack on the Black Bishop's Pawn, her would-be seducer, with these words:

The world's a stage on which all parts are play'd:
You'd think it most absurd to see a devil
Presented there not in a devil's shape,
Or, wanting one, to send him out in yours.
                                   (V.ii.19–22)

The White Queen's Pawn goes on at some length to revile him
in terms of the metaphor and her part in the play now proceed-
ing on the world's stage. Middleton, then, was quite aware of the
concept and assuredly made use of it in this play. But for the
most part he followed neoclassical criticism and, perhaps, his
own personal taste and interest. And this practice indicates a
trend.

So does the practice of Beaumont and Fletcher. Although
the various characters of *The Knight of the Burning Pestle*
(1607) are London citizens (grocers, merchants, apprentices,
barbers, soldiers, etc.), some of them play various roles, such as
knights, squires, giants, and even "the Daughter of the King of
Moldavia." Yet we are never allowed to forget that they are
London "citizens" and actors. Even Rafe's adventures as knight
errant belong to the citizens' world only. Here are no king and
court, no gentry, or lord mayor, even, as Dekker would have
provided. In *Philaster* (ca. 1610) however, the King and court
are central, with the military, the citizens who support Philaster,
and the woodsmen and clown. Yet the variety is limited if we
compare its range of characters with that of *Hamlet*, which it so
much resembles. The cast of *The Maid's Tragedy* (1611) is
made up simply of the King and his court, no more, whereas the
cast of *A King and No King* (1611) ranges from the King and
court to the military and to citizens and shopkeepers. In
Bonduca (1609–1614), though great pageantry occurs, the cast is
restricted to the Queen, the Druid priests, and to the greater and
lesser officers and soldiers, with a few servants. No tradesmen,
citizens, or professionals appear. And, except for a court physician and a panderess, *Valentinian* (1610–1614) has much the
same kind of cast. Although Fletcher suggests the degrees of so-

ciety as a whole in *Thierry and Theodoret* (Q1, 1621), with monarchs, courtiers, a priest, the military, a doctor, etc., in *The Wild Goose Chase* (1621?), a comedy, he limits his cast to gentlemen and the lower ranks, if we except the priest. And so one might continue to illustrate from these two playwrights: they seldom do more than suggest the pattern of society in the cast of a single play, no matter what its species.

With Philip Massinger it is a different matter. Although he is often praised for the effectiveness of his single plot structure and its economy, he managed pretty regularly to indicate all classes of men in his *dramatis personae*. Out of the sixteen plays attributed to him, all but three or four clearly indicate them; and even these three or four, such as *The Great Duke of Florence* and *The Picture*, though they fail to include citizens or tradesmen, do reach from the Duke or the King down to "foolish" servants, representative of the lowest class. *A New Way to Pay Old Debts* (1621?) is for comedy notable in its range of characters, especially so in that its chief model was Middleton's *A Trick to Catch the Old One* (1604–1606). Whereas Witgood, a gentleman in Middleton's play, is highest in rank among the characters, Lord Lovel, Lady Allworth, and Wellborn in Massinger's belong to the next higher class; and whereas the Courtesan in Middleton's perhaps approaches the lowest level, she is not so low or so foul as Tapwell and Froth in Massinger's. And none among Middleton's characters so well betoken the classes as Overreach, Greedy, Marrall, Parson Willdo, and Lady Allworth's delightful servants, the Steward, the Cook, the Usher, and the Porter. In Massinger's *The Fatal Dowry* (1616–1619), a tragedy, a remarkable range occurs. The rankings run from the presidents of the Parliament of Dijon and various nobility to officers, soldiers, and secretaries, to a priest, and from a priest to a tailor, a barber, a perfumer, and a singing master, and from the singing master to a housekeeper, a bailiff, and a jailer. *A Very Woman* (1634) furnishes a fine example. In it the playgoers might see upon the stage viceroys, dukes, and princes with their courtiers and other attendants, a captain and sailors, two surgeons and a physician, a slave merchant and a slave, Moors and pirates. And in what was perhaps his last play, *The Bashful Lover* (1636), a comedy, they could see the Prince of Parma and the dukes of Mantua and Tuscany, Octavia disguised as a priest, an ambassador, generals, "officers," soldiers, a doctor, and a clown. In spite of his well-known economy in plot and in characters, Massinger was careful to represent as many levels of society as possible, whether his play was comedy, tragi-comedy, or tragedy. But of course he can manage nothing so fully representative as the playwrights who opened the century.

The same generalizations cannot be made of John Ford's practice. His chronicle *Perkin Warbeck* (1622–1632?), perhaps the first play he wrote unassisted, harks back to the great chronicle period; and the range of characters, their representation of the ranks of humanity, is most notable, especially in that it comes thus late. In it appear Henry VI of England and James IV of Scotland with their nobles, ladies, and courtiers, such knights as Sir William Stanley and Sir Robert Clifford; the clergy represented by the Bishop of Durham and the King's Chaplain; a Spanish agent and a herald; officers and soldiers; citizens in the persons of the Mayor of Cork, a mercer, a tailor and a scrivener; a constable, serving men, and a maid. Such wide variety is not to be found in his other plays. In *The Lover's Melancholy* (1628) the Prince of Cyprus and his court including "an old Lord," a tutor and a physician, and various individualized servants have parts, but tradesmen, the clergy, and merchants do not. *The Broken Heart* (1627–1631) is even more restricted. *'Tis Pity She's a Whore* (1629?–1633) includes a devout friar and a cardinal, but restricts the rest to the ranks of wealthy gentlemen and citizens, their servants, and the hired banditti. Similarly, in *Love's Sacrifice* (1632?) the cast is made up of the Duke's household. Even the buffoon is an old courtier, and the fool, Roselli, is a young courtier. No professionals, merchants, or tradesmen, or "citizens" have parts. Except in *Perkin Warbeck*, Ford restricts the size of his casts and the spread of his characters among the classes.

And so does Shirley. His comedies are limited to their classes, and his tragedies to theirs. In *The Witty Fair One* (1628) the action revolves around Sir George Richley and various gentry, however foolish these upper classes may be. With these appear the witty servant, Brains, out of Jonson and Roman comedy, and various footmen and servants. The one household contains all the action. Similarly in tragedy, *The Traitor* (1631) is confined to the court of the Duke of Florence, with the noblemen, gentlemen, and servants. *Hyde Park* (1632), because of its setting and its clear anticipation of Restoration comedy of manners, ranges a little wider. In the park one may expect to find a wider representation of humanity than in a gentleman's household. Not only lords and ladies have parts in this play, but Bonavent a merchant, gentlemen, officers, bagpipers, parkkeepers, a milkmaid, and a jockey, as well as various servants. In *The Lady of Pleasure* (1635) the cast is, however, more restricted. Though Lord A. appears and Sir Thomas and Lady Bornwell, though Lord A.'s secretary and certain gallants have roles, and though a steward and even a procuress serve the others, no merchants, tradesmen, apprentices, or high officials of the government or of the Church are included in the action. The various types of plays are now becoming discrete; decorum will be regarded; the stage, the casts, and the dimensions of the action have been reduced. And though exceptions occurred until the closing of the theatres and even after the Restoration, generally the new plays were written not only for a smaller, but also for a less representative cast.[12]

Two or three general practices of the dramatists quite apart from those indicated in this survey deserve mention, but mention only, since they are obvious to anyone who reads Elizabethan plays. They reveal at once the playwrights' concern for degree and rank and for careful protocol in the presentation of their casts. The *dramatis personae* are almost invariably listed according to rank or degree, male and female roles beng separated. Kings and dukes come first, then cardinals and bishops (if required), then knights, courtiers, and gentlemen, and so downward to clowns. Perhaps more important, almost as invariably in the listing the rank or position or vocation is indicated. Sir Hugh Lacy is carefully listed as "Earl of Lincoln" and Simon Eyre as "a shoemaker." Furthermore the stage directions usually tell us the rank of the characters by the order of their appearance, especially in group entrances. These are carefully printed in the early quartos, the texts nearest the theatres' own copies. Even in a very simple entrance, protocol is almost always indicated: "*Enter* Lacie, Skipper, Hodge, *and* Firke." Lacy is the nephew of an Earl, the skipper is a wealthy ship-owner and captain, Hodge is a fine journeyman, and Firk just as fine an apprentice. Whether or not the whole of society could be represented, its form and structure could be and were observed even in the *dramatis personae* and by the stage entrances. In the Elizabethan dramatists' careful retention of these practices one is reminded of their attempt in each play to suggest the orders and degrees of mankind, the whole of the social order, reaching from crown to clown, from highest ruler to lowliest servant. All the men and women were players.

SIX

The Testing Pattern

§ PROFESSOR IRVING RIBNER has recently refined or modified two widely recognized patterns or shaping forces in Elizabethan tragedy, *hamartia* and the *casibus virorum illustrium*.[1] He prefers three somewhat different patterns, though not necessarily discrete from these two.[2] He believes that Shakespeare's tragedies (and by implication others of the period) may be grouped according to shaping forces into tragedies of a virtuous man's fall through deception, the tragedy of the deliberately evil man's rise and fall, and the tragedy of "the ordinary man's growth to maturity." These he believes have their origin in English Senecanism but are mingled with other traditions. Doubtless all these may be observed as operative in the tragedies of Shakespeare and his contemporaries. But I rather believe there is one even more basic to Elizabethan tragedy, and in comedy more obviously apparent. Perhaps it underlies Professor Ribner's three and the others. It finds expression variously.

I shall call it the testing pattern. It involves the trial or proving of a man. The play often takes something of its shape from the testing force of Providence operating within the characters of men, whether the characters ride Fortune's wheel, are frustrated by a flaw, or achieve by maturation of mind recognition and then accept their suffering. As the protagonist moves in pageant and encompassing actions across the stage of the world he is

179

proved, like Job or like Jonah, and in his proving he undergoes a testing. Often, and in the tragedies especially, this proving follows the pretty well-recognized pattern of Christian tests.[3] Divine Providence does not appear in proper person, though in tragedy it often sends ghostly agents to direct or provide the conflict. But it may, and especially so in comedy, send a vicar in the guise of the king or duke or simply the judge who settles the conflict and metes out justice, rewards, and punishments, in the last scene. In any case, God is director of the play and final arbiter at the denouement. In some plays, even tragedies, the protagonist meets the tests provided for him, passes them, and is saved; in others, even in comedy, he fails them and is punished. In comedy the testing involves a far less serious conflict, often little that can be called a struggle of soul, and the handing out of rewards and punishments, the re-establishment of justice, at the end usually results in joy for most characters, for a few some slight discomfort and reformation.

The concept of man as microcosm, discussed in Chapter II as central to the spheres of encompassing action, permits just such drama within the individual man. It provides the stage for the conflicts among the various forces which take place within the character of a man. It provides logically for the soliloquy of the tragedies and for the *commedia del arte* scenes of the comedy, as well for Launcelot Gobbo's delightful burlesque of the conflict between good and evil within a man's being—between his conscience and the fiend—as for Hamlet's consideration of suicide.

Provision for the action, the conflict, and the purpose for the testing, as already indicated in Chapter I, are parts of the various discussions of the metaphor of the world as stage. Quoting Plotinus, Philip Mornay had accounted for the existence of evil and justified God's providence in allowing it, as we have already observed in Chapter I, on the grounds that this world is but a stage-play in which the "aduersity of the godly is a gaming exercise, wherein they bee tyed to a straight dyet, that they may win the prize for which they contend," to use Sidney's or Golding's translation. And as we have also observed, Thomas Heywood, conceiving of the world as a theatre, has Jehovah sitting in the gallery of stars as spectator "And chief determiner t'applaud the best, / And their endeuours crowne with more than merit. / But by their euil actions doomes the rest. . . ." Later from Milton's *Comus* we learn of the characters that "Heav'n hath timely tried their youth, / Their faith, their patience, and their truth. . . ." God's noblest creation is free upon the stage of the world to prove himself and, according as he plays well, receive the applause of the great Director or his condemnation, the reward or the punishment. Almost every repetition of the commonplace that the world is a stage implies, if it does not state explicitly, the testing motif. In the plays themselves it is most apparent: Duke Vincentio and Prospero play God's part as director, and certainly the Prince of Verona pronounces His judgment. Leslie Hotson, as we have already observed, sees the Elizabethan stage as a place for the "trial of man's soul." [4]

The theatres provided a world for man's testing and the plays were designed to enact it, both in the Middle Ages and in the Renaissance. The mystery plays indicate it on both the macrocosmic and the microcosmic levels: in them the history of the race is enacted, with its fall and repentance, its suffering, learning, and ultimate salvation through God's grace. And many an individual is tested along the way. Among these we remember most vividly Father Abraham and the submission of Isaac his son, the first example of the struggle of the soul given by Prudentius in his *Psychomachia.* [5]

But it is in the morality plays that the basic pattern is most convincingly demonstrated. It follows the plan of testing Everyman, whereby it will be seen, not so much whether he might merit salvation, as whether he could bring himself to submit to God's will and thus gain His grace and receive the mercy that will enable him to achieve salvation. The war between vice and virtue for the possession of man's soul, the *psychomachia*, provides a course of action for the plays, but the purpose of the course of action, its conventional pattern, is to test the Christian. The moralities, indeed, are concerned, not with man's rise and fall, as on Fortune's wheel, but rather with his fall and rise.[6] If the pattern of the verse-narrative resembles a pyramid, that of the moralities resembles the letter "V"; in it the soul of man first goes down, then rises up—as Dante's did. The question is whether man can suffer redemption.

In the earliest morality extant, *The Castle of Perseverance*, a severe testing of Mankind is enacted. Announcing the banns of the play, the Vexillators indicate that the world is the stage whereunto all orders and degrees of men come naked and bare but each provided with two angels, a good and a bad, but also with freedom of will to choose "Whether he wyl hymse[lf] saue or his soul per[yll]."

A better example is, of course, the celebrated *Everyman*. The question this play really asks is that of the young man who came to Christ asking what he should do to inherit eternal life: How shall a man be saved? When Death summons him, Everyman turns to Fellowship, Friends, Kinsmen, and Riches ("Goods"). *In extremis*, almost in despair, he turns to Good Deeds, who (be it observed) tells him to seek Knowledge. In contrast to *The Castle of Perseverance*, here knowledge is paramount. Knowledge sets him on the right way—to Confession, "that clensynge ryuere," and to Penance. By such good deeds as Knowledge requires, Everyman now attains a state of grace, as Rev. John Molloy has shown.[7] Only then is the character of Good Deeds so strengthened as to attend him to the grave and beyond. (Without Grace, Good Deeds is too feeble to be of help.) Now he can put on the Robe of Contrition and get the help of Discretion, Five Wits, and Beauty. Now he can be houseled and receive Unction in preparation for the ultimate quest of the Christian soldier—the struggle with Death. Thus Everyman is saved. And though he has no substitute, as Admetus had, he does have a companion. It is worth noting here that good deeds are performed only after the summoning of Death and that they consist of the necessary sacraments—not the Seven Corporal Acts of Mercy, as Mankind had promised in his play. The sacraments are all evidences of God's grace. The doctrine of the two plays is, however, essentially the same: Through God's grace men receive God's mercy, if they ask for it. Grace is given after knowledge has brought submission to God's will through confession and penance. Thus purified, Everyman may receive the Eucharist wherein he becomes a very member incorporate in the mystical body of Christ. Thus provided he can accomplish his adventure.[8]

An even better example, apparently neglected by Professor Farnham, is John Redford's *The Marriage of Witte and Science* (1569), a school play written for the edification of the scholars. Witte is tested and proved, not that his soul may be saved, but that he may win the hand of Lady Science. His winning her hand takes him through exactly the pattern outlined above. Science will accept Witte only if Witte will slay the giant Tediousness. In his first encounter he is, like Red Cross, defeated and brought to despair. Then the reversal takes place: Reason (Science's father) calls shame down upon Witte, Witte repents, Science then asks that mercy be shown him, he receives instruction and gains knowledge, and then with the proper aid from Free Will he meets the giant and slays him. He moves from error and defeat to despair, confession, repentance, the attainment of purity through knowledge, and then the accomplishment of the quest. It is the same for Red Cross and Guyon, the same for Adam and Eve, the same (with proper modifications) for Samson, and I believe, in a more complex way, for Hamlet and for Lear.

As we move toward the plays of the secular and popular theatre of the later years of the sixteenth century,[9] we come upon the preposterous *Sir Clyomon and Sir Clamydes* (1570?), once attributed to Peele. It follows the morality play model very well and the testing motif shapes the action. Providence appears as a character to save Neronis from despair and suicide. Neronis then gains proper knowledge by reading the inscription on Clyomon's sword, so that when the tournament takes place, he, a Christian knight, will be ready for the great test. The pattern is quite obvious.

It is not so obvious in *The Old Wives' Tale* (1591–1594) assuredly Peele's play. In fact in this play the testing follows a somewhat different pattern, one more proper to comedy. The Ghost of Jack representing Providence, because of Eumenides' completely natural unselfish act (without thought of reward) in giving his last penny for Jack's burial, solves all the riddles and brings Eumenides to Delia. Apparently Eumenides does not despair, nor does he contemplate self-slaughter; but he does endure further testing when Jack asks him to keep his bargain and share Delia with him. Eumenides even agrees to this, but his unselfishness is rewarded: Jack was only testing him as Abraham was tested.[10]

The testing motif which helps to shape Greene's *A Looking Glass for London and England* (ca. 1590) follows the pattern derived from the moralities. In fact this play is a belated morality designed by its reformed author to call his people to repentance and amendment of their ways. The setting is Nineveh. Jonah, trying to escape God's command, repents, finally submits to His will, preaches to the Ninevites, and brings them to repentance. Among them is the Usurer, for example, who, following his evil angel, is moved to despair and threatens suicide; but his soul at this point is suddenly through God's grace moved to repentance, and he receives God's mercy. So are Queen Alvida and all her ladies moved. Through the Prophet, tested himself, all are tried, and by repentance and submission all become good Christian soldiers. Thus the speculum for London.

Marlowe's plays are not so simple, but the pattern emerges in some of them. It is interesting that he picked a Roman source in which the soul-struggle is implicit for his *Dido and Aeneas*, and that he made this struggle basic to his action. Aeneas is turned from his passion and personal desires, indeed from the national sin he has committed, by the will of the gods to which he accedes. Dido despairs and commits suicide. In *Doctor Faustus* the morality testing pattern is more obvious. At the very height of his career Faustus becomes dissatisfied with the knowledge he has; he wants knowledge forbidden to man. By compact with

Lucifer he is able for twenty-four years to get and use it. But it is stale and unprofitable. He would like to repent of his compact, but because of his belief in the immutable nature of his decision, he (like Claudius) cannot repent. His sin was that he, like Judas, believed his guilt greater than God's mercy. In his last hour he cries out for time to repent, but there is no faith in him. Unlike Mankind's cry in *The Castle of Perseverance*, Faustus' last cry goes unanswered. He has committed the unpardonable sin—the prideful sin of questioning God's power to forgive man under any circumstances. The pattern is obvious, but the soul through despair is lost.

In *Edward II*, however, the protagonist's soul seems not to have been lost. In weakness and error and sin Edward is brought to his knees. He repents his weakness as a king, and with the loss of Gaveston, fights back. But his cause, since he is a king, is too personal, and he loses his crown (as Shakespeare's Richard II does and in much the same way). Yet he makes a spiritual come-back. Too weak and feeble to resist the murderers at the end, he prays God to receive his soul. He dies a weak but worthy king, meriting ultimately the regard of his son. The antagonist Mortimer, on the other hand, declines morally as he rises on Fortune's wheel; and having reached the point on the wheel to which he aspired, as he himself says, he now tumbles down. Unbelieving, fatalistic, scorning the world, he goes to his execution like other Machiavellians to "discover countries yet unknown."

By various means Shakespeare tests many of his characters, but most often his protagonists. This practice of testing became a shaping force in the chronicles, where the king's worthiness as a man and a monarch is often tried. In the comedies it often operates through an agent, the duke or the prince as vicar of Divine Providence putting the protagonist or other characters to the test, or conducting actual court trials and rendering judgments in resolution of the plots. It becomes even more effective in the great tragedies, where the pattern most resembles that of the morality plays.

In most of his ten chronicle plays Shakespeare tests his mon-

archs, but with varying emphases; and in the testing he tries
other characters as well. In *II Henry VI*, for example, the corrupt Cardinal Beaufort fails his test miserably, and dies with his
king praying that "the busy meddling fiend / That lays strong
siege unto this wretch's soul," may be beaten and "black despair" purged away. On the other hand, Duke Humphrey of
Gloucester, who had good cause to despair—his wife in disgrace,
his Protectorate gone, his long and noble service to the state
scorned—apparently goes to his death with dignity and faith.
Henry VI becomes a better man than King, and Richard II
revels in despair before he comes to a noble death.[11] But it is in
the Machiavellian Richard III one finds a pattern resembling
more closely that of *Doctor Faustus* as derived from the morality play. Having at the outset "determined to prove a villain,"
having devised plots and intrigue and reveled in murder, he
comes to the unquiet night before Bosworth Field, the final test.
There is yet time, for God's mercy is infinite. But on that night
Richard is counseled to despair, not by devils or evil angels as in
the moralities he would have been, but rather by each of the
ghosts of those whom he had destroyed; and he cries out to Jesus
for mercy as he wakes from the dream. He then actually and
ironically accepts the counsel, for he recognizes that his conscience has made a coward of him. No creature loves him, and
he no creature. No man will pity him, and he can find no pity
even for himself. Incapable of repentance, he embraces despair
and sets his life upon the cast of the die, expecting damnation.

In the character of Henry V, on the other hand, a king
growing to maturity, we see a man who is thoroughly tested and
who proves himself worthy of his crown—as his father was not.
In his first play Prince Hal, if not a criminal, is well acquainted
with sin; but even in this play he wins his trial by combat with
Hotspur. In *II Henry IV* his testing runs throughout. It is revealed by his statement to his father following the episode of his
trying on the crown, in which he is moved to let his present
wildness die and make a noble change (IV.v.150–77). Before
this he had told Poins, who considered Hal to be as far gone in
the Devil's book as he or Falstaff, to "Let the end try the man"

(II.ii.48–54). The Lord Chief Justice had charged Falstaff with following the Prince "like his ill angel." The Prince's submission to the Chief Justice, his confirming this vicar of his own power in office, was a submission to justice and the will of God by which he became worthy of his crown. In the first act of *Henry V* this submission is reiterated by means of his careful investigation of the Salique Law and his reply to the French ambassadors before the French invasion: "But this lies all within the will of God, / To whom I do appeal . . ." (I.ii.289–90). And in his great prayer on the eve of Agincourt, following the knowledge he had got incognito from his soldiers and his long pondering his place and duty, he confesses, promises penance, and affirms his submission to God's will. After the battle he declares the victory God's own victory: "Take it, God, / For it is only thine." Though his waywardness may have been deliberate at the beginning of his career, it was nonetheless real. Himself little better than one of the wicked, consorting with sinners, especially "that reverend vice," "that old white-bearded Satan," the Prince through knowledge and responsibility and searching of soul became Christ's faithful soldier, servant, and vicegerent.[12]

In the comedies, too, such proved servants may appear, though not so fully realized or so outspoken. They are not often so fully tried, and the level of their action is not so high or of such wide significance. The duke or the prince will more likely act as judge or the testing agent than Divine Providence in some ghostly presence. Even in such early and Roman-like plays as *The Comedy of Errors* and *Two Gentlemen of Verona*, this character emerges as official dispenser of justice, the protagonists having been put through their trials. In *The Taming of the Shrew* the trials Petruchio puts Kate through may hardly seem to be the visitations of Providence administered by so harsh a vicar; yet by them the unruly girl has learned that it is only through submission to the will of her lord and master that she will ever have her own will. From one "who never knew how to entreat" she has been humbled to entreaty and becomes a model wife through the cruel kindness (grace) of her husband.

But perhaps the best examples from the comedies appear in

The Merchant of Venice, All's Well, Measure for Measure, and *The Tempest.* Simply to mention the plays is to recall the testings and the variations upon the testing pattern. In the first of these the motif is probably the most complicated. First, the Duke of Venice must save the economy of his state by maintaining its laws and administering them without partiality, even to the alien Jew. He stands in God's place to make final judgment. But Portia is the chief instrument of justice and mercy. She brings Shylock to the test in the trial. His demand for justice without mercy in the trial of another is met with a judgment tempered with mercy in his own trial, at least from Portia's and the Duke's point of view: he gets back his fortune provided he accepts a merciful baptism. Throughout, Antonio never wavers. But preparatory to the trial of the Jew other trials have taken place: the testing of Portia's suitors and through their tests her own. In fact the casket scenes serve as preparatory for the trial of Antonio. If Bassanio for the right reason chooses the right casket, he also for the right reason breaks his word to give the ring unwittingly to the right person. And by the ring Nerissa tests Gratiano most amusingly. But far more important is the test of the lady herself: she must accept the suitor who chooses the proper casket. To do this she must submit to the apparently irrational will of her deceased father. But he was a wise father. Her submission to his will and her recognition of his wisdom were enough to make her the wise young judge who could meet strict legality with legal quibble (for mercy is an attribute of God and beyond justice) to save her betrothed's friend.

And Helena in *All's Well That Ends Well* (1602?) is not unlike her. Like the good angel as opposed to Parolles, the Vice, she debases herself before she will give up Bertram; and though she gains him, his repentance and final change are none too convincing. The King and Countess represent the Divine power, enabling the testing, judging, and forgiving.

Measure for Measure (1604?) is perhaps the comedy most often thought of as a testing play. Vincentio, Duke of Vienna, leaves the affairs of state in the hands of his deputy, Angelo, a "just man," and disguises himself as a friar so as to test and observe the testing of his deputy and his people. He is the descendant of the Father in the morality play, here relinquishing his own vicarship to a vicar, as it were. As soon as Angelo's justice becomes too severe, the Duke reveals himself, steps in and extends mercy. Thus he tests his deputy and Angelo repents.

Of all his comedies, none better illustrates the testing force than Shakespeare's latest. In *The Tempest* Prospero represents Providence, the director of the cosmic drama as well as the masques of the play. In fact the whole drama is based upon the testing of the various characters, including Prospero himself. He tells Ferdinand that "All thy vexations / Were but my trials of thy love, and thou / Hast strangely stood the test" (IV.i.5–7). By his vexations he drives Alonzo, Antonio, and Sebastian to despair, making Gonzalo fearful that they will resort to suicide at the end of Act III. But when they have grown penitent, Prospero says that "They being penitent, / The sole drift of my purpose doth extend / Not a frown further" (V.i.28–30). Penitent and forgiven, they are enlightened; and made wise through knowledge, they now make restitution. The low characters, mere animal souls in revolt against Prospero's properly constituted government, are controlled by physical pain. But even among these, Caliban, now disillusioned, says that he will be wise and seek grace. And Prospero seeks grace too. Through the injustices done him, he has learned not only to rely upon the supernatural powers to bring about justice but himself to forgive and grant mercy. Nor must he misuse the supernatural powers. Now that he has accomplished justice and rendered mercy, he gives up the supernatural powers, as he must. And now that he has given them up, as he says in his epilogue, he would end in despair were it not for the prayer which will pierce so far as to assault mercy itself.

The whole action of *Cymbeline* (1609?), if we may look at a tragi-comedy or two, centers around the trials of Imogen and Posthumus. Deceived by Iachimo's circumstantial evidence of her infidelity, Posthumus denounces Imogen without sufficient investigation and by so doing sins; his disillusion brings him to despair. In prison, knowledge brings his repentance, and in the end he gains the hand of his lady and his own spiritual salvation as well. Imogen is more severely tested. When Iachimo comes to tempt her, she tells him she is a lady who "disdains Thee and the devil alike." Then the Queen attacks her and tries to drive her to despair and suicide; and after she discovers that Posthumus has been deceived and misled, she comes to despair indeed. Her faith, however, sustains her, and her perseverance is rewarded. In *Pericles* (1609?) also one finds more than a semblance of the motif, as Gower's speech at the end clearly indicates: the virtuous king, queen, and daughter have been "Led on by heaven, and crown'd with joy at last." Tried at every turn, like Job, Pericles is brought low by one disaster after another; he is at the point of utter despair, dressed in sackcloth, when Marina is restored to him—coming as opportunely as divine grace—and with her his wife and all he had lost are returned.

The motif as shaping force is less apparent in the earlier tragedies than in the later. It scarcely appears as *psychomachia* at all in *Titus Andronicus* (1594?); and in *Romeo and Juliet* (1594–1595?), though the pattern is certainly suggested, it does not emerge clearly. I cannot entirely agree with Professor Ribner that the two young lovers do not sin or that Romeo achieves serenity of soul before his final act, accepting and submitting.[13] His will overwhelmed by his youthful passion and controlled by it (not by reason and the will of God), Romeo is tried in the extreme and brought to despair in Friar Laurence's cell (III.iii). At this point he is saved from suicide by the instruction and sound reasoning of the Friar. Yet at Mantua he forgets, discards his knowledge and the wisdom gained, and in deliberate defiance of the stars chooses wrongly, coming in hot haste and resolute despair back to Verona and deliberate suicide. Had he waited, Friar Laurence's plan might well have worked out, and the reconciliation of the families might have been effected through the announcement of the marriage, not the death, of the lovers. He had the willpower to wait, as his patience with

both Tybalt and Paris indicated—a patience which saved their
blood from staining his hands—but not a serenity of soul or acceptance. On the other hand, as Professor Ribner suggests, the
cosmic implications of the tragedy are made manifest. The action is set in Verona *and* among the stars. "A glooming peace"
comes on the final morning of the play: "The sun for sorrow
will not show his head." The world's enmity proved too much
for Romeo and Juliet. Yet, although the waste was sickening, all
was not loss: their sacrifice corrected an ancient evil, and their
testing left the world-stage the better for their having played
upon it.

In *Julius Caesar* (1599) the pattern becomes somewhat
plainer, the force somewhat stronger. As Professor Virgil K.
Whitaker shows, *psychomachia* develops here.[14] Brutus as protagonist becomes "the first of Shakespeare's superb tragic figures
who fail through false moral choice." Brutus's reasoning is
false: he thinks the serpent (Caesar) should be destroyed in the
shell, not allowed to mature; but he cannot know for certain
that Caesar will develop into a tyrant. He has listened too much
to Cassius, has been deceived, has failed to question sufficiently.
Yet his decision to support the conspiracy comes only after
much soul-searching (II.i), and this searching continues throughout his troubled career, making him a sympathetic character.
Perhaps he trusted Cassius too much, who trusted not the stars
—only himself. Assuredly his good angel, Portia, who warned
him of the sick offence within his mind, dwelt too much in the
suburbs of his good pleasure. Hence he failed the testing and
brought himself to despair and suicide. However noble he may
seem, he probably belongs still where Dante placed him.

One does not hope ever to pluck out the heart of Hamlet's
mystery, yet whoever writes of his play is obligated to throw
what light upon it he can. Indeed the sign of Jonah is upon any
one such, as I believe it was upon Hamlet himself: "O cursed
spite, that ever I was born to set it right." The Ghost, the voice
of God, as we find out, lays upon him the difficult and most un-
pleasant task of cleansing Elsinore and all Denmark of the taint

of murder, incest, injustice, and riotous living. Even before he saw the Ghost, Hamlet's prophetic soul had been moved intuitively. He knew, or he felt he knew. But he was revolted by what he felt he knew. He comes early to despair (but is never overcome by it) and thinks of self-slaughter. He binds himself strictly to carry out the Ghost's command not to taint his soul —as any prophet must do. But trying to get the offensive task over with quickly, he acts impulsively, without sufficient knowledge or reasoning, and kills the wrong man, for which deed he must (somewhat to his relief) be sent away on a ship. But he cannot escape his assigned task any more than Jonah could: being moved by intuition—the will of the divinity that shapes our ends—he finds out the treachery intended against him and provides for the traitors, then boards the pirate ship and returns —not unlike Jonah, who cannot escape God's will even in the belly of the big fish. Following this, he accepts his divine commission, submits, accepts Providence (as Professor Bowers has pointed out); [15] and, taking advantage of occasion—the readiness being all—moves toward his work. Feeling that the fencing match may be the occasion, he disclaims any "purposed evil" toward Laertes and asks his hand in friendship. Following the pattern of the morality play, as protagonist Hamlet rallies from despair—having gained requisite knowledge—surrenders his will to Providence, cleanses himself of all malice (in love and charity with his neighbor), and thus prepared, cleanses Denmark —and with God not departed from him. That he loses his life is of slight importance. Like Jonah and the Red Cross Knight, like Milton's Samson, he accomplishes his quest. And doubtless in the audience's mind Horatio's prayer was answered: flights of angels did sing the hero to his rest, as they ministered to the Son following his triumphant overcoming of the temptations in the Wilderness.

Now, I do not think of *Hamlet* as deriving from the story of Jonah any more than I think of it as deriving from Christ's temptation in the Wilderness. I do believe it probable, however, that Shakespeare thought of the parallel; and if this is true, it helps explain, among other things, Hamlet's seeming delay, as does the whole idea of the tested hero. It will also be remembered that Greene had used the story of Jonah in his morality play in 1594—which also dealt with the cleansing of a kingdom. But my concern here is with the pattern of the morality play and its testing motif as a shaping force in the structure of the Elizabethan play.

Similarly one may illustrate the testing in *King Lear* (1605–1606). Surely no king ever suffered the testing of the gods more acutely or more fully. Indeed, if Hamlet suggests Jonah, Lear a little suggests Job. A king in name at the beginning, it is only when he has given away his kingdom and been reduced to the naked condition in which he (and Mankind) came into the world that he becomes every inch a king. He errs, he suffers, he comes soon to the recognition of his sins, he repents, he submits, and through his hard-won knowledge he is brought by grace, represented as it were in the person of Cordelia, to regeneration and redemption. He may then endure his going hence even as his coming hither, as Edgar reminds Gloucester men must.[16] And Gloucester goes through essentially the same soul-struggle. Flippant about his sin at the first, almost boastful of it in Edmund—its very incarnation—it turns upon him, deceiving and then blinding him into recognition and spiritual sight, and bringing him to despair and attempted suicide. But grace will not let him go. Naked Tom of Bedlam, his lawfully begotten Edgar, deceives him into life. His repentance unwittingly comes with the prayer before the attempt at death, and he blesses his son unaware. Not as flies—the sport of the gods—but as sparrows, are we—their care. The gods, as Edgar explains, have preserved him; and Gloucester agrees, still not recognizing the agent of his preservation, to endure his affliction. Finally, saved from despair, submitting and accepting (the ripeness being all), upon learning of his son's great love and care, his heart burst smilingly.

Othello (1604?) presents a controversial case. No one will deny that the protagonist is tested or his soul tried; whether he is saved or damned is another matter. Professor Ribner rightly suggests the pattern of the morality in the play, though I believe he overemphasizes its symbolic qualities; and I have come to doubt that "through the operation of divine grace, there is recognition of error, with consequent remorse, expiation, and promise of salvation." [17] A thoroughly noble and unsuspecting and honorable man, Othello is incapable of recognizing deceit, and he is tested by deceitfulness. His failure, his sin, derives from his very goodness. Evil in the play parades as good ("honest Iago"), Othello is duped just as Red Cross and Eve are duped, and he merits something of the mercy shown them. He cleaves to the apparent good. He does not knowingly and willingly choose to sin, as did Faustus and Macbeth; on the other hand, he is not allowed Brutus's relatively unobscured vision whereby to make his choice. (Cassius plays no Iago to Brutus's Othello.) Hence when recognition of the enormity of his deed comes suddenly upon him, he is overwhelmed; and more ancient Roman than Christian, the Moor, still doing all in honor, exacts a justice not his, according to Christian doctrine, to exact. Yet he was "great of heart," and whether he asked it or not, there was something extenuate in his story. A measure of mercy, it must be remembered, is shown to virtuous pagans. Beyond this point of hope I do not think Shakespeare goes.

Much as Faustus had been tried and failed, Macbeth was tried and failed. He chose to put his trust in the powers of darkness, evil spirits whose veracity he chose not to question or, like Banquo, to ignore. No Hamlet he to prove his spirits; he was too eager to make their predictions come true. They did not all come true; their riddles should have been suspect from the beginning. Having stepped in so far, the enormity of his crimes brings him to despair and to Richard III's realization that he is completely without friend on earth; and like Faustus, like Judas Iscariot, he thought these crimes beyond God's mercy. This, the unpardonable sin, assured his damnation.

Not so assured, however, is that of Antony, the decayed pillar of the Roman world. He was deceived by Cleopatra, though he had been warned by Enobarbus of her many dyings. *Psycho-*

machia helps shape his play. He is discovered at the opening deep in sin, revelling in the flesh pots of Egypt's lascivious court. Like Mankind in *The Castle of Perseverance* he repents and reforms, going back to Rome, assuming his responsibilities, and even marrying Caesar's sister. Like Mankind, in failing to control his will he slips back into his old sins. Then as he recognizes his own failures and Cleopatra's deceits, he despairs. But unlike Mankind, knowing of her deceptions, he tries suicide, then welcomes his punishment and expiation and concludes his life rather nobly, asking that his magnanimity be remembered. He makes a good end. In a sense he conquers at Alexandria as Julius Caesar had conquered at Philippi. Though we must leave the question of his salvation to the gods for answer, we see well enough the pattern of their testing him.

These are sufficient examples to indicate Shakespeare's reliance on the testing pattern derived from the moralities and modified as his subject required. He took a fairly rigorous pattern and adapted it to his needs, at times using only a part of it or a suggestion of it, but it was nevertheless a powerful and almost constant shaping force in his drama.

It was also a force among the works of his contemporaries, though not so great a force among his successors. A few examples, and a few are sufficient, will illustrate. Cyril Tourneur's plays retain even such allegorical names as might occur in the moralities, suggesting by the names the appropriate testing. The chastity of Castiza, as one might expect, is tried in *The Revenger's Tragedy*. She maintains her virtue, even against the will of her mother, who, threatened by Vendice, is brought to repentance and, through Castiza's testing, to steadfast virtue. In *The Atheist's Tragedy* the long-suffering Charlemont is so tested and comes to such knowledge that, while in prison, he can say, "now I am Emp'rour of the world / This little world of man. My passions are / My Subjects; and I can command them laugh" (III. iii.46–48). He and his Castabella, who has likewise suffered, come to the scaffold and to despair, but their endurance serves them well. As their executioner, D'Amville, the Vice and atheistical worshiper of nature, raises the axe to behead them, he knocks out his own brains. Providence directly intervenes.

Whoever has read Jonson's plays, the two Roman tragedies as well as the comedies, recalls as his most obvious and conventional dramatic device the numerous trials—formal trials in a court of law, such as those in *Volpone,* or those before the Roman Senate in *Sejanus* and *Catiline,* or burlesque trials, such as the court of love in *The New Inn,* or the rather informal judgments rendered by a justice of some sort, such as Justice Clement in *Everyman in His Humour,* or Lovewit in *The Alchemist,* or even Caesar in *The Poetaster.* In the comedies Jonson modifies the place of the duke or the prince as God's agent testing various of his subjects. The realistic satire of most of the plays precludes such divine connection; at best it can be implied in *The Poetaster* and *Cynthia's Revels* and a few others. *The Devil Is an Ass,* an outright morality, for example, does furnish the struggle between the powers of the devil and of God in the soul of Fitzdottrel, who ultimately tells truth and shames the devil. Indeed Pug finds the forces of evil in the world too much for him: humankind are more effective than he at producing sin. So he is taken back to hell on the back of a Vice. The burlesque is obvious. Testing is a strong motif throughout Jonson's comedies, but it is not of the soul-searching kind one encounters in the tragedies or romantic comedies, or even his own tragedies. In *Sejanus* the testing is most obvious. The protagonist is destroyed by his own overweening pride. He blames Fortune; and when her statue turns her back on him, he renounces her, becoming more and more fearful, until despair overtakes him. Even though he goes to the Temple of Apollo ostensibly to receive a new honor, he has suspected deceit, and all his protesting and denouncing Fortune and the gods are really expressions of his despair. He is rustled off and torn piecemeal by the mob, as Faustus was by the devils. Catiline in his play is hounded out of Rome by Cicero and the Senate, deserving of his fate as may be, and driven to despair. *In extremis* he turns and fights and is destroyed. Jonson most certainly does not follow in detail the *psychomachia* or have a heavenly agent obviously direct the testing of his characters; he realizes the old pattern in much more realistic and far less obvious ways, but he uses it.

It is more obvious in the plays of another satirical dramatist, John Marston. In *Antonio and Mellida* (1599), even, one may observe its operation, especially in the testing of Piero. It is readily apparent in *The Malcontent* (1604), where the displaced Duke Altofronto, a little like Shakespeare's Prospero, in the character of Malevole tests most of the other characters of the play and passes judgment on them in the last scene. Or it would be more accurate to say, hands out mercy to them all. Suffering from genuine melancholy and driven by conscience to despair, the usurping Pietro is himself robbed of his ill-gotten dukedom. But as he is just upon the point of despair, Malevole, who feigns melancholy, saves him, brings about his confession and repentance, and ultimately restores him to his despairing wife, who has likewise been tested. Revealed as Altofronto, now he saves his long-suffering Maria from the prurient Mendoza. In his great mercy he even scorns Mendoza, cringing and begging mercy at the end. He is an interesting example of the agent of Providence, for he is himself tried and tested. Displaced, fallen low, assuming the cloak of melancholy and cynicism, by means of his disguise he rises through what he learns, not merely to assert justice, but to have compassion and dispense mercy. Likewise in *The Fawn* (1604–1606) Hercules not only tests his son but is himself tested in the process. He finds out the rottenness inside the court—the effect of flattery and what a fool's paradise he has been living in. As a result he changes his ways. Dulcimel is tested by events, and actually the whole court is tried in Cupid's Parliament at the end. *The Insatiate Countess* (ca. 1610), with trials forming the business of the fifth act, furnishes another example, especially in Isabella, whose repentance and execution bring prayers from the Cardinal that angels may accompany her soul to heaven. So one might continue with Marston's plays.

Though Chapman's tragic protagonists are tested as they consciously act upon a world stage, theirs seem to resemble more often the testings required of the Stoic than of the Christian.[18] The student of Epictetus and Seneca, as well as the translator of Homer, was more likely to allow his heroes the virtues of the Greeks and Romans than those of the Christians. And yet the two are difficult to separate and the conduct of virtuous ancients is not easily distinguished from the conduct of heroic and virtuous Christians. Thus Bussy D'Ambois, recommended for a place at court purely on the basis of his personal merit, abuses his privilege through his overweening pride, seduces Monsieur's wife, and flaunts himself beyond all grace and measure. The equal of any man, he obeys no moral law beyond his own will. But then he changes: nothing in his life became him so well as his leaving it, even though accomplished with fustian and hollow heroics; and this leave-taking of life suggests the special Christian element. At the end he finds that his "divine part" does not aid his "earthly part," that life is "nothing but a courtier's breath," and he, instructed by the shade of the Friar, forgives his murderers. He dies in Christian contempt of the world, not pagan. In the sequel, *The Revenge of Bussy D'Ambois* (ca. 1610) he appears as a ghost to argue with Claremont that a man should live unto God, which

> is to do all things fitting
> His image, in which, like Himself we live;
> To be His image is to do those things
> That make us deathless, which by death is only
> Doing deeds that fit eternity.
>
> (V.i.87–91)

If this is stoicism, it is also the Christian doctrine of submission to God's will and the consequent testing it involves. Man is made in His image.

Like Faustus before him, the hero of *The Tragedy of Charles Duke of Byron* (1608) simply cannot bring himself to confess and ask forgiveness of the King for his conspiracy. His pride is too great, and he so much believes in his own superiority that he will not accept the mediation or consolation of the bishops at the end, defiantly asking them to "leave my soul alone." The implication is that he will suffer damnation. With the hero of *The Tragedy of Chabot*, such is not the case. Falsely accused of treason, Chabot is tried and convicted by the false chancelor and two false judges of the court. Recognizing the miscarriage of justice, the King uses it as further means for testing Chabot: he says he will pardon Chabot, but Chabot will accept no pardon; to do so would be admission of guilt. The King then brings the evil chancelor to trial and to justice. The judgment against him is severe. Again testing Chabot, the King asks him to review the case against the chancelor. As he dies, Chabot pleads for mercy for the chancelor, his enemy, the man who had most wronged him. Freed of all malice, cleansed of sin, he may thus meet death as the good Christian should. Though Chapman's tragic heroes are tried and though he uses trial as a basic shaping force in his tragedies, the patterns he uses are somewhat modified, perhaps through the classics, and do not exactly conform to what had come down from the moralities.[19]

Two examples from Webster must suffice. One immediately recalls how her brothers try to drive the Duchess of Malfi to despair and bring her to suicide—for that way damnation is assured—but how she, "chained to endure all your tyranny" and "because I have so much obedience in my blood," frustrates and destroys them, even as she forgives her executioners when they pull down heaven upon her. In direct contrast, one recalls how in *The White Devil* Vittoria Corombona and her brother Flamineo, a descendant of the Vice from the morality, neither repent nor forgive, and how their souls are driven they know not where.

In the anonymous *The Tell-Tale* (1605?) the Duke of Florence, jealous of his wife Victoria whom he believes to be the mistress of Picentio, leaves the government of his city to Picentio as deputy, but sets his general Aspero to spy upon his wife and the deputy. He then disguises himself and, starting the rumor that he is dead, watches what takes place. Aspero through intrigue usurps the rule and proves himself an ass, Picentio and

Victoria prove to be faithful and loyal, and the Duke finds his jealousy entirely unwarranted. He in testing the others finds himself tested. Repentant, he purges himself, and, thus cleansed, he is able justly to cleanse his city when he reveals himself. He is taught mercy by the gentle Iulio, who, though he has suffered much at the hands of the unscrupulous Aspero, begs mercy for him of the Duke when the final trial scene takes place.

Edward Sharpham, imitating Marston's *The Malcontent*, in *The Fleir* (1606) follows the same procedure. The exiled Duke of Florence, Antifront, tests his two daughters and Piso. In disguise and away from home, he yet succeeds in bringing these daughters and Piso as well to trial and to repentance. Although the tone is farcical and the characters low, the pattern is quite apparent: good deeds are accomplished only after sin and error are followed by confession, repentance, and the gaining of knowledge.

A somewhat more complicated pattern of the testing is realized in Robert Daborne's *The Poor-Man's Comfort* (ca. 1617).[20] The poor man's comfort is justice, but Justice, having gone to heaven, is unattainable except through the agents of Providence. In this case the agents are, first, the man of natural goodness, Gisbert, who assigns strict justice to his unfaithful son-in-law, the second agent. But the King, the anointed Vicar, intervenes to grant mercy to the penitent young man who now makes amends. Thus Gisbert's daughter is made happy.

Although the King only appears in V.i of *The Shoemaker's Holiday* (1599) to grant mercy in the place of justice to Lacy, perhaps the pattern can be better seen among Dekker's plays in the two parts of *The Honest Whore* (1604, 1608?) and *The Patient Grissil* (1600). In the former Bellafront, being tempted, sins, but, being enlightened, repents and is saved from her sinful ways; and Candido, tested throughout, finds his patience equal to his vexations. Infelice and Hippolito are likewise put to the test. The Duke turns judge in the end and sees to it that mercy prevails over the justice which is called for. In Part II the same testing prevails. The Duke and Bellafront's father put her to tests to see whether her reformation has been genuine, and Candido's patience is further tested. Through his stratagem, Orlando saves Bellafront, his daughter, from despair, which is "one of hells Catch-poles," and helps resolve the denouement. The Duke is judge, God's agent and dispenser of mercy again. The whole of *The Patient Grissil* (written with Chettle and Haughton) is a testing, as one would expect. But here again the trial is subtle and complicated. Not only does Gwalther test Grissil, but Gwenthyan tests Sir Owen. Grissil should have been tempted to despair; she is not. Rather, her perseverance becomes a sort of testing of Gwalther: just how far can he risk going in his inhuman treatment of his wife, whom he actually loves tenderly? Moreover, since the sycophants of the court accuse Grissil of being below her husband in rank, a beggar indeed, Gwalther's testing of his wife becomes a testing of the courtiers. They do not come out well. Laureo, Grissil's brother, is proud, his pride is bested, he is humbled, and he repents, finding that "None else but Kings can know the hearts of Kings."

Thomas Heywood, more often interested in pageantry, patriotism, and sheer story, does not emphasize the moral testing of his characters, not at any rate in the sense or by the pattern derived from the morality plays. Of his plays perhaps the early (1602?) *The Royal King and the Loyal Subject* best follows the pattern. In the last act the King suddenly sets a trial for the accused Martiall, being encouraged by the traitorous Clinton and Chester who think the King believes in the Martiall's guilt. This pair is comparable to the evil angels of the earlier plays. The Martiall is tried, and the evidence against him is obviously unfounded; yet the King, as a trap to catch the true traitors, finds him guilty. The court, except for Chester, protest the judgment. In this way the truly guilty are caught. Having tested the Martiall in all ways, having failed to drive him to despair, the monarch restores him to his place and suspends Chester and the other traitors from their places. Mrs. Anne Frankford and Susan Mountford of *A Woman Killed with Kindness* (1603) are tested, too, but in quite a different way. Susan never succumbs, but instead overcomes with her beauty and goodness her would-be seducer. Anne does succumb—to simple lust. Then out of remorse and the test of forgiveness of her husband, whose cruelty is kindness, dies. Mrs. Wimcott in *The English Traveller* (ca. 1627), much like Anne, confesses her illicit love and dies at the end. Susan was driven near despair, but persevered and saved herself; Anne and Mrs. Wimcott were driven too, but only after they had succumbed. Like the morality protagonist, however, they do repent and are doubtless wafted to their heavenly reward, however slight that reward may have been. The final judgment at the end of *A Maidenhead Well Lost* (1625–1634?) involves trial by combat. Monsieur, tutor to the Prince of Florence, fights Stroza in single combat to prove him a scoundrel. He wins the fight, Stroza confesses his crimes, and the Duke of Milan acts as judge in restoring property and order. The earlier plays of Heywood seem to make more use of the conventional pattern, though in many of his dramas, even as time went on, the scheme is discernible. In the five plays on the Four Ages of Man, indeed, the gods from Olympus laugh at the antics of both gods and men as they move through the complication and denouement of the cosmic drama.

If Heywood makes limited use of the testing motif, Middleton does not. It is paramount as a shaping force in his plays. Scarcely a one is without it; and though most of his plays deal with London low life, those of broader import manage to achieve a sort of cosmic testing, such as the moral masque, *The World Tost at Tennis* (1620) and *A Game at Chess* (1624). In the early *Blurt, Master Constable* (1601–1602), an imitation of *Much Ado About Nothing*, the Duke stands outside the main action only to step into the last scene and establish justice, acting as the vicar of Providence. And obviously the stage is burlesqued as a microcosm here, for Lazarillo drops through the trap into hell, and Curvetto tries climbing up to heaven on a rope ladder—to Simperina's balcony. Frisco, designer of their predicaments, stands aside as controller and laughs at their antics. So it is with *The Phoenix* (1603–1604), an imitation of

Measure for Measure. The son of the Duke of Ferrara, in order to prepare himself to take over his father's rule, disguises himself and observes what goes on in the dukedom. All the professions and people are corrupt—more or less. The son, Phoenix, discovers a plot against his father. At the end, the Duke sets all right, and the son has, entirely without his father's knowledge (the Duke thought he was traveling abroad) or aid, proved himself worthy to rise to his father's place. Meanwhile the corruption of the state has been revealed and justice dealt out to many who have been tried. The same sort of testing occurs in *Michaelmas Term* (1607), in which Quomodo feigns death to test his wife, son, and daughter. The final scene is a trial scene in which the judge dispenses justice. And so it goes with most of Middleton's plays, though the motif is less obvious in some of the later ones. One should notice that in *The Changeling* (written with William Rowley about 1622) Beatrice-Joanna dies unredeemed and in despair, though she acknowledges her crimes. On the other hand, De Flores, her collaborator and agent, glories in his damnation, for he has had his reward. No one will claim that Middleton carried the weight of the moral world upon his shoulders as Marston or Jonson did, or that the judgments which effected his denouements returned justice to the world graced with mercy. The best of his characters are often too badly tinged with avarice themselves to command respect as great moral agents. But the device, the scheme and pattern of testing and trial, helps give shape to his plays; and he recognized in such a play as *The Changeling* the *psychomachia,* ringing a change upon its treatment in the character of De Flores.

In every one of Massinger's seventeen plays the testing motif is present. Although as time went on it became somewhat less apparent, it was still a shaping force. In *The Virgin Martyr* (1620?), it is most prominent; working with Dekker here Massinger set his most characteristic handling of the motif. The whole play is designed as a testing of Dorothea, the martyr, and of Theophilus, her tester and torturer. Theophilus is guided first by the evil spirit Harpax; in the end he is won over by Angelo, the good spirit. He releases the Christians he has persecuted; and then, himself tortured, he sees in a vision the sainted Dorothea and dies "a soldier in the Christian wars." The same sort of testing appears in *The Renegado* (1624) in which Vitelli and his sister Paulina are tried by Francisco. Again the martyr complex is employed: Francisco, the Jesuit, manages to save the Christians from the Turks and convert Donusa. In *The Maid of Honour* (1628) likewise the martyr motif is developed. Bertoldo and Camiola are both tested. Since the former is a Knight of Malta, he must remain a celibate. It is through Camiola's efforts that he manages to do so, for his love for her and hers for him prevail over the temptations of the flesh. Camiola also saves Adorni, who has loved her to distraction—and threatened suicide. At the end she repairs to a nunnery, having given her property to charity; and King Roberto, pronouncing judgment, says that she "is a fair example / For noble maids to imitate." At the conclusion of nearly every one of Massinger's plays the prince, the duke, or the king steps in as judge, though he may not always have been director of the action and controller of it up to that point. Massinger does not greatly emphasize the *psychomachia*, though we find Bertoldo in prison consoling himself with Seneca and accepting his fate somewhat as Edward II did. The depth of the struggle has been lost.

And so one might continue with illustrations. Even though the pattern is not easily observed in Beaumont and Fletcher's plays, it appears, especially in Fletcher's *The Faithful Shepherdess* (1608–1609), where all the shepherds are tested in the end, and the Sullen Shepherd, unrepentant, suffers for his sins. In *The Maid's Tragedy* (1611), chiefly Beaumont's, the testing turns out badly. In despair Aspatia, questioning God's power to lighten her burden sufficiently for her to bear it, rushes upon Amintor's sword; and both Amintor and Evadne, for like reason, reveling in despair take their own lives. Yet Evadne indicates that by killing the King she has somehow purged herself of taint and may now go resolutely to her suicide. Amintor, because the gods will not give back Aspatia, chooses to follow her in death. He now cannot bear her loss, whereas he had only a short time before been able to marry another woman and leave her love. The nobility of an antique Roman's suicide does not emerge here.

One may see the change more readily, perhaps, in Ford's *Love's Sacrifice* (1632). The *psychomachia* is here but how changed by sentimentality. Fernando sins in that he loves his lord's wife. When he declares himself to her, he is rebuked. Later when she declares herself to him, she is rebuked. Acknowledging their sin, they repent it. But after the one is killed by the Duke, the other in despair commits suicide. The Duke himself cannot escape. He likewise fails his test, kills his wife, confesses, and is sorry, but he cannot endure: he commits suicide. It is true that Fiormonda repents, confesses to the Abbot, and accepts a chaste life. The title of the play indicates the testing motif. All the characters, including Roseilli, are tried by love and are sacrificed to it. But the sacrifice to God, if not to love (and God is love), is a broken and a contrite heart. With these characters, the second part of the Psalmist's statement is neglected, unless we think contrition requires nothing more than for one to be sorry for his sin. It seems not to require endurance, the making of amends, and a life of sacrifice. Much the same is true of another of Ford's plays which has its title from the same Biblical reference, *The Broken Heart*. In it is the same distrust of God's power to enable man to accept and bear God's just requirements, to submit to His will, to believe His mercy is sufficient. In the morality plays, in Marlowe, in Shakespeare such characters would have been lost; in Ford we are asked to be sorry for them and to believe that very possibly they will live in love hereafter (as certainly Amintor and Aspatia expect to do). With these the pattern has been perverted, and the testing motif serves a different conclusion from what it did at the high tide of the period.

Yet no sudden and complete break with the past occurred. The older pattern is basic to Thomas Nabbes's morality, *Micro-*

cosmus: A Morall Mask (1637), in which Physander, having deserted his wife Bellanima, takes up with Sensuality and is in turn deserted by her, brought to despair, then rescued by the deserted Bellanima as an act of grace, confesses, repents, makes amends, and is restored. And in *The Knave in Grain* (1638?), written perhaps by John Day, the Duke as judge in the final scene tempers his justice with mercy—even for the false Julio. Here, then, are the two aspects of the pattern, for tragedy and for comedy, in the years just before the closing of the theatres.

PROVIDED FOR in the ancient concept of the world as a stage, this testing motif developed into a pattern in both the mystery and the morality plays and descended as a shaping force in the Elizabethan drama. Although it is apparent in all sorts of plays, it was perhaps most effectively used in tragedy. In those tragedies in which the protagonist succeeds in his quest, though he loses his life, one may discern the special pattern of the career of the Christian hero, a Dante, a Red Cross or a Guyon, Adam and Eve, a Jesus in *Paradise Regained*, or a Samson.

I suggest, moreover, that the pattern of their lives and of the plays they live in resembles the basic pattern of liturgy. The Morning and Evening Prayer of Cranmer's Book of Common Prayer most easily illustrate. The participant comes to the service soiled by sin, verging upon despair, "and there is no health in him." He confesses his sins; he is given absolution; he receives doctrine, gains knowledge, and then renders praise; thus purified, he makes his petitions and goes forth on his quest.

I suggest that this pattern is present in many of the comedies, romantic comedies, tragi-comedies, and chronicle plays, where protagonists stand their tests successfully and conclude their action, if not with divine vision, with at least a recognition of God's mercy and grace. It is even more effective in many of the high tragedies of the Elizabethan period. And I suggest that the katharsis achieved through this pattern was of a power scarcely conceived of by the Greeks, except in such plays as *Oedipus at*

Colonus. For, although the heroes in the finest Elizabethan tragedies through their error, defeat, despair, and suffering arouse our
fear and pity; through their confession, submission, gaining of
knowledge, and ultimate triumph, even in death, they bring the
swell of admiration to our hearts and veneration to our spirits.
These are the final feelings produced by the protagonists of the
noblest tragedies.

$\mathcal{N}otes$

INTRODUCTION

1 Sidney berates the dramatists for not following the rules, for using the narrative structure of history rather than the "rules of poesy" in writing tragedy, and for mixing comedy with tragedy as well as clowns with kings. Eliot remains conditioned by the ideal of classic form: he speaks, for example, of Chapman as having the most classical mind among the Elizabethan dramatists, his drama being "the most independent in its tendency toward a dramatic form" ("Four Elizabethan Dramatists," *Elizabethan Essays* [London, 1934], p. 19).

2 For example, see W. J. Lawrence, *The Elizabethan Playhouse and Other Studies*, 2nd Ser. (Stratford-on-Avon, 1913), pp. 151, 153.

3 *Shakspere's Five-Act Structure: Shakspere's Early Plays on the Background of Renaissance Theories of Five-Act Structure from 1470* (Urbana, Ill., 1947). Although as Dryden had pointed out and as Baldwin fully demonstrates, Terence doubles his plots, it is difficult on this ground to defend the Elizabethan tripling and quadrupling of plots. Furthermore, as Baldwin shows, the structure of the morality plays lies back of Lyly's plays and of such plays of Shakespeare as the early *Love's Labour's Lost,* a different sort of structure to be sure, but fundamental. The studies of the influence of Plautus, Terence, and Seneca on Elizabethan dramatists are too well known to be listed here, and the frequent references of the dramatists to the Romans, as well as to the classical strictures (Jonson, Heywood, Chapman, and others), are equally well known.

4 *Shakespeare and Five Acts* (New York, 1960).

5 *The Medieval Heritage of Elizabethan Tragedy* (Oxford, 1936).

6 *Induction to Tragedy* (Baton Rouge, La., 1939).

⁷ "The Medieval 'Cycle' as History Play: an Approach to the Wakefield Plays," *Studies in the Renaissance*, VII (1960), 76–89.

⁸ "Notes on the Dramatic Structure of the York Cycle," *Studies in Philology*, XXVIII (1931), 433–49.

⁹ *Patterns in Shakespearean Tragedy* (London, 1960).

¹⁰ *Shakespeare and the Allegory of Evil* (New York, 1958).

¹¹ *From Mankind to Marlowe: Growth of Structure in the Popular Drama of Tudor England* (Cambridge, Mass., 1962).

¹² Although it was not her direct intention, Miss Jocelyn Powell illustrates this point very well in her article "Marlowe's Spectacle" (*Tulane Drama Review*, VIII [1964], 195–210) in which she shows that the characters of Marlowe's plays are "ambivalent, fluctuating between personality and personification." When Mephistophilis, for example, offers Faustus the dagger, he becomes the immediate personification of Suicide, recognized at once by the audience as such.

CHAPTER ONE

¹ T. W. Baldwin, *William Shakespere's Small Latine & Lesse Greeke*, 2 vols. (Urbana, Ill., 1944), I, 654; Sister Miriam Joseph, *Shakespeare's Use of the Arts of Language* (New York, 1947), p. 12; Jean Jacquot, " 'Le Théâtre du Monde' de Shakespeare à Calderón," *Revue de Littérature Comparée*, XXXI (Juillet–Septembre, 1957), 341–72. Neither one of the three has noticed that Horace seems to have been aware of Democritus' use of the figure (See *Epistles* II, i.). Ben Jonson uses as epigraph to the first edition of *Bartholomew Fair* (1631) a garbled quotation from the epistle in which Horace refers to Democritus as looking and laughing at the human spectacle passing before him, more comic than the shows the people attend at the theatre. The chief implications suggested by M. Jacquot that involve dramaturgy stem from the concept of the gods' creating and producing the human comedy, as revealed in the play-within-the-play device particularly. Miss Anne Righter has gone much further than Jacquot in showing how this device develops from Democritus' figure in *Shakespeare and the Idea of the Play* (London, 1962), *passim*. It is readily observed in such schemes as the Induction to *The Taming of the Shrew*, more subtly used by Calderon in his secular *La vida es sueño*, and Prospero's masque in *The Tempest*. A second sort of illustration Jacquot suggests is the obvious sort one encounters in those remarkable late Corpus Christi moralities, Calderon's *autos sacramentales*, especially *La vida es sueño* and *El gran teatro del mundo*. It should be noted here that I had completed this chapter in more extensive form before the appearance of M. Jacquot's

article and had covered essentially the same appearances of the metaphor among the philosophers, the Fathers, and the humanists. I have, of course, covered far more extensively than he its appearance in the writings of the Elizabethans.

Ernst Robert Curtius briefly sketches the development of the metaphor from Plato through the Middle Ages, and mentions its impact upon Calderon and then upon Hofmannsthal, who seems to have had it from Calderon. He emphasizes John of Salisbury's use of the figure in the *Polycraticus* and cites Luther's and Ronsard's references to it. I think he is wrong in his unqualified statement that Calderon was "the first poet to make the God-directed *theatrum mundi* the subject of a sacred drama" and in his contention that the English and French drama know no "theo-centric concept of human life" (See *European Literature and the Latin Middle Ages*, trans. from the German by Willard R. Trask [London, 1953], pp. 138–44, especially p. 142).

[2] Trans. A. M. Harmon, Loeb Classical Library (London, 1925), IV, 99–101.

[3] Trans. Leonard F. Dean (Chicago, 1946), p. 66.

[4] Jacquot, " 'Le Théâtre du Monde,' " pp. 348–49.

[5] See chap. xiii, p. 213.

[6] *Trewnesse of the Christian Religion* (London, 1587), pp. 197–98.

[7] *Trewnesse of the Christian Religion*, pp. 220–21.

[8] *Marlowe's Tamburlaine: A Study in Renaissance Moral Philosophy* (Nashville, Tenn., 1941), pp. 125–26.

[9] Jacquot, " 'Le Théâtre du Monde,' " p. 350.

[10] *Ioannes Coletus Super Opera: Two Treatises on the Hierarchies of Dionysius*, trans. J. H. Lupton (London, 1869), p. 7.

[11] *History of the World* (1614), sigs. D_1^v–D_2^r. The metaphor was a favorite of Ralegh's. I have casually noted six other appearances of it in the *History*.

[12] See her *Mountain Gloom and Mountain Glory: The Development of the Aesthetics of the Infinite* (Ithaca, N.Y., 1959), p. 138.

[13] " 'Le Théâtre du Monde,' " p. 352.

[14] Quoted by Baldwin, *Small Latine & Lesse Greeke*, I, 675, from St. Chrysostom (Paris, 1581), V, 322. See Jacquot, " 'Le Théâtre du Monde,' " pp. 353–54, for full analysis of the three passages.

[15] Marcellus Palengenius, *The Zodiacke of Life*, trans. Barnaby Googe with Introduction by Rosamond Tuve, Scholars' Facsimiles & Reprints (New York, 1947), sig. Gii^r. Palengenius refers to the metaphor in at least two other places, sigs. D_7^v and N_1^v, mentioning in the one especially the laughter of the gods as they look at the "staged Comedy" which is the life of man. Jacquot gives a full account of Vives' treatment of the figure (" 'Le Théâtre du Monde,' " p. 357).

¹⁶ See *Elizabethan Critical Essays*, ed. Gregory Smith, 2 vols. (Oxford, 1904), I, 7.

¹⁷ I use the edition of 1581, "Imprinted at London by Thomas East."

¹⁸ See ¶ iiiʳ.

¹⁹ See ¶ iiiʳ. In this connection see also Thomas Sackville, *The Complaint of Henry Duke of Buckingham*, ed. Marguerite Hearsey (New Haven, Conn., 1936), stanza 86, in which Buckingham's grandsire says he stepped onto the stage of the world, where he was taught that "no state maie staye," that Fortune is fickle—the medieval concept of tragedy.

²⁰ See sig. Sviiʳ.

²¹ The figure is likewise basic to another "theatre," Jan Van der Noot's *A Theatre, wherein be represented as wel the miseries and calamities that follow the voluptious worldlings as also the greate joyes and plesures which the faithful do enjoy* (1569), the poems of which were translated into English by Edmund Spenser; and yet to another, *Wits Theatre of the Little World* (1599), a *nosce teipsum* collection of exempla in which the microcosm, man, may see the two-fold course of his life in the virtuous examples he may choose to follow and the vicious he should eschew.

²² Iohn Davies, *Microcosmos: The Discovery of the Little World, with the government thereof* (Oxford, 1603), p. 81.

²³ See John Davies, *Nosce Teipsum: This Oracle Expounded in two Elegies* (London, 1619), pp. 78–79.

²⁴ Peter de la Primaudaye, *The French Academie* (London, 1618), p. 334.

²⁵ I quote from the notes in the New Variorum edition of *As You Like It*, ed. H. H. Furness (Philadelphia, 1890), p. 123. Likewise in 1586 the first complete edition of Pettie's translation of Guazzo's *Civile Conversation* "introduces the saying of some philosopher 'that all this world was a stage, we the players which present the comedie.'"

²⁶ *Poems by Henry Lok, Gentleman: (1593–1597)*, ed. Rev. Alexander Grosart, Miscellanies of the Fuller Worthies Library (London, 1871), pp. 186–87.

²⁷ *The Fall of Man, or the Corruption of Nature, Proved by the Light of Naturall Reason* (London, 1616), pp. 20–21.

²⁸ Bacon casually uses it in his discussion of the active and the contemplative life in *The Advancement of Learning*, saying, "But men must know, that in this theatre of man's life it is reserved only to God and angels to be lookers on." And in his discussion of the *Idola Mentis* in the *Novum Organum* (1620) he speaks of the Idols of the Theatre as "but so many stage-plays, representing worlds of their own creation after an unreal scenic fashion."

²⁹ Noted by M. Jacquot. See *The Sermons of John Donne*, ed. George Potter and Evelyn M. Simpson, 10 vols. (Berkeley, Calif., 1953–

1959), I, 207. The metaphor is basic to Donne's Sermon XXIII, Folio of 1640, preached at St. Paul's on Easter Day, 1628.

[30] *The Poetical Works of William Drummond of Hawthornden With a Cypresse Grove*, ed. L. E. Kastner, 2 vols. (Manchester, 1913), II, 84.

[31] *The Works of Sir Thomas Browne*, ed. Charles Sayle, 3 vols. (Edinburgh, 1927), I, 60, 66–67.

[32] *The Selected Poems of George Daniel of Beswick, 1616–1657*, ed. Thomas B. Stroup (Lexington, Ky., 1959), p. 1.

[33] Milton's plans for a morality play with the heaven and the earth as the stage ultimately became *Paradise Lost*. As one might expect, Henry Vaughan, the Neoplatonist, liked the figure and set such poems as *The World* and *The Constellation* on the cosmic stage. Likewise the mystical Traherne makes use of it, notably in *A Thanksgiving and Prayer for the Nation*. In it he thinks of the world as a jewel case as well as "A silent Stage, / A Theatre for Actions, / Made for innumerable ends," and extends the two conceits for some twenty lines, praying God to spare "those Persons on thy Stage."

[34] *The Practical Works of John Bunyan*, ed. J. Newton Brown, 8 vols. (Philadelphia, 1852), VIII, 264.

[35] *Works of John Bunyan*, VIII, 178.

[36] Thomas Heywood, *An Apology for Actors*, Scholars' Facsimiles & Reprints (New York, 1941), sig. a4^{r-v}. M. Jacquot, not having seen this work, merely refers to it.

[37] Anne Righter, *Shakespeare and the Idea of the Play* (London, 1962) finds that the metaphor lies back of all Shakespeare's use of play images. And she points out (*passim*) his remarkably frequent use of stage imagery. She believes it is essentially a technique of "maintaining contact with the spectators" (p. 89). Similarly Charles R. Forker in "Shakespeare's Theatrical Symbolism and Its Function in *Hamlet*" (*Shakespeare Quarterly*, XIV [Summer, 1963], 215–29), finds the metaphor basic in his analysis of the dramatic theory which shapes *Hamlet*.

[38] Shakespeare's other direct references (the indirect are far too many to record) to the world as stage are these: *Winter's Tale*, V.i.55–61; *II Henry VI*, I.ii.63–67; *Macbeth*, II.iv.3–6 and V.v.23–26; *King Lear*, IV.vi.186–87; *Henry V*, Prologue, 1–4; *Richard II*, V.v.31–40; *II Henry IV*, IV.v.196–99; *Antony and Cleopatra*, V.ii.76–86; and *Sonnet XV*, 1–4. Unless otherwise noted, throughout this study my references are to *The Complete Works of William Shakespeare*, ed. G. L. Kittredge (Boston, 1936).

[39] Other allusions may be found in Chapman's *The Tragedy of Charles Duke of Byron*, III.i.43–48, and at the beginning of "Vigiliae Quartae & Vltimae" in his long poem *Eugenia*. See *The Plays and Poems of George Chapman*, ed. Thomas Marc Parrott, 2 vols. (London, 1910–1913), and *The Poems of George Chapman*, ed. Phyllis Brooks, MLA

General Series, XII (New York, 1941), pp. 295–96. Future references to Chapman will be to Parrott's edition.

[40] I quote throughout from *The Works of Thomas Middleton*, ed. A. H. Bullen, 8 vols. (London, 1885).

[41] The famous declaration in the Prologue to *Everyman in His Humour* implies the figure as it had shown itself in earlier plays, especially in the histories. Jonson does not, in spite of his declaration of independence, abandon the idea; rather, he modifies it in shaping his plays. He was well aware of the commonplace and its origins.

Unless otherwise noted, references are to *The Complete Plays of Ben Jonson*, Everyman Edition, 2 vols. (London, 1910). For my study this edition, with scene markings following the Gifford edition of 1816, is more convenient than the Herford and Simpson edition, although I have frequently used this brilliant work and cited its text in notes when I quote stage directions. Since the Herford and Simpson edition follows, for the earlier plays especially, the Folio of 1616, dropping as it does many of Jonson's earlier directions from the quartos and adopting his new and non-Elizabethan scene divisions, its use without modification would destroy the uniformity of practice in my handling my material.

[42] See *The Duchess of Malfi* in *The Complete Works of John Webster*, ed. F. L. Lucas, 4 vols. (London, 1927). Future references to Webster's plays will be to this edition.

[43] See *Beaumont and Fletcher*, ed. J. St. Loe Strachey, Mermaid Series, 2 vols. (London, 1950), I, 355. Unless otherwise noted future references to Beaumont and Fletcher's plays will be to this selection from their works. They are representative enough for my purposes.

[44] See *A Critical Edition of Massinger's "The Roman Actor,"* ed. William Lee Sandige, Jr. (Princeton, 1929).

[45] As quoted in the Furness Variorum *Hamlet*, II, pp. 131–32.

[46] See *The Dramatic Works of Thomas Dekker*, ed. Fredson Bowers, 4 vols. (Cambridge, 1953–1961), IV. Future references to Dekker's plays are to this edition.

[47] See Jacquot, " 'Le Théâtre du Monde,' " p. 362.

[48] *Shakespeare's Wooden O* (London, 1960), p. 187.

[49] *From Art to Theatre* (Chicago, 1944), *passim*.

[50] In his *The Idea of a Theatre* (Princeton, 1949), p. 116.

CHAPTER TWO

[1] E. M. W. Tillyard, *The Elizabethan World Picture* (London, 1943), p. 77.

² *Shakespeare's History Plays* (New York, 1947), p. 17.

³ See *Essays and Studies 1960* (London, 1960), p. 71.

⁴ Theodore Spencer, *Shakespeare and the Nature of Man*, 2nd ed. (New York, 1949), p. 60.

⁵ Spencer, 62.

⁶ Spencer, 78.

⁷ Spencer, 92.

⁸ Spencer, 96.

⁹ Jean Paris, "The Three Sons of *Hamlet*," *The Atlantic*, CCII (June, 1959), 68–76.

¹⁰ *The Question of Hamlet* (New York, 1959), pp. 161–64. A fuller and a more explicit statement has recently been made by Professor Levin in his paper "The Shakespearean Overplot" read before the Shakespeare Section of the Modern Language Association of America, meeting on December 28, 1964.

¹¹ See *Dramatic Essays by John Dryden*, Everyman Edition (London, 1912), p. 34. I wrote this passage in 1957. In January of 1963 Miss Jean Calhoun published (*Renaissance News*, XV, pp. 281–98) a very stimulating article "*Hamlet* and the Circumference of Action," in which she based her reading of the play on essentially this same pattern. From the domestic concerns of Polonius to the state affairs of Claudius to the unearthly realm of the Ghost, Hamlet moves—from the private life to the national to the "undiscovered country." "The many circumferences radiate concentrically from the characters' actions and intentions to encompass ever wider scenes until they embrace the ultimate possible scene of human action—the eternal, cosmic, or divine scene" (pp. 282–83).

¹² For a sufficient statement of the concept of man as microcosm, see Tillyard, *Elizabethan World Picture*, pp. 60–73.

¹³ My references throughout are to *The Complete Plays of Christopher Marlowe*, ed. Irving Ribner (New York, 1963).

¹⁴ See *The Works of Cyril Tourneur*, ed. Allardyce Nicoll (London, [1929]). Further references to Tourneur's works, unless otherwise indicated, will be to this edition.

¹⁵ See *The Plays of Thomas Nabbes*, ed. A. H. Bullen, 2 vols. (London, 1887), Act II, p. 174. Future references to Nabbes's plays will be to this edition.

¹⁶ All references are to *The Complete Works of John Lyly*, ed. R. W. Bond, 3 vols. (Oxford, 1902).

¹⁷ *Endymion*, because of its allegory dealing with Elizabeth and the court (perhaps the love of Leicester for the Queen and the complications involving Mary of Scotland), does reveal the conflicts between personal affairs and public duties; and the gods on the outside, forces of right and wrong, rule the inside conflicts.

[18] All references are to *The Works of George Peele*, ed. A. H. Bullen, 2 vols. (London, 1888).

[19] M. Jean Jacquot suggests that the Induction to *The Taming of the Shrew*, and by implication such encompassing areas of action as are here discussed, derives from the metaphor of the world as stage (See *Revue de Littérature Comparée*, XXXI [Juillet–Septembre], 1957, 343–45).

[20] Unless otherwise indicated, all references to Kyd are to *The Works of Thomas Kyd*, ed. F. S. Boas (Oxford, 1901). The structure of Senecan tragedy in some parts adapts itself easily into the pattern I am describing. The Elizabethan playwright, for example, made the chorus a more functional device than it was in Seneca's plays and fitted it to his special use, as in this play.

[21] Anne Righter, *Shakespeare and the Idea of the Play*, pp. 80 ff., comments fully on the effective use of the play-within-the-play in *The Spanish Tragedy*.

[22] I refer throughout to *The Plays and Poems of Robert Greene*, ed. J. Churton Collins, 2 vols. (London, 1905).

[23] I use the version of this play published in *Elizabethan and Stuart Plays*, ed. C. R. Baskervill, Virgil B. Heltzel, and Arthur Nethercot (New York, 1934). This anonymous play was one of the most popular of the entire period and was revived by Cowley after the Restoration as *The Cutter of Coleman Street*.

[24] I refer to the Malone Society reprint of this play, 1923.

[25] I use the text of this play found in *The School of Shakespeare*, ed. Richard Simpson, 2 vols. (London, 1878).

[26] Felix E. Schelling, *Elizabethan Playwrights* (New York, 1925), p. 41.

[27] Though the fairies in *The Merry Wives of Windsor* (1602) are mock fairies, they serve the same purpose as those of *A Midsummer Night's Dream* (1595): they resolve the two inner plots, serving as the supernatural sphere. In *The Merry Wives* the court is far distant (Bardolph goes there for horses for the "Germans"), but the commercial realm is well represented by the Host of the Garter. In *All's Well that Ends Well* (1602) Helena's love for Bartram is involved in state affairs, and the state affairs reach out through the war with Florence to international affairs. The King, drawn into the private action by illness, nevertheless stands mostly outside and as God's vicar judges and resolves the complications. In *Winter's Tale* (1611) Time, "that pleases some and tries all," as chorus appears once to assure the audience of his controlling presence outside the main action; inside, the state affairs involve an international situation; and within the state affairs come the almost disastrous double private action and the Autolychus plot. Less

obvious in Shakespeare's other comedies, the pattern of concentric spheres of action still underlies the plays.

[28] Harold S. Wilson, *On Design in Shakespearean Tragedy*, Univ. of Toronto Dept. of Eng., Stud. and Texts, No. 5 (Toronto, 1957), p. 123.

[29] Even in a play like *Epicoene*, though the spheres of action are not evident, this concept of life as make-believe is evident. Not a single person in the play is what he seems; everyone parades as somebody he is not; and the whole action is a set of hoaxes. Similarly, Face, Brainworm, and Mosca are protean hoaxers, revealing the world as a fraud, or at best a vanity and a dream. Such practice sets every play within a play, and to separate one from the other becomes impossible. C. G. Thayer suggests that Jonson regularly writes plays within plays: a group of fools at the center of his great comedies are surrounded by a group of sharpers who control them, and some kind of induction directly relates their action to the audience (*Ben Jonson: A Study in the Plays* [Norman, Okla., 1963], *passim*).

[30] The same sort of induction and outside frame is used in *The Magnetic Lady* (1632), but with the playhouse conceived of as a shop where plays are sold. Damplay and Probee as audience are introduced to the play proper by the Boy, and they comment upon the action throughout.

[31] I use the version of *The Fleir* published in *Materialen zur Kunde des älteren Englischen Dramas*, ed. W. Bang (Band 36, 1912); I use the edition of *Cupid's Whirligig*, ed. Allardyce Nicoll (London, 1926). Similar to the action in *Measure for Measure* also is that in Robert Daborne's *Poor-Man's Comfort* (ca. 1617). The extremely complicated plot, got from Sidney's *Arcadia* in part, involves the simple shepherds' lives and world, the court, the international area, and the spiritual—in which the King acts for God, tempering justice with mercy. I have used the 1655 quarto of this play (London, printed for Robert Pollard).

[32] I refer throughout to *The Plays of John Marston*, ed. H. Harvey Wood, 3 vols. (Edinburgh, 1943).

[33] Much the same pattern may be observed in *The Wonder of Women* (1606) where the Senecan ghost and an enchantress stand outside, and the conflict between jealous lovers for the hand of Sophonisba becomes involved with their duty to Carthage and to Rome. The private, national, international, and supernatural realms are apparent. Even in Marston's *The Dutch Courtesan* (1605) the pattern is at once recognizable: Sir Lyonell Frevill appears at the end as judge to settle everything in the courts. And in *What You Will* (1601) one finds the familiar role of the Duke as judge, standing outside and watching and then like a god stepping in to assert justice at the end. In *Histrio-Mastix* (1610) the spheres are clearly defined. At the center are the rustic players; next

and encircling them, the Lords of the Hall; outside both these, the Queen and her power; and at the end she in the costume of Astrea metes out justice. Surrounding all are the allegorical characters of Pride and her train.

³⁴ Exceptions which prove the rule are Chapman's imitations of Plautus, Terence, and Piccolomini. In these the spheres do not extend beyond the domestic, the home. I refer especially to *All Fools* (1604?) developed from Terence's *Heautontimoroumenos* and *Adelphi*, and *May-Day* (1601–1602) from Piccolomini's *Allesandro*.

³⁵ Heywood's plays have not been collected and edited in a modern edition; hence I have read them in various places ranging from carefully edited recent editions of single plays to poorly done quartos of the seventeenth century. Since textual problems and quotations are not often involved in this study, the edition of a particular play of Heywood that I have read (and sometimes I have read two or three) is not important. These are sufficient for the plays directly referred to here: *I* and *II Edward IV* and *The Golden and Silver Ages*, Shakespeare Society Publications (London, 1842, 1851); *The Iron Age* (London, 1632, pr. N. Okes); *The Brazen Age* (London, 1613, pr. Okes), *II Iron Age* (London, 1632); *A Challenge for Beautie* (London, 1636, pr. R. Raworth); *I Fair Maid of the West* (London, 1631); *II Fair Maid of the West* (London, 1631, pr. Richard Royston); *The English Traveller* (London, 1633, pr. R. Raworth); *A Mayden-Head Well Lost* (London, 1634, pr. Nicholas Okes); *The Four Prentices of London* (London, 1632, pr. Nicholas Okes); *The Wise Woman of Hogsdon* (London, 1638, pr. Henry Shephard); *The Royal King and the Loyal Subject* (London, 1637, pr. Nich. & John Okes); *Fortune by Land and by Sea* (London, 1655); *The Late Lancashire Witches* (London, 1634, pr. Thomas Harper); *If You Know not Me You Know No Bodie* (*The Dramatic Works of Thomas Heywood*, 6 vols. [London, 1874]); *A Woman Killed with Kindness* and other plays (*Thomas Heywood*, ed. A. W. Verity, Mermaid Series [London, n.d.]); *The Captives*, ed. A. C. Judson (New Haven, Conn., 1921); and *The Rape of Lucrece*, ed. Allan Holaday (Urbana, Ill., 1950).

³⁶ The domestic, state, and international forces are indeed apparent in *A Maidenhead Well Lost* (1625–1634?), but not the supernatural. *Love's Mistress* (1634) is a series of pageants from the Cupid and Psyche story presented by means of a chorus.

³⁷ Both the international and the spiritual areas are fully developed in Rowley's play. Out of the spirit world provided by the angel and the spring of St. Winifred come the salvation of England and provision for her future. The domestic center formed by the shoemakers becomes involved with the state, the state with Rome, and Rome with the church

and indirectly with the supernatural powers. Thus Albion [Alban], converted, becomes the first English martyr. Rowley also provides the pattern in *All's Lost by Lust* (ca. 1620), though with a difference: at war with the Moors, the tyrant Rodorique sends Iacinta's father to the battlefront because of his lust for her; but he fails to reckon with the supernatural powers represented by the enchanted castle and by a vision of his fall.

[38] Essentially the same was true of the earlier *Patient Grissil* (1600), in which three plots are encompassed by the court of Pavia, the spiritual force being represented by Gwalter, God's instrument as dispenser of ultimate justice and rewards. Similarly in *Sir Thomas Wyat* (1602): the love of Jane and Guildford is caught up in the conflict within the kingdom, and the international power represented by Spain conditions the action. No supernatural or spiritual power is made explicit.

[39] I quote from F. L. Lucas's edition of Webster's plays (vol. IV), Lucas having included the play among Webster's—without good reason.

[40] Similarly in *The Maid's Tragedy* (1610–1611) the supernatural is not made explicit, and again the emphasis falls upon the personal interests of the characters: it is the King's desire to hide his illicit amour with Evadne and keep her as his mistress, not any concern for the state, which perpetrates the tragedy. Tangential to this center is the vague conflict between Calianax and Melantius, and equally vague is the war from which the latter has returned. In *A King and No King*, to pick at random, the supernatural sphere has no place, though the domestic, national, and international are distinguished. In *Thierry and Theodoret* the only evidence of the spiritual or occult is the false astrologer. But Thierry does regard himself as a microcosm, and the private lust of the evil mother of two good kings involves the state in international difficulties. By the time of Fletcher's *The Wild Goose Chase* (1621) we have a play better suited to the Restoration: only the households of urbane and witty ladies and gentlemen are involved in the action.

[41] Evidence of the concentric spheres of action, sometimes considerably sophisticated, may easily be noted in Middleton's *A Chaste Maid in Cheapside* (domestic affairs encircled by commercial), *Anything for a Quiet Life* (Beaufort's authority controlling all), *The Witch* (the Governor as arbiter controlling from the outside), *More Dissemblers Besides Women* (the Cardinal standing outside to direct the action), *A Mad World My Masters* (Penitent Brothel as microcosm, visitation of the Devil in Mrs. Harebrain's shape, play-within-the-play), and *The Mayor of Quinborough* (Hygden as Induction, the dumb show, the personal affairs of Horsus, Vortiger, and Roxena running counter to the welfare of the city, the welfare of the city conflicting with that of the state, and the two with Saxony). An excellent example also is *The*

World Tost at Tennis, best described as a moral interlude and called a "Courtly Masque." In it Jupiter presents a play for the benefit of a soldier and a scholar, in which such allegorical characters as Simplicity and Deceit appear.

[42] Except as noted otherwise, throughout this study I refer to *The Plays of Philip Massinger,* ed. W. Gifford, 4 vols. (London, 1805). In *A New Way to Pay Old Debts* the lines between spheres of action have faded. The plot of Lovell and Lady Allworth does surround and shape the Overreach-Wellborn plot, and the Tapwell-Froth affair is conditioned by the latter plot; but the international area is barely suggested by the career of Lovell and the aspirations of Tom Allworth. Lines between individual, home, and state are not drawn. If we allow the King or the Duke his vicarious sphere as divine agent, however, all areas are pretty well defined in such plays as *The Maid of Honour, The Emperor of the East, The City Madam* (much like *Measure for Measure*), *The Guardian,* and *The Bashful Brother.*

[43] "The Play within a Play," *Essays and Studies,* 1960, pp. 44–46.

[44] Except as otherwise noted, references to Ford's plays in this study are to *John Ford,* ed. Havelock Ellis, Mermaid Series (London, n.d.).

[45] Unless otherwise noted, all references to Shirley's plays in this study are to *James Shirley,* ed. Edmund Gosse, Mermaid Series (London, n.d.).

[46] The best known of these is, of course, Milton's *Comus* (1634). The supernatural and moral sphere is represented by the Attendant Spirit and Sabrina, as well as Comus' rout; the state by the setting, the occasion, and the actors as referred to in the text; the personal and domestic by the Lady and her two brothers.

[47] I refer to *The Knave in Graine New Vampt,* Q 1640, as reprinted by the Malone Society, 1960 (1961). This version is attributed to Day, but obviously much of it had existed in earlier forms, going back perhaps as far as 1599.

CHAPTER THREE

[1] *Play within a Play: The Dramatist's Conception of His Art: Shakespeare to Anouilh,* Yale Romanic Stud., 2nd Ser., V (New Haven, 1958), p. 30.

[2] In this connection see Hereward T. Price, "The Mirror-Scenes in Shakespeare," *Joseph Quincy Adams Memorial Studies,* ed. James G. McManaway, et al. (Washington, 1948), pp. 101–13.

[3] See especially Harry Levin, *The Overreacher: A Study of Christopher Marlowe* (Cambridge, Mass., 1952), pp. 47–53.

[4] "The Staging of Elizabethan Plays at the Rose Theater, 1592–1603" (unpubl. doctoral diss., University of Kentucky, 1958), pp. 128–29.

⁵ *The Dutch Courtesan, The Fawn, What You Will,* and *The In-satiate Countess* are all, each for its kind, rich in these dramatic materials, but especially the last with its procession to the Senate, the trial, and the scaffold scene.

⁶ Other Roman plays, not so rich as *Antony and Cleopatra,* have yet a great deal of the same sort of pageantry. In *Julius Caesar* 13 entrances at least and 10 exits require procession or formal organized movement, and 5 or more ceremonies take place in it, if we include the two great funeral orations. In *Coriolanus* an audience would see something like 23 formal entrances and 20 such exits, as well as 5 ceremonies, including a military parley (I.iv), Coriolanus' public petitions for the consulship (II.iii), a challenging of the watch (V.ii), and the banishing of Coriolanus (IV.i). In *Pericles,* if one may place it among the Roman plays, 12 formal entrances are required and 8 such exits. About 6 ceremonies take place, including the ceremony of coming aboard ship (V.i).

⁷ Formal entrances, processions, ceremonies, and rituals occur as frequently almost in Shakespeare's other tragedies. *Romeo and Juliet,* basically a domestic play, has fewer of these than most. Yet the 3 entrances and exits of the Prince are made formally, with his train attending; his acts (the quelling of the feuding, the banishing of Romeo, and the final judgment and reconciliation at the end) are public and formal acts. The appearance of the Nurse and Peter (II.v), however comic, is formal: Peter acts as gentleman usher. The Nurse's and Lady Capulet's keening (IV.v) for Juliet's supposed death, with the echo of the *Dies Irae* is ritual, as is Juliet's kneeling to beg pardon (IV.ii) for having refused the hand of Paris. The masque and the ball are ceremonious and formal. In *King Lear* 28 entrances and exits are indicated as formal. The opening scene is a formal holding of court in a room of state, the ceremony involving the division of the kingdom and the rejection of an heir. The herald's announcements and the ceremony preceding the duel between Edgar and Edmund are notable (V.iii), as is Lear's prayer before the hovel (III.iv). In *Macbeth* at least 22 entrances and exits are formal, consisting frequently of soldiers marching in formation on and off the stage, or of the King and his accompanying train. The witches present at least 4 rituals, and 2 banquets occur, one behind the scenes and one onstage. In *Othello,* more nearly a domestic tragedy, the pageantry is less. Yet 20 or more entrances and exits require formal presentation, with "flourishes" and attendants or soldiers in military formation. The ceremony of the Senate meeting is here (I.iii), and the herald reads a formal proclamation (II.ii). As time went on, Shakespeare made less, but more effective, use of such devices.

⁸ Marked IV.v in the Herford and Simpson edition, the direction for the entrance is a little simplified, but sufficiently full to indicate the procession: "Avocatori 4, Bonario, Celia, Voltore, Corbaccio, Corvino,

Mosca, Notario, Commandadori." The second trial scene (marked as V.x in the Herford and Simpson edition) has the entrance indicated thus: "Avocatori 4, Notario, Commandadori, Bonario, Celia, Corbaccio, Corvino, Voltore, Volpone."

⁹ This entrance in the Herford and Simpson edition is marked "Praecones, Flamen, Ministri, Seianvs, Terentivs, Satrivs, etc." The description of the ritual is the same in all editions.

¹⁰ *Caesar and Pompey* (1613?) is similarly crowded with formalities. At fewest a dozen entrances and a like number of exits require observance of order and degree in their staging. The entrance which opens Scene ii of the play takes place before the Temple of Pollux and is carefully described: "*Enter some bearing axes, bundles of rods, bare, before two Consuls;* Caesar *and* Metellus, Antony *and* Marcellus, *in couples;* Senators, People, Soldiers, *etc.* . . ." In the Senate the statesmen speak formal orations, and the announcement of the herald is ceremonial.

¹¹ So does *Satiromastix* (1602). It opens with a ceremony: two gentlewomen scattering flowers before the house of a bride returning from her wedding. The second entrance of the play, that of Sir Quintilian, is a burlesque of the formal; so is that of Sir Adam, who enters with a light being carried ceremoniously before him; and the whole party go off stage in procession—all this in Scene i. Much the same may be noted for the rest of the play: in II.i Sir William and the others enter in formal order, and in the same scene the King is heralded by trumpets and followed by his train as he comes on for the stately dance. III.ii opens in the same fashion; IV.i with a banquet; and the final scene is a masque. *The Famous History of Sir Thomas Wyatt* (1602), in which Webster probably collaborated, is about as ceremonious and pageant-like as any. A procession, for example, opens I.vi, and in the scene Wyatt kneels to Arundel to present the case for Princess Mary. II.ii is made up of a series of ceremonies in which Northumberland is arrested.

¹² Although Cyril Tourneur's *The Revenger's Tragedy* (1607) has no excessive amount of pageantry, the procession of the court (I.i), the trial scene (I.ii), and the banquet and two masques in the final scene of the play are very effective. *The Atheist's Tragedy* (1611) is, however, both rich in these devices and quite as effective in their use. Again the play opens with a formal entrance and in I.iv another such entrance occurs; Act II opens with "*Musicke, a banquet. In the night.*" Then a procession takes place, during which ceremonial drinking is required. The funeral procession for Montferrers opens Act III, with a dead march playing, and the final scene is a trial scene with two judges presiding.

¹³ For example, *The Fair Maid of the West* (both parts) is really a series of processions. In Part II 10 entrances such as this occur: "*Enter*

Mullisheg, Iaffer, and Alcade, Spencer, Goodlack, Besse, and the rest,"
or this: *"Flourish. Enter Florence, Mantua, Farara."* The exits are likewise formal. Such pageantry, as everyone who has read them knows, is
required by such plays as *The Four Prentices of London, The English
Traveller,* the two parts of *King Edward the Fourth,* and *If You Know
not Me You Know No Body.* *The Captives,* adapted from Plautus, is
especially notable, for Heywood sets Plautus' plot within much burlesqued pageantry, ceremony, and ritual.

¹⁴ And the definition of scene is clearer than in the earlier plays. For
example, *The Maid's Tragedy* has only 12 scenes, all well defined, as
opposed to 26 in Marston's *The Malcontent,* including the Induction;
Philaster has 16, as opposed to 20 in *Hamlet; A Wild Goose Chase* has
16; *Thierry and Theodoret* has 13, as opposed to perhaps 24 in *Romeo
and Juliet;* and *Bonduca,* chronicle though it is, has 18 as opposed to 23
in Marlowe's *Edward II.*

¹⁵ It is especially well adapted in such a "low" play as *The City
Madam* (1632?), in which Lady Frugal's household has "grown a little
court." Thus the Lady and her household with the astrologer enter "in
several postures, with looking-glasses at their girdles." A burlesque procession of a justice of the peace, a constable, watchmen, etc. opens III.i;
in IV.ii the Sheriff makes an arrest and takes off his prisoners in procession; and in V.iii a procession of servants crosses over the stage to serve
a banquet. A masque is given in the same scene.

¹⁶ His *'Tis Pity She's a Whore* (1629–1633), apparently not set at
court, does not, except for the Cardinal, involve a prince and his entourage. Hence formal entrances and processions and ceremonies are not
so much required. But there are the fatal banquet (V.vi) and one other
(IV.i), the betrothal ceremony (III.vii), and the fine *tableau vivant,*
with Annabella kneeling before a table with waxed lights on it making
confession to the Friar (III.vi).

¹⁷ Such is not true of his masques, of course. *The Triumph of Peace*
is perhaps as elaborate a piece of pageantry as was produced in the whole
period. Something of the same sort of distinction occurs in Thomas
Nabbes's work: whereas his *Microcosmus: A Moral Maske* is pure pageantry, his *The Bride, A Comedy* (1638) requires only one formal
entrance, a scene in which a betrothal takes place, a ceremony of confession with Theophilus on his knees in the final scene. Yet Henry Glapthorne's *The Tragedy of Albertus Wallenstein* (1634–1639) requires
about 15 formal entrances and exits and 3 ceremonies at least. One must
agree, however, that this play rather looks forward to the heroic play
of the Restoration than backward to Jacobean tragedy.

¹⁸ See Vol. I, pp. 106–7. Alice S. Venezky elaborates Chambers' statement, though not directly, showing that the plays furnished much pag-

eantry: "The procession was a striking symbol. Moral implications of the transience of pomp and earthly glory were expressed by the juxtaposition of a victory march and a funeral, or by the presentation of a triumphing hero who later was cast down by Fortune" (*Pageantry on the Shakespearean Stage* [New York, 1951], p. 61).

CHAPTER FOUR

[1] The substance of a part of this chapter appears as "The Scenes in Shakespearean Plays" in *All These to Teach: Essays in Honor of C. A. Robertson* (Gainesville, Fla., 1965).

[2] "The Medieval 'Cycle' as History Play: An Approach to the Wakefield Plays," *Studies in the Renaissance*, VII (1960), 76–89.

[3] *The Defense of Poesy*, ed. A. S. Cook (Boston, 1890), p. 48.

[4] In the Prologue to the 1633 quarto of this play Heywood boasts that he has changed to a different type. Here, he says, is a play in which "We vse no Drum, nor Trumpet, nor Dumbe Show. . . ." He wants to see whether he can get along without these and other such aids, among which are obviously the numerous places of action.

CHAPTER FIVE

[1] *The Dramatic Works of William Shakespeare*, ed. Dr. Johnson, G. Steevens and others, revised by Isaac Reed, 6 vols. (New York, 1850), I, 28.

[2] See Chapter I, pp. 14–17.

[3] *The Growth and Structure of Elizabethan Comedy* (London, 1955), p. 12.

[4] Perhaps the trend may be seen as early as Webster's two great tragedies: *The Duchess of Malfi* (1613–1614) has only 15 speaking characters, though many mutes in the background, and *The White Devil* (1612) only 19. Late in the 1630's Glapthorne's plays range from 14 to about 21.

[5] Though the clergy are represented, they are less frequently put upon the stage than representatives of the other estates. Since Kyd, for example, had been charged with atheism, he may have been unwilling to risk a cleric in *The Spanish Tragedy*, though the plot could well have provided for one. Doubtless the dramatists found themselves somewhat restricted in their presentation of the clergy by the various licensing and censorship requirements of the government. These requirements, though indirect with regard to the representation of the clergy, might easily lend themselves to repressive interpretations and thus persecution under the law. (See V. C. Gildersleeve, *Government Regulation of the Elizabethan*

Drama [New York, 1908], especially pp. 19–20, 91–92, 110, and *passim*.) In the chronicle plays they appear almost invariably where the poets are protected by history, and in later plays set mostly in wicked Italy, where the Roman clergy could be treated with whatever disrespect the dramatist desired. The lower orders, especially the friars who had traditionally been regarded as dissolute, were frequently put into the cast, and occasionally one of the Puritan brotherhood, as in Jonson's plays, to be lampooned.

⁶ A good example of the customary setting forth of the estates and degrees within them occurs in Gascoigne's *Steel Glass*. Following ecclesiastical practice, the poet divides society, and subdivides it, into princes and kings, "Nobility and Councillors," clergy, "All Learned," and then "the Commonality," or "the common people, each in his degree," into which group he places all tradesmen, farmers, shipmen, and merchants, all producers and laborers, the first being the plowman.

⁷ "*The Alchemist:* Jonson's 'Estates' Play," *Renaissance Drama*, VII (1964), 37. Mr. Dessen points out also that Jonson in *The Staple of News* (1625/26) directly explains to his audience how he has transformed the allegorical characters of the moralities into the realistic characters of his comedies. They are dressed as "men and women o' the time," but they still retain their original allegorical qualities.

⁸ The restrictions imposed by classical or neoclassical criticism, especially the unities, are of course prominent in *Epicoene*, *The Alchemist*, *The Magnetic Lady*, and *The Staple of News;* yet in each one Jonson carefully indicates an entire social order, a unified society. And *Volpone* has as wide a spread of characters upon the social spectrum as one can expect to find in any Elizabethan comedy: from the Commandadori of the court and Sir Politic Would-be, to the advocate, the merchants, the waiting women, to Volpone and Mosca (the parasite), and to Volpone's dwarf, eunuch, and hermaphrodite, his entertainers. Lacking only are the Doge of the city and the clergy.

⁹ See the "Prologue to the Stage," *The Royal King and the Loyal Subject* (London, 1637).

¹⁰ *A Challenge for Beautie* (London, 1636), sig. A3ʳ.

¹¹ See Chapter I, p. 23.

¹² It is interesting, for example, to compare Henry Chettle's *Hoffman* (1602) with Henry Glapthorne's *Albertus Wallenstein* (1634–1639). In the one not only do the dukes of Prussia, Saxony, and Austria have parts, but certain lords, a hermit, heralds, soldiers, citizens, and various attendants; in the other, only the Emperor of Germany, the King of Hungary, various dukes, a marshal, two colonels, a captain, an executioner, and a guard. It is likewise revealing to notice the much wider representation Edward Sharpham manages in his *Cupid's Whirligig* (1607) than what

Glapthorne manages in his *The Hollander* (1636), both derived from Roman comedy. Sharpham fetches in a Welsh courtier and an Alderman Vintner, as well as a pedant, an Inns-of-Court man, and a midwife.

CHAPTER SIX

[1] The substance of parts of this chapter was published as "The Testing Pattern in Elizabethan Tragedy," *Studies in English Literature, 1500–1900*, III (Spring, 1963), 176–90.

[2] See Ribner's *Patterns in Shakespearean Tragedy* (London, 1960), especially pp. 11–12 and 35. Professor Willard Farnham, *The Medieval Heritage of Elizabethan Tragedy* (Berkeley, Calif., 1936) emphasized the fall of the protagonist as inherited from medieval narrative verse tragedy as the more frequent shaping force, as did Professor Howard Baker in his *Induction to Tragedy* (Baton Rouge, La., 1939).

[3] I am fully aware that the nature of dramatic conflict very often, if not always, involves some sort of testing of characters. I am equally well aware also of what might be called a testing motif similar to that I am discussing in Greek tragedy, especially in the plays of Aeschylus and Sophocles. In them, however, the protagonist is more often punished for a stubborn violation of eternal decrees or wilful prying into secrets better left hidden than being tested to see whether he can carry out an assignment or perform a duty without loss or destruction. Prometheus, a god himself, heroically maintains his defiance of a seemingly unjust Zeus, who is punishing him. Oedipus at Colonus, having endured his suffering, now achieves a peace of soul resembling that of Lear, it is true; he comes close to the Christian hero being tested. And in Aeschylus' *Eumenides* Orestes through a legalism is brought relief from his suffering in the guise of justice—really mercy. But here the dramatist does not set out to provide a test for Orestes; rather he examines man's dilemma when caught between two conflicting eternal decrees. In drama since the seventeenth century the pattern I suggest has been pretty well lost— though plenty of testing occurs. An interesting recent case may be observed in Dürrenmatt's *The Visit*: the impersonal, inevitable exacting of the moral debt of the protagonist. It is an eternal law as inevitable as a law of nature; it cannot be avoided. But it is not a test. The protagonist is not in the play handed his *donné*, assigned his duty, to see whether or how well he can perform it. The Mayor of the town is no agent to pronounce God's judgment, though the town's people take the punishment into their hands. Here is an assertion of moral law, not a scheme for the testing of a man's soul, not a *psychomachia*, though the struggle much resembles it.

[4] *Shakespeare's Wooden O* (London, 1960), p. 187.

[5] See *Prudentius, with an English Translation*, 2 vols., Loeb Classical Library (London, 1949), I, 275.

[6] Perhaps the clearest statement of the war of the soul as it emerges in the morality and bequeaths its "soldiery of the Devel" (the Vices) to the later drama is that set forth in Bernard Spivack's *Shakespeare and the Allegory of Evil* (New York, 1958), pp. 60–95. David Bevington in *From Mankind to Marlowe* (Cambridge, Mass., 1962) takes into account the *psychomachia* as he traces the mutations of structure from the moralities through Marlowe's plays, but his main concern is the pragmatic solution of the structural problem by the acting troupes.

[7] *A Theological Interpretation of the Moral Play, "Wisdom, Who is Christ"* (Washington, 1952), p. x.

[8] The pattern is equally apparent in Henry Medwall's *Nature* (1486–1500) and in *Mundus et Infans*. In the latter, Infans is saved from suicide by perseverance (as Hamlet is later) and thus attains mercy. Similarly Skelton, the humanist, in *Magnyfycence* brings his Prince to despair and the threat of suicide before he allows him to be saved by Good Hope. So it is with Lusty Juventus, in the play which bears his name, who falls into sin but who through contrition wins forgiveness. One finds the same pattern in John Bale's plays. And John Milton displays more than a casual acquaintance with it in *Paradise Lost*.

[9] Some little evidence of the motif, though hardly of the kind derived from the morality plays, may be observed in Lyly's plays. In *Endymion*, for example, Endymion undergoes considerable testing, and so does Eumenides; and in *Gallathea* Neptune standing outside the action controls and tests the people who evade his demands. The conclusion is not satisfactory, however.

[10] In Peele's *David and Bethsabe* the pattern of sin, despair, and repentance may be observed in the character of David, who is moved to acceptance and reconciliation at the end.

[11] Both Henry VI and Richard II are tested as monarchs and men; both fail as kings, Henry abdicating his power just when he had become most nearly worthy of it. As God's anointed he merited the death he received, but as a man, the salvation he surely enjoyed. Perhaps the same can be said for Richard. Several good examples of testing are to be noted in *Henry VIII*. Wolsey, caught as he acknowledges at the top of Fortune's wheel, faces and knows himself for what he is, submits, repents, and gains peace before death. Buckingham, whom Wolsey had ruined, is brought to the edge of despair at his trial, where the false surveyor testifies against him; nevertheless, he submits, accepts, forgives all, and goes to his grave attended by angels, so he prays (II.i.55–136). Similarly Queen Katherine, who refuses to be tried in Wolsey's court, dies forgiving even him, having a vision of her salvation.

[12] See *Certaine Sermons or Homilies appointed to be read in Churches, in the time of the late Queene Elizabeth* (London, 1623), p. 277, for the official statement of the position of the crown: the king or queen is named as God's vicar; King Edgar in *A Knack to Know a Knave* (1594) says in his very first speech (Scene i), "Then as I am Gods Vicegerent here on earth . . ." (Malone Society Reprints, 1964 for 1963).

[13] *Patterns in Shakespearean Tragedy*, pp. 25–35. Ribner does not recognize the *psychomachia*.

[14] *Shakespeare's Use of Learning* (San Marino, Calif., 1953), pp. 234–50.

[15] "Hamlet as Minister and Scourge," *PMLA*, LXX (Sept., 1955), 740–49.

[16] See R. B. Heilman, *This Great Stage: Image and Structure in King Lear* (Baton Rouge, La., 1948), p. 278, for a statement concerning the suffering and maturing of Albany and Kent; for a long note on Christian traditions and practices in *King Lear*, see p. 331.

[17] *Patterns in Shakespearean Tragedy*, p. 115. I cannot agree with Paul N. Siegel that Othello is damned. See his "Damnation of Othello," *PMLA*, LXVIII (Dec., 1953), 1068–78. His iteration is not evidence, and his parallel between Othello and Adam would be more convincing if he had carried it further—at least to the harrowing of Hell. Nor do I agree with Granville-Barker (*Prefaces to Shakespeare*, Series IV, London, 1945, pp. 183–84); nor with Arthur Sewell (*Character and Society in Shakespeare*, Oxford, 1951, pp. 94–97); nor with S. L. Bethell ("Shakespeare's Imagery: The Diabolic Images in *Othello*," *Shakespeare Survey* 5, pp. 62–80). I more nearly agree with H. S. Wilson (*On the Design of Shakespearean Tragedy* [Toronto, 1957], p. 67) that Shakespeare "avoided any judgment concerning Othello's ultimate fate. . . ." M. D. H. Parker (*The Slave of Life* [London, 1955], pp. 156–58) argues well for Othello's salvation. Roland M. Frye (*Shakespeare and Christian Doctrine* [Princeton, 1963], p. 30) asserts that "there is no major element of either Roman or Reformed theology which would venture to assert with Mr. Ribner's confidence the salvation of anyone who committed suicide in the manner of Othello." For the Moor I believe Shakespeare suggests hope, nothing more.

[18] See in this connection Travis Bogard's *The Tragic Satire of John Webster* (Berkeley, 1955), pp. 26–34. Bogard points out that Chapman's heroes, all "Senecal men," are tested; but being "complete," they do not change, cannot change.

[19] Among Chapman's comedies the pattern is perhaps best observed in *The Gentleman Usher* (1602?), wherein Alphonso, seeing himself as he actually is, repents and gives Margaret to Vincentio; in *Monsieur D'Olive* (1604), where the Duke stands outside the action as judge; and

in *The Widow's Tears* (1603–1609), in which Lysander tests his wife by spreading the rumor that he is dead, sending back his presumed body to a tomb, and then returning in his proper person and wooing his widow in the tomb.

[20] Robert Daborne, *The Poor-Mans Comfort* (London, pr. for Rob: Pollard, 1655).

Index

231